DEALING WITH UNWRITTEN RULES

Creating Openness in Policy Development

Max E.J. Herold

ISBN: 978-90-812022-3-7

Uitgeverij Managementissues.com
Noordwijk zh

info@managementissues.com / www.managementissues.com

Coverdesign and layout: Loes Kema, GVO drukkers & vormgevers, Ede

Printed by: GVO drukkers & vormgevers, Ede

DEALING WITH UNWRITTEN RULES
Creating Openness in Policy Development

Omgaan met ongeschreven regels
Hoe beleidsambtenaren zélf ruimte kunnen creëren
voor openheid in de beleidsontwikkeling

Doctoral thesis

At Erasmus University Rotterdam
On the authority of the
Rector Magnificus

Prof.dr. H.A.P. Pols

And in accordance with the decision of the College for Promotions.

The public defence will take place on

Thursday October 5th 2017

At exactly 15:30 hr

by

Max Eugene Johannes Herold

Born in Roermond

Erasmus University Rotterdam

Table of contents

Preface

Mapping and advising about unwritten rules is not a new thing. Take Machiavelli. He was a fan of great monarchs. Based on careful observations, he provided monarchs with insight into ways in which they could rule their kingdoms *and* preserve their power. The methods he described in his book 'The Prince' (Il Principe) were a mixture of coping strategies ('how-to') and unwritten rules that applied to the level of a monarch at the time. The following is an example of that:

Unwritten rule: "Every prince, no matter how strong his army may be, needs the favor and collaboration of his citizens. The people have to be the prince's friends. The prince needs to try and win the people's favor. This will not be difficult, because the people will happily put themselves under his protection. A prince who can count on the people's favor has little to fear of conspiracies."

Coping strategy: "Let others impose hard measures, but be a benefactor yourself."

Machiavelli made a distinction between the top segment and the people. He thought in terms of top-down management. But there are ministries with civil servants who play a role in management based on policy development. These civil servants have to deal with unwritten rules that affect policy development. How can civil servants deal with those unwritten rules, when they want to do justice to what the 'people' want (bottom-up) instead of what the 'prince' wants? How can the knowledge and wisdom of the people be used to improve the quality of policy? And how can civil servants make that possible?

For me, finding answers to these questions has been an end to a lengthy research journey. One that has not always been easy, but that was always extremely fascinating and highly educational. This promotion project has proven to be a way not only to serve science, but to improve my own knowledge and skills in a domain that has interested me for many decades.

Max Herold,
January 2017

Acknowledgements

A promotional study is not something one does on one's own. And without the support of many, this thesis would never have been written. There are a few people I want to mention in particular.

First of all, I would like to thank my two promoters: Geert Teisman and Mathieu Weggeman. And I should certainly add Peter van Hoesel. His numerous insights have taught me a lot.

And then there is that other true research expert: Daan Andriessen. Daan, I want to thank you for your expert advice and your ever-present willingness to be my sparring partner.

Annemieke Roobeek, you were one of the first to suggest I should think about writing a thesis. Something which I had never really thought about before. Thanks for allowing me to reflect with you on the process as it developed.

I also want to thank Mirko Noordegraaf. The few conversations we had at the start of this research improved my understanding of concepts that were fundamental in this research.

Jaap Uijlenbroek and Roel Bekker, thanks for your reflections on the various draft versions. Your experiences as Director-General and Secretary-General helped deepen my understanding. The same applies to Mark Frequin. Thanks for your questions and reflections with regard to the concept of unwritten rules and in particular my own relationship with the concept.

All the people who took part in this study, thanks! Without your input and trust in me as a researcher, I would not have succeeded.

Furthermore, I want to thank Bram Castelein, Loubna Zarrou and Marlies IJpma. For your contributions in conducting the interviews. And Bram and Loubna also for checking the final text and our discussions about the intermediate results. Carola van Zijl, thank you for checking the English translation of the summary.

Mirjam Sabir, thank you for your critical observation of the various coping strategies. Your experience as a civil servant and project leader at a policy department has helped me tremendously. The same goes for Jan van Dommelen and Boudewijn Nouwens, for reading and, where necessary, commenting on the first drafts of my thesis.

Cees WIllemse, I would like to thank you for reading the thesis and your enriching insights based on your management experience. And the same goes for Guy Noordink and Sandra Franssen.

Krispijn Beek, Saskia Böttcher, Teun Guijt and, at a later stage, Margo Stam, Jeannine de la Bursi and Sarah Lee Tilly. When I started this research at the end of 2009 and beginning of 2010, and later as well, I had very useful talks with you about the subject of this thesis. I want to thank you for that. Even though you worked at a different Ministry (Economic Affairs), it turned out that we were on the same page with regard to Open Multi-Stakeholder Policy Development, and it was a rewarding thing to know.

I also want to thanks all the students of the Open Masterclass From the Outside In. Over the years, your participation in the Masterclass and the questions you asked me have helped me enormously to improve my insights into Open Multi-Stakeholder Policy Development and unwritten rules.

In addition to the colleagues from the Learning and Development plan of the Ministries of Education, Culture and Science, Social Affairs and Employment and Health, Welfare and Sport, there is one group that cannot go unmentioned. A group of people with whom I have shared a flex-work spot for years. Next to Fouad, they include the 'cappuccino loves' of the Social Affairs and Employment Agency, as Social Affairs and Employment Agency colleague Liz Verhoef told me to call them: Nazish Jamal, Roos Garretsen, Louisa Afenich, Reyhan Cephe and, of course, Liz Verhoef.

I want to thank you all for the warm relationship over the years, for better and for worse. A relationship that managed to soften adversity and allowed me to put successes into perspective.

Joan van Aken, Marcel Weber and other members of the Design Science Research Group, I want to thank you all for the discussions about subject-oriented research. I have learned a lot from you. It has made me more aware that Design Science Research can offer a valuable contribution to policy trajectories in which a practical product (scan, benchmark, etc.) for a certain target group is one of the end results. And Marcel, thank you for your comments to my manuscript. It gave me confidence to know that you considered it a solid story.

Carine Bolijn, thanks for the energy and comments that reached me, thanks to you. Without it, I probably would not have succeeded.

Thanks to my mother and brothers. In particular Ruud. Your comments as a chemical scientist regarding the intermediate results and the end product were very valuable. Not to forget, your comments about similarities with multinational companies.

And Harrie Muermans, who deserves a place in my story. I want to express my immense gratitude for your hospitality. It gave me the time I needed to continue with this research.

Finally, a special thanks to Vivian Muermans. You are my sister and I never really thanked you for your extraordinary positive attitude, your never-ending faith in the final result and for encouraging me during our numerous conversations about this promotional research.

Summary

DEALING WITH UNWRITTEN RULES

Openness in Policy Development and related Coping Mechanisms in the Dutch Government

This research started with my fascination about the tension between vertical (government) and horizontal (governance). A lot of research has been done about this tension. However, the influence of unwritten rules on the degree of openness in policy development (horizontal) and how to deal with unwritten rules as a policy advisor, has never been a part of it.

This study presupposes that the tension vertical-horizontal should be considered as a tension that cannot be changed, but can be dealt with in a clever way. It requires in practice specific coping strategies, which are the core of this research.

The study focuses primarily on policy advisors working in the ministries of Social Affairs & Employment, Economy and Education, Culture & Science. These are ministries, which perform functions beyond the night watchman state. Kuiper (1992) says about the development of the government:

> *'The function of the government in the nineteenth century watchman state was limited to defense, maintaining law and order and taking care of the infrastructure (water management and traffic). All other tasks were, in principle, seen as private initiative of individuals and societal connections. During the twentieth century the welfare state developed, in which the government considers itself responsible for the collective social welfare for citizens'*
> (Kuiper, 1992: 137).

Statements in this study therefore mainly relate to the governmental domain of those 'other duties', although the impression is that the observed findings also relate to the traditional tasks of the night watchman state and other levels of government such as municipal. The empirical evidence however, says something about the way national governments operate that were part of the development of the welfare state.

Unwritten rules, as an expression of 'vertical', have been studied with a variant of the method of Scott-Morgan (1995). My research focuses on hard-unwritten rules that are an expression of elements that form the heart of an organizational culture. They are hard to change, not by staff nor by leadership.

The many concepts that are mentioned in the literature discussing 'horizontal policy development' have been reduced in the study to the variable 'openness' (participation level and degree of exclusion-inclusion).

The premise, that hard-unwritten rules impede openness, has been tested and confirmed. An important additional limitation is that this study focuses on coping strategies which help to get openness in policy development accepted. Not on holding a policy process open, once it has been started. The following conceptual model shows the relationship between the variables are as follows:

Scheme: Conceptual model with three core variables

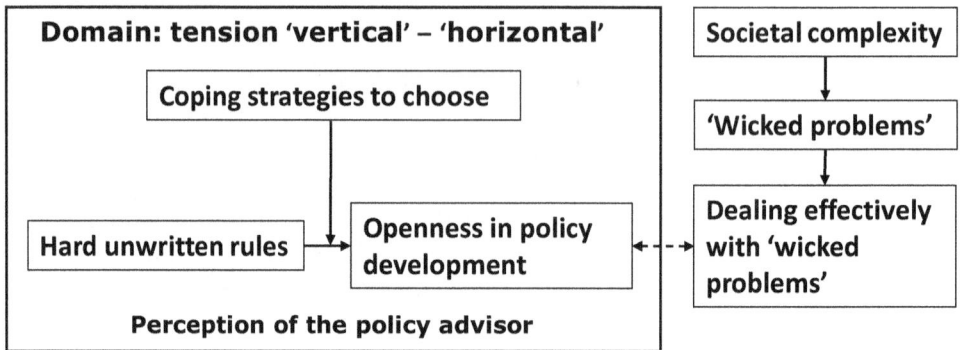

Domain: tension 'vertical' – 'horizontal'		Societal complexity
Coping strategies to choose		↓
		'Wicked problems'
		↓
Hard unwritten rules → Openness in policy development	←--→	Dealing effectively with 'wicked problems'
Perception of the policy advisor		

The added value of this research for the public administration theory and research methodology is:

- *Research method 1*: Adaptation of the method of unwritten rule analysis (Scott-Morgan, 1995). Scott-Morgan does not focus on causal relations (and explanations) between hard-unwritten rules and a dependent variable.
- *Research method 2*: Systematic skill analysis using a newly developed method based on work study / business perspective.
- *Research method 3*: Hard unwritten rules and skill analysis combined is a new way of analyzing organizational cultures.
- *Public administration theory 1*: With the analyzing of hard unwritten rules this thesis adds a new element to the existing literature of organizational cultures and the tension between vertically and horizontally.
- *Public administration theory 2*: A matrix and policy typology that shows you when a policy development approach is open or not.
- *Public administration theory 3*: The mismatch between hard unwritten rules and the degree of openness in dealing with wicked problems

- *Public administration theory 4*: Insight in coping strategies which can make openness possible in policy development, from the policy advisors perspective.

The following key terms are used in this study:

- *Openness*
  All concepts that have to do with horizontality are reduced to a single measurable theoretical variable in policy development: openness, which has been made operational by (1) the level of participation (how actors participate) and (2) the degree of exclusion – inclusion (who participate).
- *Open Multi-Stakeholder Policy Development (OMSPD)*
  A policy development process, containing a sufficient degree of openness, is called Open Multi-Stakeholder Policy Development.
  OMSPD is about harnessing the collective knowledge / intelligence in a network or helping it to improve its efficacy (Roobeek, 2014). This in function of the quality of the policy.
- *Hard written rules*
  Fundamental formal aspects that determine the design of an organization. Think of generic (bureaucratic) characteristics as mandates and standard procedures. Mandates for example, create a top-down, hierarchical stratification with corresponding accountability.
- *Unwritten rules*
  A resultant of written rules and the manner in which management behaves. The result is reflected in the way both, written rules and the way managers behave, are interpreted by people in everyday life (Scott-Morgan, 1995: 30).
- *Hard-unwritten rules*
  Collectively shared and recognized unwritten rules that are difficult to change. Unlike the definition of Scott-Morgan of unwritten rules, they cannot be influenced by the style of leadership.
- *Coping strategy*
  Principles out of which is handled (operating principles) and a structured set of actions for dealing with a problem or achieve a goal.

There are four research questions formulated. The starting point is in the literature about the relevance of openness in policy development and the relation to wicked problems. The first sub-research question is:

1. Why does tackling wicked problems require openness in policy development?

With the eyes of the present, the world in the 50s and 60s was more clearly and understandable for citizens, entrepreneurs and policy advisors.

But the world has changed in many ways. Internet, individualization, media, globalization, loss of information monopolies, etc. have created a different type of society with changing, often higher, and perhaps more erratic and contradictory demands on industry and government. The world has become more diverse and more pluralistic as described by many authors. Among others by Dijstelbloem (2008), with reference to Habermas (1985), who at that time already spoke of a new 'clutter 'and complexity in society. Or Frissen (2002) who used the words 'pluralism', 'variety' and 'fragmentation'.

This has led to a different playing field for public organizations which Noordegraaf (2004: 50) outlines with the following societal conditions: *'Diffuse knowledge, individuals thinking in their own way and powerful corporations.'* More and more players can, if they wish, influence governmental policy development. Habermas (1997) argued that the complexity of the society makes it necessary to reconsider the relationship between the government and the various 'publics' in society (Dijstelbloem, 2008: 156; Habermas, 1997). The revision of the relationship is reflected in policy development. In the solution of policy questions the mutual dependence between people and parties increases, in a context of decreasing validity and reliability of knowledge. Policy items get characteristics of 'wicked' problems (unstructured problems).

Dealing with wicked problems requires openness in policy development, says the WRR (2006) in its report 'Learning government: A Plea for Problem-Oriented Politics' (Dutch: De lerende overheid, een pleidooi voor probleemgeoriënteerde politiek). It is desirable to 'match' policy development with a social context where more actors have influence. That desire is in accordance with Ashby's Law of 'requisite variety' and Graves insights (see Annex 2). Ashby (1956) and Graves (1970) provide empirical evidence of this need to 'match'. Both of these scientists show that changes in the context, in the direction of increasing social complexity, require a change in organization paradigms and related methods of problem solving. Requisite variety is according to Hendriks:

> *'An inevitable feature of the decision-making system that has to deal with variety and complexity, with wicked problems which are disputed both empirical and normative. Intensive networking among decision makers*

*and between decision makers and the environments in which they oper-
ate, are considered here as right in functional learning policy and quality
in decision making'*
(Hendriks, 2012: 73).

DIAGRAM: OPEN MULTI STAKEHOLDER POLICY DEVELOPMENT (OMSPD)

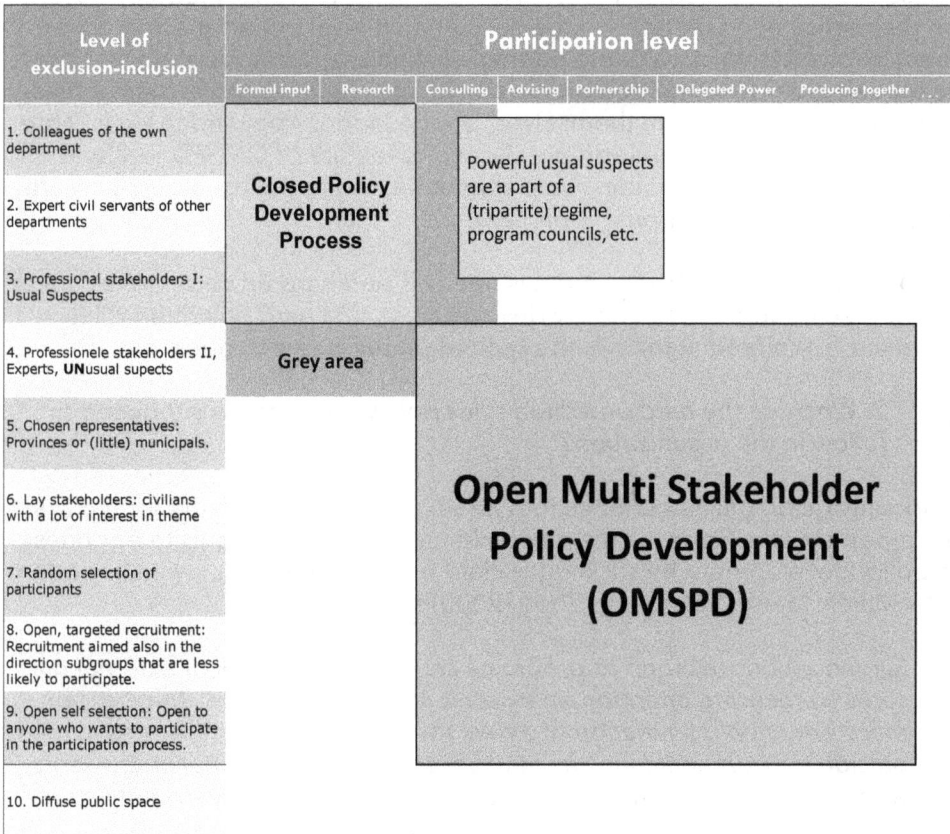

Level of exclusion-inclusion	Participation level						
	Formal input	Research	Consulting	Advising	Partnership	Delegated Power	Producing together
1. Colleagues of the own department	**Closed Policy Development Process**		Powerful usual suspects are a part of a (tripartite) regime, program councils, etc.				
2. Expert civil servants of other departments							
3. Professional stakeholders I: Usual Suspects							
4. Professionele stakeholders II, Experts, **UN**usual supects	**Grey area**						
5. Chosen representatives: Provinces or (little) municipals.		**Open Multi Stakeholder Policy Development (OMSPD)**					
6. Lay stakeholders: civilians with a lot of interest in theme							
7. Random selection of participants							
8. Open, targeted recruitment: Recruitment aimed also in the direction subgroups that are less likely to participate.							
9. Open self selection: Open to anyone who wants to participate in the participation process.							
10. Diffuse public space							

The required openness in policy development, and its necessity, receives
much attention in the literature. Mostly this is known as 'interactive policy
development'. Interactive policy development involves early engagement
and joint development of policies with a range of stakeholders such as citizens, businesses and interest groups (De Bruijn, Full Heuvelhof and In 't Veld,
2002). This study uses the term openness because also 'closeness' is made
visible in policy development. Openness is operationalized, in this study, in
two sub-variables:

- Level of participation (<u>how</u> are the actors involved?).
- Degree of exclusion-inclusion (<u>who</u> is involved and who is not involved).

This research has summarized policy processes, which are open under the header Open Multi Stakeholder Policy Development (OMSPD).

These are characterized by the level of consulting at the very least or beyond on the participation ladder. On the consultation level politicians and government involve actors as valuable partners. Politicians, administrators and policy officials are not committed on the consultation level to the results of these talks. They still can decide themselves. Up the ladder / beyond there is more space for joint policy development. A second feature of OMSPD is that at least professional stakeholders who do not belong to the usual suspects are part of the policy development process.

If openness in policy development is needed, and hard unwritten rules affect the degree of openness in policy development, first hard unwritten rules need to be explored. It follows the second partial research question:

> *2. What are the hard unwritten rules policy advisors are supposed to follow in the organization?*

If administration officials choose for OMSPD, the space available for it plays an important role. Does the inside of a Ministry allow the requisite openness in policy development for tackling wicked problems? Rules play an important role. March, Martin Schulz and Zhou (2000) state that:

> *'Organizations respond to problems and react to internal or external pressures by focusing attention on existing and potential rules. The creation, modification, or elimination of a rule, then, is a response to events in the outside environment (such as new government regulations) or to events within the organization (such as alterations in internal government structures)'*
> (March, Martin Schulz and Zhou, 2000: cover of their book).

They establish a link between internal rules and external pressure. Internal rules specify how problems should be addressed in a context (outside environment). Rules give officials therein direction. An important step in this research is the focus on a particular type of rules which are the unwritten rules. Unwritten rules are:

'A logical way of acting, given the explicit formal rules and behavior of the management of an organization. They show the true behavior of employees and arise from the way the leadership of an organization behaves - their actions and their statements - as well as the way employees interpret written rules that are enacted or maintained' (Scott-Morgan, 1995: 30).

An important step in this research is the focus on a specific set of unwritten rules. This study shows the existence of hard unwritten rules that are interpretations by employees of hard written rules that belong to the internal politics, but regardless of how leaders behaves. The latter means that these rules are difficult to change.

Hard unwritten rules have a relationship with what Zuboff and Maxmin (2002: 19), analogous to (Gersick, 1991: 19), call the 'deep structure' of an organization:

SCHEME: RULES AND HARD UNWRITTEN RULES

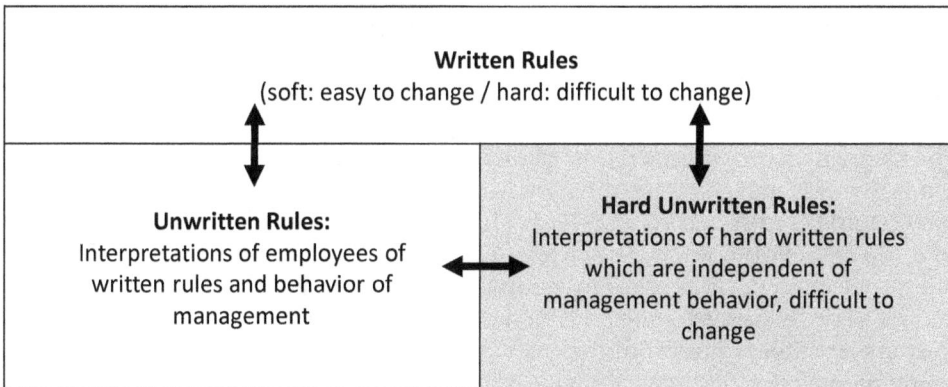

Written Rules (soft: easy to change / hard: difficult to change)	
Unwritten Rules: Interpretations of employees of written rules and behavior of management	**Hard Unwritten Rules:** Interpretations of hard written rules which are independent of management behavior, difficult to change

The reconstruction of (hard) unwritten rules appears to be a challenging task. They are not recorded on paper, but are embedded in the culture. That necessitates doing thorough in-depth interviews. These were held with policy advisors in the salary scales 11, 12 and 13 (multiple interviews of 1½ hours) in policy departments within the three selected ministries.

For this study, the method Scott-Morgan is slightly modified to obtain the necessary data, from the perception of respondents. Namely:

1. Eliciting what they saw as hard unwritten rules.
2. Their assessment of the impact of separate hard written rules on the level of participation.
3. Their estimation of the effect of specific hard unwritten rules on the degree of exclusion / inclusion.
4. Their explanations for the effect of specific hard unwritten rules on participation level and the degree of exclusion / inclusion.5. Coping strategies to create openness (how they thought that openness can be achieved).

To find the hard unwritten rules and the relationship with openness at least two interviews per interviewee were held. In the first interview, the unwritten rules were central. Then the focus was on finding unwritten rules in general and hard unwritten rules in particular. In the second interview, the relationship between what the respondent perceived as main hard unwritten rules and openness was explored. Also respondents have been asked how according to them a greater degree of openness could be realized looking to the unwritten rules they mentioned. Then, the result from the interviews in the first round were presented to other policy advisors; if they recognized these and/or if they thought something should be added. All respondents were asked whether they knew people who had actually managed to achieve openness in policy development. Of these new respondents skill analysis are made in phase II. This is also done through in-depth interviews.

The interviews provides a range of unwritten rules. Everyone puts them in their own way just because they are unwritten (see Chapter 7). Nevertheless, they could be reduced to a core of four hard unwritten rules by making use of three selection criteria. These are (1) simple counting how many times they are mentioned, (2) to answer invariably the question which unwritten rules can be seen as derivative from which other unwritten rules and (3) whether they are an interpretation of the main hard written rules of the Dutch government, namely the political primacy, ministerial responsibility, the rule of trust and the civil loyalty. The core of four hard unwritten rules that emerged in this study are:

1. *Remember, we have to serve the minister (and hierarchy)*
    This unwritten rule shows that the focus is mainly 'upwards'. A policy advisor must always remember that he is a servant, a representative of the minister. The unwritten rule expresses law-abidance and hierarchical loyalty.
2. *Be visible in the direction of the hierarchy*
    The essence of this unwritten rule is that, if you are not visible to the hierarchy, doubts may arise about what you're doing. Especially about your value to next-higher-ups in line and finally the minister.

3. *Get your schedule*
   Delaying your time schedule with respect to a dossier, especially one
   that is important politically, is missing the momentum that you can score
   visible.
   If a policy advisor misses that momentum, the minister may suffer in politics. As a result the hierarchy within the ministry has a problem and so
   does the relevant policy advisor.
4. *Your network is crucial (especially with the usual suspects)*
   Managing your network, especially with the usual suspects, is important.
   Without this network, it is difficult for a policy advisor to do his work because the usual suspects have political influence. Policy development
   takes much faster shape if you talk with recognized stakeholders and not
   with others.

Looking to these hard unwritten rules, Kupchan (2012: 62) is worth mentioning. He speaks of a mismatch between the increasing demand for good
governance and the ability of politicians and governments to deliver that.
In line with his insight, it was hypothesized that hard unwritten rules impede
openness. Then for the scientific theory, and for policy advisors in practice,
the following sub-research question becomes important:

> **3. *What is the mismatch between the required transparency in the poli-
> cy development and the internal hard unwritten?***

Hard unwritten rules make sure that not enough unusual suspects become
part of the policy development, in the eyes of the respondents. Open policy
development (unusual suspects involved) can yield results which the minister
does not want, or are against the policies the hierarchy wishes. Moreover,
they can demand external action and questions, which are not helpful to be
visible in a positive way internally. In addition the time schedule is often tight.
That is another reason to reduce the number of actors involved. The underlying idea is that more actors ask more time. So the hard unwritten rule 4, 'your
network is crucial', seems at first a call for openness, but respondents say that
it mainly means involvement of usual suspects. Particularly with politically
sensitive issues the usual suspects (level 3) are only involved. With parties
that are seen as 'More Exclusive' (other ministries and the usual suspects),
sometimes policy development is beyond the level of participation 'consult'
going to partnership.

TABLE: EFFECT OF HARD UNWRITTEN RULES ON THE DEGREE OF OPENNESS

HARD UNWRITTEN RULES	OPENNESS	
	LEVEL OF PARTICPA-TION	LEVEL OF INCLUSION / EXCLUSION
Remember, we have to serve the minister (and hierarchy)	Only consulting. In order to maintain control over the end result.	Only the usual suspects are of interest. They have political power which the ministers (and hierarchy) have to take into account.
Be visible in the direction of the hierarchy	Only consulting in order to maintain control over the end result, in line with the wishes of the minister and thus to score in a positive way.	A policy advisor is visible in a positive way to the hierarchy as he shows that the usual suspects have been consulted.
Get your schedule	Limit to mere consulting so you can more easily decide about the result yourself.	Only consultation of the main usual suspects. Under time pressure this is safe and responsible.
Your network is crucial (especially with the usual suspects)	With key persons / institutes that affect politics and the field, the policy advisor has to go beyond consulting (formal and informal). Then partnerships are formed.	Bad relationships, or insufficient coordination in the usual suspect network may pose political risks for the minister. Sometimes experts are consulted which are no part of the usual suspects for new ideas.

The research shows, as hypothesized, that there is a mismatch between hard unwritten rules and the necessary openness in policy development. This is in line with the many literature speaks of a voltage between vertical and horizontal.

By making a comparison with other literature, which unwritten rules of the past provides insight (among them Peter, 1985; Peter & Hull, 1969 Packard, 1963); Parkinson, 1955), are strong indications that the hard unwritten rules have not changed in recent decades. They therefore express what Mintzberg (2010) refers to as system inertia. An additional conclusion is supported by this research project. The hard unwritten rules can undermine moral thinking and acting of civil servants. The government has a social function in which not only a responsible weighing of interests must take place. The government must provide open and accurate policy information to the Parliament. Just as a municipal organization has to provide to the City Council. Closed policy networks operate more one-sided, and therefore less correct information can be more easily presented, at the expense of tackling wicked problems. Knowledge integrity is at stake.

Moreover, there is a tendency to hierarchical political-administrative nepotism. Luyendijk (2015) offers in-depth understanding for this problem. He makes a distinction between immorality and a-morality as he writes:

> 'A-moral does not mean bad or immoral. Amoral means that the terms 'good' and 'evil' do not appear in discussions. We do not look if a plan is morally wrong, but how much 'reputational damage' it carries' (Luyendijk, 2015: 88).

The unwritten rules sec. hinder not only openness but undermine the own moral and promote a-morality. This is because 'looking upwards in the hierarchy' and 'abiding' are the most important. So what to do when openness is required and unwritten rules impede this? What are coping strategies to deal with this mismatch in practice? Therefore the central research question is:

> *4. What coping strategies are available to policy advisors in order to deal with given hard unwritten rules and make openness in policy development possible?*

Ledeneva (2001) shows that (unwritten) rules can be followed, but also can be used for own purposes. A policy advisor can choose one or more coping strategies to enable openness in policy development while connecting with hard unwritten rules.

Coping strategies are analyzed in this study using a self-developed method based on a work analysis / scientific management perspective. A coping strategy (How-To) is a specific skill and in this study defined as:

'A structured set of actions, and underlying (operating) principles, for the benefit of dealing with a problem or achieving a goal.'

'Operating Principles', as part of a coping strategy, are underlying assumptions, often crucial dos and don'ts that are considered essential for the successful operation of a (coping) strategy. The skill analysis method for analyzing coping strategies, is a technique which is helpful in making implicit mental knowledge processes explicit. The underlying idea is an insight of Miller, Galanter & Pribam:

'Skills are normally tacit, but by careful analysis and investigation we are often able to discover the <u>principles</u> underlying them and to formulate <u>verbal instructions</u> for communicating the skills to someone else' (Miller, Galanter & Pribam, 1986: 143).

The author of this thesis has published the method in the Manual of Design Science Research (Dutch: Handboek Ontwerpgericht Wetenschappelijk Onderzoek), edited by Van Aken and Andriessen
(Van Aken and Andriessen, 2012; Herold, in Van Aken and Andriessen, 2012: 345-360).

This research shows that policy advisors have opportunities to make openness in policy development possible through dealing smart with the hard unwritten rules. This leads to an open policy paradox:

1. *Hard unwritten rules impede openness in policy development.*
2. *Policy advisors can respect and use the same rules to get openness accepted in the organization.*

There are 62 coping strategies found. They help, separately or combined, to respect internal hard unwritten rules' <u>and</u> make openness possible in policy development. The caveat here is that the coping strategies are as respondents have presented them. No formal α-test (test within the organization / group of developers) and β-test (multiple users in everyday life) have been done (Magnée, Cox, & Teunisse, 2015). The coping strategies found, can be divided into two main categories.
The first main category is the 'directly-influencing coping strategies'. A policy advisor analyses, as OMSBO is desirable in his eyes, how the hierarchical structure can be influenced without immediately thinking of colleagues or engaging third parties. Then the situation, and the hierarchy, is analyzed with the following question in mind: 'How can I get acceptance for openness from the Director-General (highest manager) as the key to the politics?'
The second main category is playing the game 'via the band'. In this case

other individuals are used. Doing so, a distinction can be made between 'via-the-internal-band and 'via-the-external-band'. A policy advisor can mobilize conscious internal colleagues and / or external stakeholders to exert pressure on the hierarchy and political leaders to ensure openness.

The research finally showed three operating principles, which provide an underlying attitude to perform (combinations of) the coping strategies successfully. For the detailed explanation of the operating principles (Chapter 8) the comments of the respondents have been used.

1. *Be (policy) entrepreneurial*
   Being (policy) entrepreneurial means to have guts as a policy officer, and to be stubborn and loyal at the same time.
   This means sticking one hand to an OMSPD approach. On the other hand, it means staying open to new insights. With in mind the ultimate goal of getting an OMSPD plan accepted, in which the relevant actors have been taken into consideration.
2. *Be convinced of the value of OMSBO*
   A policy advisor with a policy entrepreneurial attitude believes in his OMSPD product. That means being really convinced of the value of OMSPD. That it is valuable to involve parties other than the usual suspects, in policy development.
   Even though working for ministers (secretaries of state), and executing a 'grand policy, the importance of 'field reality' should be seen. Then a policy advisor finds implementation, which primarily represents the 'hands and feet' of the policy implementation, as important as the pre-shaping of a policy. That means for a policy advisor to develop an inherent curiosity about how policy works in practice.
3. *Be convinced of the importance of respectful long-term relationships*
   Being convinced of ones own networking qualities is important. A policy advisor has to build long term relationships with the policy playing field. The better a policy advisor succeeds in improving the quality of relationships with external parties, the less chance there is for political risk. This means that actors have to trust the policy advisor. Improving network relations also means that a policy advisor is respectful towards all parties including unusual suspects. This means demonstrating equality between policy and field, without distinction of rank and position, and when dealing with 'strange ducks in the bite'. The relational key question is: 'How are you as a person?' Networks is a people business.

Recommendations

Partly based on the findings of Acemoglu and Robinson (2012), it is recommended to embed OMSPD institutionally within the Dutch government. That could be realized, for example through the creation of an Institute for Participatory Democracy. That is a governmental organization that periodically checks the quality and professionalism of OMSPD within government organizations, e.g. by means of visitations based on an Appreciative Inquiry-thought (Cooperrider, 1987). This should be given a legal basis. If the hierarchy is asked to take care for openness, they too will ask their policy advisors to make this happen. The four hard unwritten rules are then in support for this form of policy process innovation.

Also Future Centers (FC) can offer a helping hand. At the Ministry of Social Affairs & Employment almost a decade such a Future Center has been active which made an effective contribution to the design and realization of more open approaches. Dvir, Schwartzenberg, Avni, Lettice & Webb (2006) write about Future Centers as follows:

> 'The first future center was conceptualized by Leif Edvinsson and established by Skandia, a Swedish insurance company, in 1997 (Edvinsson, 2003). Since then, additional public and commercial future centers have been created. Although little has been written on them in the literature, future centers are known in practice as facilitated working environments, which help organizations prepare for the future in a proactive, collaborative and systematic way. They are used to create and apply knowledge, develop practical innovations, bring citizens in closer contact with government and connect end-users with industry. They are used by government organizations for developing and testing citizen-centered, future-proof policy options with broad acceptance by stakeholders'
> (Dvir, Schwartzberg, Avni, Webb & Lettice, 2006: 111).

A Future Center helps with practical applications and is a knowledge center for openness in policy development. Castelein (2011) says:

> 'An FC offers organizations the option of working out of the box to work on important developments ... it provides for business as unusual that adds value to the primary process'
> (Castelein, 2011: 25).

With an FC challenging process questions for open policy development can be designed and executed. A policy recommendation is to consider the Ministerial Responsibility. Lubberding (1982) argues that this law provides the main guarantee to maintain the quality of democracy. However, this law also has to give this guarantee in increasing complex, changing social contexts.

The question in tackling wicked problems is: here the minister is responsible for? He is not only accountable for the results, but also for the (open) quality of policy development. The latter must, even if established stakeholders / usual suspects have trouble with it, explicitly included in the Ministerial Responsibility Act. Such a change in the law would create a huge momentum for openness in policy development.

Chapter 1

Introduction

Chapter 1   Introduction

This chapter shows how the author, based on his own fascination with the tension between vertical management and horizontal management, is working towards a question and conceptual model, via an exploration of concept in literature.

1.1   Origin of this research

The starting point of this research is curiosity about the functioning of government in relation to the outside world. Curiosity because I had learned to think in terms of 'bottom-up' and 'outside-in', while working in a vertical organization. Growing up in an entrepreneurial family and working in a medium-sized company, I assumed that 'you cannot make an effective product without knowing the market'. For me, market exploration was more than science and statistics. It also included with so-called '(un)usual suspects' and experiencing things in practice. Staying connected to where and what is 'really' happening. And now, I worked at a government organization where the own requirements took center stage. That caused friction, even in the eyes of the people inside the Ministry.

In 1998, I took part in a project at the Ministry for Social Affairs and Employment (SAE), which emerged from a departmental program called 'The windows open', the aim of which was to improve the quality of legislation by reinforcing the contacts with the outside world. One of the characteristic statements at the time was: 'No bad law will be passed here'. 'The windows open' was followed by a program 'Relationship management'.

A policy project in which I was involved later was aimed at evaluating a part of the then Social Security Act: Social Security for Self-Employed. This project used the so-called Klinkers Method, an interactive research-like method in which a large number of 'unusual suspects' were consulted (Klinkers, 2002). It was an in-depth exploration of the influence of the vertical organization on policy development trajectories, in particular the ones that involve an open, outside-in approach. I noticed a tendency on the part of the hierarchy to want to control the results of the open policy trajectories. I got the suspicion that there is a tension between open policy approaches on the one hand, and the way the policy directions of the Ministries normally operate. The Klinkers method turned out to have added value in the approach of the social security problem, a 'wicked problem', in which an increasing number of actors play a role in a context of diminishing knowledge certainty. Later again, I was involved in facilitating stakeholders in the design and development of policy trajectories. In many cases, so-called Group Decision Rooms were used more than 40 times per year. In a Group Decision Room (GDR), participants answer questions on a laptop. The answers of all the participants are displayed anonymously on their own laptops and on a big screen, allowing the participants to discuss the results and conduct electronic voting rounds about the input.

The above-mentioned experienced provided be a deeper insight into what civil servants consider to be relevant and into the 'do's and don'ts' of policy development, and in dealing with external stakeholders with political influence. They are rarely excluded from the process.

In addition, for the Learning and Development Square of the Ministries of Education, Culture and Science (ECS), Social Affairs and Employment (SAE) and Health, Welfare and Sport (HWS), I developed the Open Masterclass Outside In, which provided an overview of open policy development approaches. Since 2005, the masterclass is organized annually. One of the elements is the discussion of the organizational culture and its effect on openness, with the participants sharing comments on do's and don'ts like: *"Max, a good method, but my boss will not allow me to use it".* The answer to the question 'why not' was often: *"There's a chance it could yield information that is unpalatable to the line' or 'image it will produce a result that the Minister doesn't like'.* When the answer *'the boss will not allow it'* was followed up, the response was always *'That is how things are done here'.*

That revealed a paradox. When a government is faced with complex issues involving a variety of actors, knowledge is not unambiguous (so-called 'wicked problems') *and* open policy development is desirable, it frequently does not fit the established departmental 'policy production processes'. I kept being fascinated by the question '<u>How</u> does it work <u>exactly</u>?' What does that mean for open processes and how should civil servants deal with the paradox between open policy development and 'that's how it is done here'? With regard to 'that's how it is done here', this research focuses on a specific category of so-called unwritten rules, namely hard unwritten rules, which are the heart of the organizational culture. They are hard to change, either by employees or by the leadership.

The core reasoning underlying this research can be summarized in three hypotheses that need to be examined:

1. <u>Openness</u> is needed in policy development to solve 'wicked problems'; these are problems in which increasing numbers of actors play a role and where there is diminished knowledge certainty.
2. <u>Hard unwritten rules</u> restrict <u>openness</u> in policy development.
3. There are <u>coping strategies</u> (How-to's) that civil servants can use, if they want, to facilitate openness.

These three hypotheses have been translated to the following research (sub) questions:

1. Why does the approach to 'wicked problems' require open policy development?
2. What are the hard unwritten rules that civil servants are expected to observe within their own organization?
3. What discrepancy is there between the required openness in policy development and those internal hard unwritten rules?

The core concepts of 'unwritten rules', 'openness' and 'coping strategies' are explored and defined as a theoretical framework in chapters three through five. The 'why' of open policy development, the need for it, is answered on the basis of a literature review in chapter two.

The hard unwritten rules that civil servants are expected to observe within their own organization and the discrepancy with required openness in policy development are examined empirically using a variation of the method published by Scott-Morgan (1995), which makes it possible to detect unwritten rules and examine the effect they have on the level of openness. To that end, openness needed to be made measurable. In chapter seven, the effect of the hard unwritten rules we detected on the level of openness is described.

Finally, at the core of this research, we detected and examined coping strategies that answer the question as to how a civil servant can shape open policy development in the face of hard unwritten rules. The central research question, which is answered in chapter eight, is:

> Which coping strategies are available to civil servants to deal with hard unwritten rules and allow for openness in policy development?

By identifying hard unwritten rules, the aim of this study is to add a new element to scientific literature about organizational culture and the tension between vertical and horizontal management. The coping strategies designed to make openness in policy development possible, given the hard unwritten rules, are a second addition to managerial theory formation.

A third addition is the more exact definition of the concept of openness: when can we talk of openness and when can we not?

The aim of this study is also to what the coping strategies are for civil servants wanting to apply open policy development, while recognizing and using the hard unwritten rules to match the level of openness to unstructured 'wicked' problems, the ultimate goal being to apply open policy development where it should be, but is not applied due to the aforementioned tension, and thus reduce a discrepancy in terms of (problem-solving) policy development and the type of policy issue.

1.2   Explorations in literature I: the tension between vertical – horizontal

In literature, The abovementioned paradox between 'that's how it's done here' and open policy development is called the tension between vertical and horizontal, or between 'government' and 'governance'(Stoker, 1998, and others). In addition, governance is related to values like integrity, transparency, legitimacy, etc. (De Graaf & Huberts, 2011). To accentuate the coherence with horizontal approaches, I want to introduce the term knowledge integrity.

Box: Knowledge integrity
In the future, policy development approaches that are too closed (with limited interactivity) can be designated as integrity transgression. Karssing & Spoor (2010) describe the development of thinking about integrity in three phases. With integrity 1.0, the emphasis is above all on fraud and corruption. Higher civil servants are expected to be loyal to the wishes of and carry out the rules that are devised by their political masters. With integrity 2.0, attention shifts to the administrator who has accepted responsibility and has to be willing to be held accountable. He has to provide open information and show that he is operating independently. There is a lot of attention to issues like conflicts of interest and procurement, confidential information, accepting gifts, administrative expenses, declarations, credit cards (behavior top). In addition, integrity is included in standard reports. Integrity 3.0 transcends things like open information and independence, and includes questions like 'Am I doing my job well?' and 'Am I a good civil servant?' In concrete terms, it also includes open approaches to developing policy. How and from whom has the policy information collected? How were considerations made? In a general sense: which methods and techniques are used with which issues and from what basic attitude?

Should integrity 3.0 become more important, the expectation is that policy development methods that are more closed will be marked as approaches in which there may be doubt about a responsible collection of information. For instance, has the collection of information been too one-sided, by primarily only talking with the usual suspects, to allow for a balanced consideration of interests? Integrity 3.0 then becomes knowledge integrity, which connects to the concept of knowledge democracy used by In 't Veld (2010)

and thinking about 'democratic validity' and the extent to which all the rele-
vant actors have been involved in the research process
(De Bruijn & Westerhuis, 2013: 41, Anderson & Herr, 1999: 16).

The line of reasoning is that 'wicked problems' demand a horizontal and open approach to policy development (chapter 2), while civil servants are faced with a vertical, hierarchical organization that has a tendency to solve problems in a closed way.
This creates tension and discrepancy between 'that which requires a changed context' versus 'that which a government offers' in terms of open prob-lem-solving approaches. A *"discrepancy between an increasing demand for 'good governance' and the ability of politicians and governments to provide it"* (Kupchan, 2012: 62). Becoming stuck in that discrepancy can have conse-quences. Graves (1970, 1974) states that a system that does not adapt to an increasing environmental complexity, in terms of the way it thinks and deals with issues, risks succumbing to entropy. Entropy is a measurement of 'dis-order'. Existing thoughts and actions create such chaos that a fundamentally different approach is required. Failure to adopt that different approach will result in the death of the system. If a changing context and the associated issues require more open approaches, that requires a different frame of mind of problem-solving principles with associated skills. In appendix 2, we focus on the relationship between 'context – problem-solving methods – frame of mind'.

Many studies describe the tension between 'vertical versus horizontal' in an abstract sense and outline how bureaucracies should develop into network organizations. The underlying assumption is that the tension will be resolved once government bureaucracies make such a transition. But we are not there yet. For now, the tension is a given. Transitions face tenacious obstacles. Zuboff & Maxim (2002: 19) see a 'deep structure' that, as they argue, helps organizations offer resistance to change. They refer to Gersick, who states: *"It generates a <u>strong inertia</u>, first to prevent the system from generating alter-natives outside its own boundaries, then to pull any deviations that do occur back into line"* (Zuboff & Maxim, 2002: 19; Gersick, 1991: 19). That is why a literature survey about transitions of bureaucracies lies outside the scope of the research domain 'tension vertical – horizontal'. For those who are interest-ed, it is include in appendix 1.

Other studies about the tension between vertical – horizontal focuses on political and civil administration. Most of the work, however, including that in coordination with the outside world, is done by civil servants, who, with their files and policy work, are at the center of the tension described above. It is interesting to examine who, in particular, civil servants involved in policy deal with the operations of vertically functioning government organizations and the desire to adopt a more horizontal approach in policy development. In this thesis, verticality is approached from bureaucratic characteristics like the ones described by Rainey (2009: 29):

- An authority hierarchy with supervision from higher over lower ranks.
- Demarcate (legal) areas of responsibility through rules that officially lay down

rules and divide them among fixed positions and departments. Diefenbach & Todnem (2012) make an additional observation with regard to the continuity of bureaucratic characteristics in organizations:

> *"Despite the constant introduction and re-introduction of 'new' business concepts and change rhetorics, key principles and mechanisms of management and organization do not change: the hierarchical order of social relationships, the dominance of superiors, their prerogatives and privileges as well as the well-functioning, obedience and tight control of subordinates via all sorts of physical and virtual bureaucratic means continue whatever the actual change initiative (seemingly) suggests"* (Diefenback & Todnem, 2012: 4).

'Key principles' can be translated into hard written rules that generate hard unwritten rules, the core of 'that's how we do things here'.

> 'Key principles' translated into hard written rules within the national government are 'political primacy', 'ministerial responsibility', 'the confidence rule' and 'official loyalty'
> (Nieuwenkamp, 2001).

Horizontality is about involving actors in policy development and has been translated into one theoretical variable that needs to be made measurable: openness. Openness is about 'participation level' (how actors are involved) and the 'level of exclusion-inclusion' (who is and is not involved). Policy development that is sufficiently open is called Open Multi Stakeholder Policy Development (OMSPD). What is meant by 'sufficiently open' is discussed later. Analogous to Roobeek (2014), it concerns the ambition to utilize collective knowledge/intelligence in networks and/or let it do its job as a network in service of the quality of policy.

1.3 Explorations in literature II: unwritten rule – analysis

The focus on 'that's how it's done here' crossed another personal experience line, in that I had also been interested in thinking about organizational cultures for many years. To make the idea of 'that's how it's done here' concrete, culture analysis methods that describe profiles or identify general cultural characteristics are less suitable. Profiling methods fail to capture the culture of an organization accurately in the words, experiences and decisions of the employees. The method proposed by Scott-Morgan (1995), on the other hand, is able to do just that and makes it possible to map specific unwritten rules from the perception of civil servants themselves, in particular unwritten rules that determine their decisions. Initial practical experiences with the method of Scott-Morgan were collected in 2006, together with a colleague who currently is working at the Ministry of Economic Affairs, during a study into the organizational culture of a department within a ministry. And further in 2011, during a study into unwritten rules and policy quality at the Ministry of ECS. Scott-Morgan (1993: 1) gives the following example of an unwritten rule:

> 'As an Englishman, I had this lesson brought forcibly home the first time I tried driving a car in Boston. The driver's manual says that when you get to a rotary the cars already on the rotary have the right of way. I'm supposed to slow down, wait my turn, and merge courteously with the flow of traffic. I tried that, and I never got onto the rotary. The unwritten rule of the road in Boston says that when entering a rotary, you avoid eye contact and speed up. You don't wait your turn, because it's nobody's turn. And you try to shoot ahead of the cars already on the rotary before they can either shoot ahead of you or crash into you. So if I want to be pragmatic and get onto that rotary, I need to understand the unwritten rules.'

A written rule like 'the cars already on the rotary have the right of way' in everyday traffic leads to the following unwritten rule:

> 'You avoid eye contact and speed up. You don't wait your turn, because it's nobody's turn. And you try to shoot ahead of the cars already on the rotary before they can either shoot ahead of you or crash into you.' (Scott-Morgan, 1993: 1).

According to Scott-Morgan (1993: 1), organizations have their own unwritten rules:

> 'We all know that corporations also have unwritten rules. And if you're behind the wheel of a corporation, it pays to understand its unwritten rules.

> *Knowing the Rules of the Game is another way to be street smart about your business. In fact, every CEO I've met has had an intuitive grasp of the unwritten rules of his or her organization. You can't get to the top without understanding the unwritten rules.'*

March (2010) calls unwritten rules 'informal rules' and describes their relationship with written rules as follows:

> *'Routines, procedures, conventions, roles, strategies, organizational forms, and technologies around which political activity is constructed. We also mean the believes, codes, paradigms, cultures, and knowledge that surround, support, elaborate and contradicts those roles and routines ......* Rules are codified to some extent but the codification is often incomplete.'*
> (March, 2010: 22).

Scott-Morgan (1993: 33) gives an example of an unwritten organizational rule that follows from a written rule. *The written rule is 'to become a top manager, you need to have experience in various positions within the company (product development requires a helicopter view'.* An unwritten rule that can follow from this is: *'To get to the top, you need to change jobs as often as you can: go job-hopping'.*

According to Scott-Morgan (1995), unwritten rules match the internal politics of an organization and often start with the way leadership behaves. Unwritten rules are the result of written rules *and* the way leadership behaves. The result is expresses itself in the way in which the rules that an organization's management devises are interpreted and implemented by employees in everyday practice (Scott-Morgan, 1995: 30).

There is something to be said against this perspective. Employees make comments like *'Ministers are passing ships'*, that refer to unwritten rules that, contrary to what Scott-Morgan (1995) claims, do not depend on what management does. These unwritten rules are robust and underlying. Managers have no influence on them. It was in this direction that remarks at a ministerial culture change process pointed, like: *'We have discussed the items of the culture agenda, now we can get back to work'.* In addition, it can be observed that, if one manager prefers behavior A, and the next manager prefers behavior B, people changed their behavior accordingly. *'Do what your manager wants'* is a basic unwritten rule that does not depend on the person in charge. This is in line with a comment found in literature that points to a similar fundamental (hard) unwritten rule:

'The President does not want 'yes men' and 'yes women' around him. When he says no, we all say no"

Statement from Elisabeth Dole, assistant of President Ronald Reagan (Peter, 1985: 77).

Many studies confirm the suspicion of (deeper) unwritten rules, as shown in the literature overview presented below about (1) departmental cultures, (2) top management and (3) civil servants implementing policies.

Re 1. Practical characteristics Dutch departmental cultures

Relationship politics – media – civil service

In the 'Nieuwspoort Code', Luydendijk (2010) describes an interesting aspect of political-administrative culture, namely the existence of an informal code or unwritten rule about how journalists, Members of Parliament, lobbyists and (top) civil servants meet and share information.

In 't Veld (2010) states that the disappearance of dominant and consistent ideologies turns political parties into economic actors, whose main aim is to get as many votes as possible at the next elections, making personalities rather than programs the main distinguishing feature of the political party. Personalities that are 'sold' via the mass media. The media need politicians for a news production that gives them a competitive edge.

Structural mutual dependence between politicians and media, as In 't Veld (2010) indicates, has thus become a feature of our society.

Teisman (2005) points to the reward and assessment regimes in the public domain, including politicians being rewarded for the share they manage to acquire of the state's treasury in favor of the administrative organization. The number of new rules that a cabinet member manages to pass through Parliament also plays a role in the competition with other Ministries. As Teisman (2005) indicates, cabinet members are rewarded for shielding and divisive behavior. The studies suspect the existence of unwritten rules (without using that term) in the political circuit. Unwritten rules for civil servants and the relationship with openness are not described.

The inside: the practice of Dutch cultures

Literature on Dutch departmental cultures describes their practical character-istics (Hakvoort & Heer, 1994; Veenswijk, 1996). Additional studies focus on the internal processes inside specific Ministries. Metze (2010) writes about the state of affairs inside Department of Waterways and Public Works, which is part of the Ministry of Infrastructure and Environment. Other authors use the term 'office politics', a term that can be used to describe a certain type of unwritten rules that involve the interests of Ministries. Korsten (1999: 5), refer-ring to Rosenthal, Geveke & In 't Veld (1994: 309), describes them as follows:

> *'If services within a government organization surrounding a policy issue or complex compete with each other from different positions and inter-ests, and also have a different perception of an issue and may possible desire a different direction for solutions, the term office politics is some-times used. Office politics involves the competition of interests in the civil service machine, which is expressed in the political processes and behav-iors initiated by civil servants and institutions'.*

Re 2. Top Management

The way Dutch top civil servants operate

There are culture studies into the way Dutch top civil servants operate. Nieuwenkamp (2001) examined the relationship between ministers and top civil servants at Ministries, and the associated sensitivities. He started from certain standards of the democratic state, to wit 'political primacy', 'ministerial responsibility', the 'rule of trust' and 'civil loyalty'. He also mentions Article 125a of the Civil Service Act, which states:

> *'... that the execution of the right of freedom of speech must not lead to a situation whereby a good execution of his tasks or the proper functioning of the public service, insofar as related to the execution of his tasks, would not in all reason be ensured'*
> (Nieuwenkamp 2001: 111).

Nieuwenkamp (2001: 112) describes the tension between these standards and the actual situation and refers to Noordegraaf (2000: 198), who encountered top managers who see it as their duty to protect the Minister from negative media exposure, and to that end facilitating positive media exposure to create an image of success.

Noordegraaf (2000, 2004) examined managers based on the following questions:

- *How do public managers allocate attention (actor attendance, actor attention, issue attention) amidst ambiguity?*
- *What rules to they follow?*
- *What mental maps do they have?*
  (Noordegraaf, 2000: 259)

Noordegraaf (2000: 259) draws the conclusion that public managers manage 'issue flows' in political arenas, observing that there are 'major problems' with different interpretations. These interpretations cannot be prioritized on the basis of objective facts. There is a *'conceptual struggle over labels'.*

Furthermore, he observed that the work of the managers is led from meetings and paper and that their work is driven by *'politics, incidents and publicity'.* Managing *issues* in an ambiguous context takes place through the production of written or spoken texts (Noordegraaf, 2000: 261-263).

Management styles and horizontal (open) approaches

Management styles have been studied in relation to interactive (open) approaches. Within the framework of this thesis, a management style can be seen, in accordance with the insights of Pröpper & Steenbeek (1999), as the way in which management is given shape in terms of the level of participation (or: openness). Management styles are a *'continuum from interactive to non-interactive styles'* (Klok, 2009). The authors themselves have the following to say:

> *'Interactive policy (or: horizontal approaches) can be seen as a certain style of management, a way in which government interacts with target groups of policy and with possible (other) initiators'*
> (Klok, 2009; Pröpper and Steenbeek, 1999: 50).

Edelenbos, Teisman & Reudink (2003), based on Pröpper & Steenbeek (1999: 52-53), mention four management styles:

1. Facilitating: Management provides support (time, money, expertise, material resources).
2. Cooperative: Management works together with other parties on the basis of equality.
3. Delegating: Management authorizes participants to make decisions or implement policy within certain parameters.

4.   Participation: Management openly asks for advice, with room for discussion and input. Participants can indicate their own problem definition and proposed solution.

Whereas Pröpper & Steenbeek (1999) emphasize management and its style with regard to the organization and external actors, Tops places management within a broader coalition of actors, and speaks of a regime, with reference to the regime theory proposed by Stone (1989). A regime is:

> 'A working coalition of political and non-political actors between whom there is a hierarchical relationship'
> (Tops, 2007: 8; Stone, 1989).

Actors are seen as:

> 'Part of a complex network that is characterized by fragmentation, a lack of consensus and mutual dependence'
> (Tops, 2007: 22).

A regime has the following characteristics:

> 'informal (there is no hierarchical structure), relatively stable and long-lasting (regime partners try to organize long-term relationships and are not focused solely on short-term gains), a coalition of actors (who maintain their autonomy, while recognizing their mutual dependence) with parties that usually have an institutional basis (they have their own domain of 'authority').
> (Tops, 2004: 5)

In this theory, the organization of management capacity is not presupposed, but 'has to be created and maintained' (Tops, 2007: 23).

Actors can include professional organizations with which strong ties are maintained in policy development, professional organizations that are somewhat further removed from policy and, of course, citizens themselves, for whom there is little attention in classic regime theory (Tops, 2007: 27). However, according to Tops (2007: 28), referring to Bang (2002a, 2002b), public organizations:

> '... are no longer able to manage and control their environment with only their own resources. They are increasingly dependent on the everyday knowledge and the direct involvement of citizens'
> (Tops, 2007: 28; Bang, 2002a, 2002b).

An 'executive-centered' regime manages on the basis of authority, a 'network-centered' regime on the basis of policy networks (Tops, 2007: 26). Tops (2007) draws a second distinction on the basis of 'policy management' and 'frontline management', which connects to the discussions about horizontal approaches. Policy management is political management, aimed at control and accountability. There is a design logic. Frontline management is based on 'the work itself', the 'primary process' or the 'public' work floor. Here, there is an action logic (Tops, 2007: 36). Studies on management styles shed additional light on what managers can do to stimulate openness in policy development, on 'managing with open approaches'.

Re 3. Executive civil servants

For management by executive civil servants, De Jong et al. (2008) refer to studies by Crozier (1964) and Lipsky (1984), which show how executive civil servants, at the counter or behand the front door, implement policy in everyday practice. Crozier (1964) shows that rules and guidelines that are meant to manage individual civil servants, become typical behavioral strategies.

'Ritualism' is a behavioral strategy in which civil servants impose rules and guidelines on reality to make it fit the boundaries of the rules (which are not subject to discussion). *'Retreatism'* is a behavioral strategy in which civil servants shut off the outside world (De Jong et al., 2008; Crozier, 1961). *'Profiling'* is a behavioral strategy to categorize people quickly into rules and target groups as seen from the civil servant's own service with associated rules. *'Creaming'* is selecting customers with whom one can score quickly and easily (De Jong et al., 2008; Lipsky, 1984).

Looking at the literature review presented above, it is striking to see that a mix of unwritten rules, codes and coping (behavioral) strategies are used interchangeably, making it impossible to answer the question as to which hard unwritten rules apply to civil servants in their daily work, or what their effect is on (the level) of openness in policy development civil servants choose.

1.4 Explorations in literature III: openness

Question three focuses on the discrepancy between the required openness in policy development and the internal hard unwritten rules. The underlying hypothesis is that hard unwritten rules restrict openness in policy development. To be able to examine that, we have to be able to measure openness in concrete terms. When can we speak of openness and when not?

In studies about open processes, there are three themes that regularly appear:

- How are actors involved, expressed in participation levels.
- Who is (and is not) involved in policy development.
- The transparency of the policy development process itself.

With regard to 'how actors are involved', various participation ladders have been developed by Arnstein (1969), Schiphorst (Veen, 2005) and Edelenbos (2005b). A combination of these ladders results in the participation ladder presented below, which was used as ordinal measuring tool in this study. An expanded version, with the various levels of three participation ladders juxtaposed, is included in the appendix. Table 1 contains all the levels that are mentioned in the three participation ladders. To make the question 'who is involved' measurable, the included-excluded scale by Fung (2006) provides enough direction. That scale is used in this study as a second measurement for openness. We diverged slightly from Fung and have described levels 3, 4 and 5 from a departmental perception. See table 2.

With the axes 'how' and 'who', openness in policy development can be measured concretely. In closed policy development, Ministries themselves decide what happens (level of actor participation), involving only the usual suspects (who). The result is an exclusive network.

Policy development is open when it meets two criteria in at least one of the policy development phases (preferably as early as possible):

- On the participation ladder, the consultation level (4) or higher.
- On the inclusive-exclusive scale, level 4 (professional stakeholders, Unusual suspects) or higher.

Literature mentions transparency of policy development as a third important issue regarding open policy development. Transparency has not been included as a research variable, based on the assumption that a policy development that is open in terms of 'how' and 'who' is automatically transparent. The higher the level of equality between actors in the policy development, the clearer the set-up of the process itself will be to the parties involved and how they can influence the process and content.

Literature talks about involving unusual suspects at an early stage in open policy development. It is a hard condition for an open approach. That implies that these actors 'are allowed' to participate in policy development (broad inclusion). This presupposition is not self-evident in open policy development.

TABLE 1: OVERALL PARTICIPATION LADDER: PARTICIPATION LEVELS AND DESCRIPTIONS

Participation level		Descriptions
1	Informing	Politicians and government set the decision-making agenda and inform the parties involved. No further communication.
2	Formal input	At the end of the policy process, stakeholders can respond to proposed policy decisions. Decision-makers display try to 'convert'.
3	Research	Especially through questionnaires, neighborhood/actor meetings and public hearings.
4	Consultation	Politicians and government set policy agenda, but consult parties involved in policy development. Politicians are not committed to outcomes talks.
5	Advice	Politicians and government in principle determine policy agenda, but allow parties involved to point out problems and formulate policy solutions. Politicians are in principle committed to results of the policy development, but can deviate when making decisions.
6	Partnership	Actors and civil servants shape part of or overall policy together. Actors are part of program councils, planning committees and processes. Ground rules are laid out and observed.
7	Delegated power	Actors involved hold the main cards to make the policy program successful. In case of disagreements, politicians and government start a negotiation process.
8	Joint production	Within a framework, the policy-maker gives responsibility for both the development process and the content of policy/plans to external stakeholders.
9	Joint decisions	Politicians and government leave policy development and decision-making to stakeholders. Politicians accept proposed policy solutions as binding.
10	Free market	No intervention from government.

TABLE 2: EXCLUSIVE-INCLUSIVE (AFTER FUNG, 2006).

Exclusive Inclusive	Who to involve in policy development?
More ex-clusive	1. Fellow civil servants of one's own Ministry.
	2. Experts from other ministries.
	3. Professional stakeholders I: *Usual suspects (officially recognized stakeholders).*
	4. Professional stakeholders II: *Experts who are not aiming the ministries' usual suspects.*
	5. Elected representatives: *Political representatives of province and small municipalities.*
	6. Lay stakeholders: *Unpaid citizens with a deep interest in a certain policy area.*
	7. Random selection of participants.
	8. Open, focused selection: *Focused selection, including subgroups who have a lower tendency to participate.*
	9. Open self-selection: *Open to anyone who wants to take part in the participation process.*
More in-clusive	10. Diffuse public space: *mass media, organizations not directly involved in policy, informal meetings.*

Literature on openness presupposes a relationship between the level of openness and integrity. In the future, overly closed policy development approaches can possibly be designated as lacking integrity, because a closed approach makes the information to be provided one-sided and incomplete. The insights provided in this thesis regarding open policy development are aimed at preventing this one-sidedness and incompleteness.

1.5   Explorations in literature IV: coping strategies

As mentioned, literature provides no insight into what civil servants do to realize open approaches in policy developments involving 'wicked problems', given the (hard) unwritten rules under which they have to operate.
This question became relevant for me via a third area of personal experience. As an organizational consultant, I was involved in knowledge management and knowledge processes, in particular the question: 'How can implicit knowledge be made explicit?' A systematic analytical technique of the **mental knowledge processes** of civil servants (in other words: coping strategies) was lacking. I have designed a skill analysis method based on the managerial labor analysis, which uses the method proposed by Gilbreth (1917), who combined the analysis of physical/manual processes with the organization of the workplace and Taylor's stopwatch. Gilbreth introduced the (micro-) movement analysis, with which hand movements and the order in which they occur can be recorded in detail. That made it possible to eliminate inefficient and redundant movements and increase the efficiency in physical actions.
My skill analysis method is based on an insight by Miller, Galanter & Pribam, which emphasizes making implicit knowledge explicit:

> *'Skills are normally tacit, but by careful analysis and investigation we are often able to discover the principles underlying them and to formulate verbal instructions for communicating the skills to someone else'* (Miller, Galanter & Pribam, 1986: 143).

They conducted psychological research and argued (as an axiom) that behavior is organized hierarchically and can be divided into a plan that contains a goal and a hierarchy and order of (sets of) instructions. In it (or below it) are strategies and tactics. That entirety is part of the mental image or reality of a person carrying out a certain action (Miller, Galanter & Pribam, 1986: 17-19). A concrete execution of a plan possesses a TOTE (Test-Operate-Test-Exit), a cybernetic mechanism whereby each action (operate) and the feedback (test) is analyzed to get closer (exit) to the desired goal (Miller, Galanter & Pribam: 1986: 27),

Analogous to Gilbreth, and using TOTE, mental skill knowledge can be made explicit. The method has been published (Herold, in Van Aken and Andriessen (eds.), 2012: 345-360). See also Chapter 5 of this thesis[1].

1.6   Central research question and sub-questions

Surrounding the three central variables of this research, to wit hard unwritten rules (vertical), openness (horizontal) and coping strategies (handling), three sub-questions and a central research question were formulated. The sub-questions are:

1.   *Why does the approach to 'wicked problems' require open policy development?*
2.   *What are the hard unwritten rules that civil servants are expected to follow in their own organization?*
3.   *What discrepancy is there between the required openness in policy development and the internal hard unwritten rules?*

The central research question is:

What <u>coping strategies</u> are available to civil servants to deal with <u>unwritten rules</u> and allow for <u>openness</u> in policy development?

The three central variables have been defined as follows:

* *Openness*
  Concepts that have to do with horizontality have been reduced to one theoretical variable to be made measurable in policy development itself: openness. This has been operationalized via the participation level (<u>how</u> actors participate) *and* the level of exclusion – inclusion (<u>who</u> participate).
* *Hard unwritten rules*
  Collectively shared and recognized rules in an organization that are hard to change. They can be seen as interpretations of fundamental written rules by employees and, contrary to the definition of Scott-Morgan, are not in part determined by leadership style.
* *Coping strategies*
  Principles on the basis of which people operate (operational principles) *and* associated structured sets of actions designed for dealing with a problem or achieving a goal.

The words *'allow for'* in the central research question signify: <u>getting</u> openness accepted in policy development by the vertical line. For the conceptual model, see the diagram.

---

[1] Prior to this research, the skill analysis method was demonstrated tot wo scientists, who considered the interview protocol useful and valid for the analysis of coping strategies.

DIAGRAM 1: CONCEPTUAL MODEL WITH THREE CORE VARIABLES

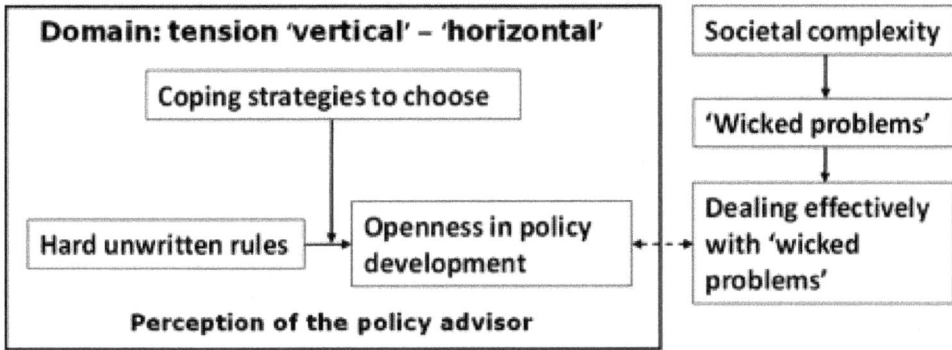

```
┌──────────────────────────────────────────────┐   ┌──────────────────────┐
│ Domain: tension 'vertical' – 'horizontal'     │   │ Societal complexity  │
│                                               │   └──────────┬───────────┘
│   ┌──────────────────────────────┐            │              │
│   │ Coping strategies to choose  │            │   ┌──────────▼───────────┐
│   └──────────────┬───────────────┘            │   │ 'Wicked problems'    │
│                  │                            │   └──────────┬───────────┘
│                  │                            │              │
│ ┌───────────────────┐  ┌───────────────────┐  │   ┌──────────▼───────────┐
│ │ Hard unwritten    │─▶│ Openness in policy│◀─┼─▶│ Dealing effectively  │
│ │ rules             │  │ development       │  │   │ with 'wicked         │
│ └───────────────────┘  └───────────────────┘  │   │ problems'            │
│                                               │   └──────────────────────┘
│        Perception of the policy advisor       │
└──────────────────────────────────────────────┘
```

1.7   Structure of the thesis

In the next chapter, the research question is discussed: 'Why does the approach to 'wicked problems' require open policy development?'. Next, the theoretical framework is addressed. The variables 'openness', 'unwritten rules' and 'coping strategies' are discussed in Chapters 3, 4 and 5 respectively. In Chapter 6, we take a closer look at the research method, the target group of the research, the research philosophy, the way the research results were analyzed, and the validity, reliability and generalizability (external validity) of the results.

Chapters 7 and 8 contain the research results. The effect of hard unwritten rules on openness in policy development is discussed in Chapter 7, the answer to the central research question in Chapter 8. Finally, the conclusions are presented in Chapter 9, with recommendations on how to implement the results in the afterword.

Chapter 2

The relationship 'wicked problems'
openness - governance

Chapter 2   The relationship 'wicked problems' – openness – governance

The first sub-question of this research is: 'Why does the approach to 'wicked problems' require open policy development?'

To answer that question, this chapter explores social <u>changes</u> and their consequences for the policy issue (<u>problem</u>). Paragraph 2.1 discusses the new reality of lack of clarity, complexity, 'wicked' or even 'super-wicked problems' and multiple rationality. Paragraph 2.2 addresses the shift from government as an organization (government) towards a combination of organizations and stakeholder (government). Paragraph 2.3 shows the shift towards chains and networks and horizontal methods in the private sector.

The dominant thinking is that these changes encourage more open policy processes. In paragraph 2.4, I show that government is unwilling to accept a secondary role in a governance system without putting up a fight. Government 'fights' back and it does so through internal rules, often hard rules, legitimized by concepts like ministerial responsibility and political primacy. That is a prelude to the hard unwritten rules that occupy a central place in this thesis. In paragraph 2.5, I explore the instruments civil servants use to deal with this situation, as a prelude to the coping strategies that occupy a central position in this thesis. Paragraph 2.6 contains a summary of this chapter.

2.1   The new obscurity

The world, which, in the 1950's and 1960's, seemed fairly clear to the average citizen, company and civil servant, has changed. The Internet, individualization, media, globalization, the loss of information monopolies, etc., have created a society with changing demands on business and government. Dijstelbloem (2008) refers to Habernas (1985), who spoke of a 'new lack of clarity' and complexity in society. Frissen (2002) talks about the changing context using words like pluralism, variety and fragmentation. Bekkers (2007) speaks of 'fragmentation' and draws a distinction between a structural and a politico-cultural dimension. When he talks about structural fragmentation, Bekkers (2007) refers to an increasing number of organizations and stakeholders. The relatively autonomous stakeholders embody partial rationalities and perspectives on reality. The politico-cultural dimension involves process of depillarization, individualization and loss of ideology, which affect the role that institutions play with regard to the transfer of values and the organization of the public domain. They create a clash of reference frameworks. Politico-cultural fragmentation

> *'is also connected to the meaning of values in our society, the way these values are mobilized and translated into political controversies, and are used as decision-making criteria'*
> (Bekkers, 2007: 33).

This creates a playing field for public organizations, which Noordegraaf (2004: 50) outlines with three conditions: *'diffuse knowledge, headstrong citizens and powerful companies.'* Although more actors could influence policy development, should they wish to do so, they do not control the end results, as argued by In 't Veld (2010), referring to Zygmunt Bauman, who, in 'Society Under Siege' (2002), comments that, as a result of the increased global interdependencies, everyone can create possible butterfly storm effects, but that, on the other hand, we have above all been reduced to bystanders. A bystander is a spectator who watches from the sidelines. But it is not just that. It goes further. We are no longer just bystanders, but also participants in that world with its increased interdependencies. It is the fairway, the context in which we live. As far as governments and civil servants are concerned, that means that they can no longer design and govern society from 'above' and in a 'distant' way. They stand in the middle of the fairway, with all its dynamic currents and whims.

2.1.1 The shift from complicated to complex society

Sargut & McGrath (2012: 45) see a development *'from complicated to complex* social *systems'.* Complicated systems have moving parts that interact a lot, but that have a knowable and known pattern, allowing researchers and other observers to make accurate predictions about how the system behaves.

That is no longer the case with complex systems, which contain functions that may function according to certain patterns, but whose interactions change continuously. Complex systems have the following characteristics (Sargut & McGrath, 2012: 47):

*   Unpredictable with regard to what happens when different parts of the context interact. The same starting conditions can lead to different results.
*   Apparently simple acts can have unexpected consequences.
*   Managers are no longer able to cognitively comprehend all aspects of 'the business', but find it hard to acknowledge their own cognitive limitations.
*   Rare events can become more significant and occur more frequently than people think compared to regular events.

Taleb (2012: 4) complements Sargut & McGrath (2012) and In 't Veld (2010). He identifies two characteristics of complex systems:

*   Countless mutual dependencies that are hard to detect.
*   Non-linear reactions.

Bekkers (2007) refers to Van Gunsteren and Van Ruyven (1993), who called this phenomenon TUS: The Unknown Society. There is 'information overload', because the quantity of information that politicians, citizens, civil servants and administrators have to deal with has increased exponentially. The result is a structural rationality shortage. The cognitive abilities of people and organizations to fathom the complexity and then take targeted action are by definition insufficient (Bekkers, 2007; Luhmann, 1984).

2.1.2 Complex, unstructured 'wicked' problems as the norm

A second idea is that complex societies have complex problems, which are different from complicated problems. Complicated problems can be dissected and structured into causal diagrams and schematics, after which targeted solutions can be devised. It is possible, by taking the time to study complicated problems, to understand their inner workings and composition, creating indisputable expert knowledge of the logic contained in the problems, patterns and solutions involved.

Complex problems are different. Although it may be possible to determine the starting conditions, the consequences are unclear. Rittel and Webbers (1973) conclude that many social problems cannot be solved and tackled through linear analysis. They called them unstructured 'wicked problems', in contrast to what they called 'tame problems'. The transition towards complex problems crosses a boundary where no individual person, or organization, is able to comprehend the problem on their own (Sarguth & McGrath, 2012).

Tame problems are the same as what Sargut & McGrath (2012) call complicated problems. Although they are technically complex, they can be defined and structured. It is still possible to devise and implement a targeted effective solution. That is to a lesser extent the case for 'unstructured' problems, which are harder to define. Problem descriptions that are proposed involve partial sub-aspects (Australian Public Service Commission, 2007). None of the descriptions is the complete problem description.

When the number of stakeholders increases, it is to be expected that there will be less consensus about values. Schön & Rein (1994) speak of a *'intractable policy controversy'*.
Differences in values, from which actors approach an issue, lead to a difference in explanations and solutions. To characterize unstructured problems, we compared the findings of Rittel and Webbers (1973: 161-167), Schön & Rein (1994) and the Australian Public Service Commission (2007) (Appendix 3), which has provided the insight that unstructured problems can be expressed on two dimensions:

Knowledge:
- The problem cannot be described clearly.
  It is complex and *'the boundaries of the problem are diffuse, so it can hardly be separated from other problems'* (Hisschemöller & Hoppe, 1995: 43).
- It is not exactly clear what relevant knowledge is.
- There are no clear directions for solutions.

Stakeholders:
- There are many stakeholders.
- The stakeholders have different standards and values, and think differently about means and ends.

According to the Australian Public Service Commission (2007), the practice of many policy problems is situated on a continuum between structured and unstructured problems. The division into four categories by Van Heffen (1993), translated into a table by Hisschemöller, visualizes the continuum. Some problems move along this continuum over time.

TABLE 3: TYPES OF POLICY PROBLEMS (HISSCHEMÖLLER, 1993: 253; HISSCHEMÖLLER & HOPPE, 1995; 44)

		Certainty of knowledge	
		Yes	No
Consensus about values and norms	Yes	Structured problems	Averagely structured problems/goal concensus
	No	Averagely structured problems	Unstructured problems

Box: Super-wicked problems

Metze & Turnhout (2014: 4) point out that recent literature talks about super-wicked problems. These add four elements to the division by Hisschemöller (1993, 1995):
* *Transcend disciplinary, territorial and administrative boundaries, as a result of which there are no authorities to address the problems.*
* *Are tenacious, because they are stuck in systems that are difficult to change.*
* *Have a time dilemma and the need to solve them is high, while at the same time providing lots of stimuli to postpone measures.*
* *It is not possible to define the problems precisely, never mind approaching them in innovative ways.*
It is with these elements that face civil servants applying open policy approaches in practice. Administrative boundaries, authority and problem definitions have to do with mandates and responsibilities. Time dilemmas on the one hand point to urgency and, on the other hand, to political risks regarding certain social problems. If a politician tries to tackle them, he can get into trouble. For instance because unpopular measures have to be taken. As a result, a problem can be parked.

2.1.3   Complexity and opacity

Non-linear responses in the case of complex systems cast doubt on the concept of cause. Causes are almost impossible to detect or define (*Taleb, 2012: 53*). Or, as Taleb formulates it:

*'In a complex system, it is simply impossible to determine causal relation-
ships. There is a causal opacity, which means that it is hard to detect an
arrow from cause to effect. As a result, many conventional analytical systems and standard logics cannot be used'*
(Taleb, 2012: 54).

Where Taleb (2012) speaks of causal opacity, In 't Veld (2010) detects a problem for science when he states that causality as a cause-effect relationship
and generally valid causal relationships fall short as explanation of or support
for social dynamics. In his view, in addition to causality, dialectics, reflexivity
and serendipity also play a major role.

- *Dialectics*
  Each change starts with an impulse or starting point that already contains
  the opposite starting point. As the impulse becomes change, the opposite force already gains momentum.
- *Reflexivity*
  Acquiring knowledge, learning from it and changing ones behavior as a
  result, immediately making the knowledge in question potentially obso-
  lete.
- *Serendipity*
  Being alert to what comes along; 'seizing the coincidence' and doing so
  successfully. This is an intuitive method, not a cognitive notion.
  It involves developing a sixth sense for recognizing coincidences and the
  potential added value they can have in one way or another
  (In 't Veld, 2010).

That involves paying attention to dialectics, reflexivity and serendipity in the
policy development itself by translating these three insights into process reflection questions.

What are the opposing forces and how can we deal with them constructively?
Who will potentially learn something if we do X and how can we deal with
that? What happens at the same time if we are engaged in open policy development and how can that be utilized in a constructive way?

Van Hoesel (2008) puts it more simply when he indicates that the available
knowledge about social problems virtually always is to a greater or lesser extent limited. Even if a lot of information were available, it is not easy to determine which of the information is relevant to an issue. In addition, information
is in many cases dated.

According to Van Hoesel (2008), social dynamics play a role in that. Social problems are subject to change, because society itself changes constantly. As a result, good policy measures may become ineffective over time. Not only because the nature of problems can change in a changing society, but also because various stakeholders manage to adapt or respond creatively to earlier policy measures.

All that does not mean that a good analysis is not useful. Van Hoesel (2008) comments:

> 'A basic condition for the development of good policy is, therefore, that available scientific knowledge, but also practical knowledge that has not been added to science, is used to optimize the operation of the policy instruments to be used'
> (Van Hoesel, 2008: 57)

The notion of the relevance of practical knowledge is an extension of Scott (1998), who protested against the exclusion of local, practical knowledge. Scott uses examples to show that a one-sided combination of (bureaucratic) government and science leads to abstract thoughts and actions, and results in an irresponsible disconnection from practice.

2.1.4   Multiple rationalities in addition to opacity of rationality shortage

Houppermans (2011) does not speak of causality and opacity, but of singular and multiple rationalities.

A singular rationality is associated with solution-oriented methods that assume there is one optimal approach for the solution of problems. In the case of multiple rationalities, there are multiple perspectives, problem descriptions and potentially related (partial) solutions with certain policy themes that have to be taken into account. As Houppermans (2011) formulates it:

> 'The belief in the existence of one correct approach to the solution of problems is making way for multiple perspectives (multiperspectivity), perceptions and rationalities to problems and solutions. The traditional singular rationality makes way for the multiple rationality. Although government is part of society, and can in that sense be characterized as post-modern, government uses a predominantly singular rational government approach to policy, when it involves the formal and institutionalized procedures and methods regarding policy preparation, policy and the policy cycle' (Houppermans, 2011: 3).

The insights and associated concepts from Taleb, Rittel & Webbers, Sargut & McGrath, Bekkers, In 't Veld, Hisschemöller & Hoppe, and Houppermans can be represented in an ordinal scale:

TABLE 4: LEVEL OF STRUCTURE OF PROBLEMS

Structured problem → → → → unstructured problem		
Not wicked	**Wicked**	
Uncomplicated è	Very complicated è	Complex
Singular rationality è	Multiple rationality è	Opacity
One person can grasp it on their own è	One person can no longer grasp it on their own è	Transcends rational comprehension/rationality fails
Experts/professional stakeholders (mostly usual suspects) è	Experts/professional stakeholders (also unusual suspects) è	Usual and unusual suspects (also non-professional)
Structured è	Moderately structured è	Unstructured

So whenever a problem is called 'wicked', these insights can be added to those provided by Van Heffen (1993) and Hisschemöller (1993). They have a multiple rationality and can no longer be grasped by one person. 'Wicked' transcends the rational.

2.2 'Wicked problems' and openness

Houppermans (2011) connects 'wicked problems' to open policy development. Openness brings relevant 'tacit knowledge', practical experiences and relevant knowledge to policy development. Houppermans (2011: 283) speaks of a 'respectful participation'. She states that:

> 'It has become clear that the optimization of the quality of policy preparation in favor of the effectiveness of policy is possible by adopting a multi-perspective approach to policy, with equal importance being assigned both to singular-rational elements and multiple-rational elements. The two elements are not opposites, but are integrated, and multiple-rational does not mean irrational, but different from traditional and singular-rational'
> (Houppermans, 2011: 310).

In terms of simple rational elements, Houppermans (2011) thinks of scientific support for policy. See Table 5. Houppermans concludes:

> *'The more open the interactivity, the more room is available for the rele-*
> *vant knowledge, the more possible it is to gather the relevant knowledge,*
> *the more actors are open and receptive to using that knowledge and ar-*
> *rive at a shared need and common interest for the policy and to take the*
> *time, and the greater the influence of that knowledge is on policy … . The*
> *more the policy is scientifically supported with 'tacit knowledge' and prac-*
> *tical research, the greater the insight into clues for policy in practice, like*
> *the actors' openness to change and the state of affairs of their knowledge*
> *level and the better the match between policy and practice will be'*
> (Houppermans, 2011: 313)

In the case of multiple rationality, the presumption remains that reality exists and can be understood. A closed approach can still be successful. The policy-maker does, however, need to make a greater effort to understand the complicated issue, but effective policy is still possible through collecting knowledge. In a situation involving opacity, that is only possible to a limited extent. Collecting knowledge will not eliminate the lack of rationality. As soon as reality cannot be comprehended rationally, a different approach is needed (Sargut & McGrath, 2012). The idea is, if there is a structural lack of rationality, for 'acting from system morality' to play a more dominant role. Policy-makers need to open up to the system in which they operate and fully take that system on board in a respectful way, keep an eye on the long term *and* organize policy processes as self-unfolding processes of 'right actions'. Although it is still possible to use detailed pre-determined steps, they need to be adjusted as soon as the process unfolds in a different way. That has consequences for the approach. Openness becomes a quality of policy development.

TABLE 5: SINGULAR (SCIENCE) AND MULTIPLE RATIONALITY/INTERACTIVITY (HOUP-PERMANS, 2011:105)

	Cluster 1: Singular rationality	Cluster 2: Multiple rationality
Indications	Execution of ex-ante evaluation; quality of policy theory; rational decisions	Connection to historically grown rules, norms and values in society
	Presence of learning loops	Exchange of argumemts between actors involved; controllability; intersubjectivity and rationality of arguments in an instrumental normative, social and expressive sesne; the link to norms and values in society
		Link to the action theory of the target group; interaction between and support from actors involved; the use of tacit knowledge
		Exchange of and insight into various reference frames and shared experiences between actors involved in policy
		Mutual independence
		Stimulating relationships between actors
		Action- and innovation-oriented
		Idelaism, creativity and innovation
		Flexibility
		Naming-, framing and re-framing
		Communication between and within the target group of the policy and society about the policy
Factors	**Scientific substantiation**	**Interactivity**

2.3   From government to governance

Literature on changes in government overwhelmingly sees a change 'from government to governance'. Stoker (1998) characterizes this development as follows:

> 'There is however an agreement that governance refers to the developing of governing styles in which boundaries between and within public and private sectors have become blurred. The essence of governance is its focus on governing mechanisms which do not rest on resource to the authority and sanctions of government'
> (Stoker, 1998: 119).

Governance diffuses the line between governments, but also between public and private. The group of parties who are involved transcends the 'usual suspects', the acknowledged parties who are consulted as a matter of course. The circle of participants widens, changes and becomes less top-down. According to Arend (2007), that has consequences:

> 'From government to governance is from top-down, central, technocratic management in a representative democracy, to bottom-up, interactive, responsive network management in a direct deliberative democracy' (Arend, 2007: 18).

In her perspective, network management is a logical response. Castells (2000) sees information and communication technology as important catalysts in the development of a networked society:

> 'New information/communication technologies allow networks to keep their flexibility and adaptability, thus asserting their evolutionary nature. While, at the same time, these technologies allow for co-ordination and management of complexity, in an interactive system which features feedback effects, and communication patterns from anywhere to everywhere within the networks' (Castells, 2000: 15).

Governments have to adapt to this new context, if they want to remain effective, as shown by Ashby's Law of Requisite Variety: 'Variety can destroy variety' (Ashby, 1956: 207). Hendriks (2012: 73) describes requisite variety as:

> 'Inevitable characteristics of decision-making systems that have to deal with variety and complexity, with 'wicked problems', which are disputed both empirically and normatively. Intensive networks between decision-makers, and between decision-makers and the environments in which they operate, are considered functional here for policy-oriented learning and for high-quality decision-making' (Hendriks, 2012: 73).

Hendriks (2012) states that open networks can provide a key for dealing effectively with unstructured problems. A network society calls for network governments. Frissen (2002: 51) states,

> 'that, in a network society, government will also have to take on a network shape'.

Governance from open network concepts means other relationships and forms of interaction in policy development practice. Nederland, Huygen & Bouttelier (2009) indicate that governance presupposes a vision

> 'on collaboration with social organizations, and sometimes with private enterprises, and on the participation of citizens in the formation and implementation of policy. Government has to be able to relate to a variety of actors'
> (Nederland, Huygen & Bouttelier, 2009: 12)

The concepts of 'governance' and 'policy networks' go hand in hand (Peters & Pierre, 2001; Kickert et al., 1997; Van Kersbergen & Van Waarden, 2004). It is based on the notion that government policy is developed with a complex force field of mutually dependent, yet relatively autonomous public, private and social parties. Researchers Sørensen & Torfing (2004) speak of 'governance networks', bringing together the management style of governance and policy networks as an organizational form. Such a network (multi-actor) approach, according to In 't Veld (2010) does justice to the variety and dynamics of policy formation.

2.3.1   Government <u>versus</u> governance

It is interesting to problematize the way 'from government to governance'. Is it actually happening and is it possible? Is there no 'fight' between governance and government? Unlike the authors cited above, in this thesis, my assumption is that it is not so easy to change 'government', when discussing the tension between the openness that is required and the (hard) unwritten rules that create a tendency towards closedness and asking whether the theory about governance, which seems logical when we look at the changing shape of social problems, can and may be translated into a culture of government organizations within which civil servants have to adopt more governance-like approaches.

However, that is far from an easy process. Various authors mention the 'tension' that exists between vertical management mechanisms, developed in a representative democracy, and horizontal approaches, as an expression of a participatory democracy (Van der Arend, 2007; Nuys, 2006; Van der Heijden, 2005; Paauwe, 2004). Noordegraaf (2004: 26) concludes:

> 'The collective approach to social issues has itself become an issue.

Edelenbos & Monnikhof (1998) describe the increasing tensions at municipalities as a result of increasing interaction with citizens, including clashes between the mandate of councilors and mandates that fellow citizens (claim to) have. Edelenbos, Domingo, Klok & Van Tatenhove (2006) show a similar tension among Ministries involving interactive processes (and their outcomes) in an existing institutional environment. Interactive processes to do fit in with 'normal' departmental decision-making procedures. The report 'Learning government, a case in favor of problem-oriented politics' of the WRR (2006) describes the tension as a vertical (government) <u>versus</u> a horizontal tradition (governance) of political thinking. In the vertical tradition

> 'the focus is on making legitimate decisions, with politicians being the ones making the decisions .... In the horizontal tradition, on the other hand, the politician is the manager who develops new forms of collective action in which divergent views are reconciled'
> (WRR, 2006: 10).

This translates to the civil servant's reality. In a report by the Department of Waterways and Public Works (1995: 9), the following (vertical) motives are mentioned:
1. The desire on the part of those preparing policies to reason towards a certain predetermined outcome. The 'solutions' are presented to the other parties involved in a 'ready-made' form.
2. A fear that opponents are handed ammunition for criticism and resistance.
3. The assumption that the social sectors are represented sufficiently in the 'usual suspect network' and that opposing views can be reconciled that way.
4. The assumption that enough information and inventiveness is available to find the solution largely on their own.

Whereas de WRR (2006) seas politicians as innovators developing new forms of collective action within the horizontal tradition, this study emphasizes civil servants as innovators towards more open policy development.

Schrijver (2013) illustrates the contrast between government (vertical) and governance (horizontal) within the national government through two observable thought patterns of two boards within the Ministry for Internal Affairs and Kingdom Relations (BZK), one of which has a more vertical, government-like approach, and the other a more horizontal, governance-like approach. In the table, the names of the boards have been replaced by the words government and governance.

TABLE 6: TWO THOUGHT PATTERNS JUXTAPOSED (SCHRIJVER, 2013: 53-54)

Vertical/Government	Tending towards Horizontal/Governance
Based on management model or doctrine	Based on multiform management practice
Coherence between phenomena attributed by the model	Coherence between phenomena experience by parties involved
Uncertainty and complexity reduction as main activity for the sake of manageability realization objective	Uncertainty and complexity as beneficent given; manageability only on level of values and purpose
Planned preparation of clearly defined product; FPTP (From Policy budget to Policy preparation)-proof	Open search based on problem definition and time frame, let yourself be surprised. FPTP has to be achieved through linguistic tricks
Do not be distracted	Side effects are as least as education as main track
Rational-causal management model	Constructivist management approach
Input from outsourced research	First and foremost based on own research and observations
Politics comes first: instruction comes from above, civil servants elaborate and implement	Politics comes last: civil servants present alternative perceptions to politicians, who select
Individual civil servant subordinate and interchangeable	Individual civil servant and his personal motivation, network and perception determine the result
Organization speaks with one voice, is like a pyramid	Organization is multiple network, works together within and without
Things 'happen' at the top of the organization	Things 'happen' at the boundary of the organization
Structures and rules are determining	Approach and content are determining

A comment can be added to the table that, in the case of open policy development beyond consultation, there is not much to choose for politicians and they have to follow the field, keeping in mind that, at a certain level of problem complexity, there is and never was an all-encompassing solution, but rather a continuous interplay of partial solutions, presented and executed by many (instead of some) actors, in a continuous mutual open coordination.

That should have consequences for the management style. If openness is necessary for dealing with 'wicked problems', that requires a different kind of management. Management needs to create room for a higher degree of openness in policy development. Both insights by Graves (1981, see Appendix 2 for explanation) regarding more specific forms of problem-solving in relation to type of issues, and more recent remarks by Roobeel (2014) about the need to utilize collective intelligence, support these ideas.

This room for openness in policy development should have been created earlier. While there is now increasing pressure to make policy development more open, according to Hoesel in 2014, that should have happened earlier, even with problems that appeared to be more clear-cut. At the time, politicians and government got away with not doing this; in part based on thoughts and actions from vertical organizational paradigms. In addition, the adverse effects of many policy decision were not experienced by the decision-makers themselves and could be postponed to a future date.

2.4   Looking at the neighbors: businesses and complexity

The tension between vertical and horizontal is not unique to government. In an interview with Robbins (2014), Kottler states:

> 'The basic strength of hierarchies is that if they are designed well – the departments/silos make sense in light of your business strategy and your competition, there aren't too many levels, the rules that accompany the hierarchy are smart and sensible – hierarchies can be an incredibly efficient and reliable way to get work done. In fact nobody has found a more efficient and reliable way ...... The problem is that hierarchies change slowly to changing conditions, to new rapid-fire strategic challenges, to technological discontinuities. They're not agile, they can't jump to the left or to the right quickly. In today's world you have to be fast and agile, but you also have to be efficient and reliable'
> (Robbins, 2014: 1).

Roobeek (1994) does not speak of a tension, but of too much verticalization, indicating that pyramid-like structures are an obstruction to fast and open communication and a resulting ability to act in an alert and innovative manner. Limited openness can be an obstruction to dealing with complex issues. Roobeek states that lots of things can go wrong due to the greater distance between the top and bottom in large organizations (Roobeek, 1994). In her view, the vertical tradition is closely related to Fordism:

> *'An intensive accumulation of monopolistic regulation, to a large extent*
> *replacing market mechanisms by institutional rules and agreements.'* ...
> *'In a Fordist constellation, the top of the organization decides. The execu-*
> *tion is "top-down"'*
> (Roobeek, 1992: 132; 98).

Governance and the horizontal tradition are related to Roobeek's (1996) managerial model of 'Strategic Management from the Bottom Up'.

> *'Strategic management from the Bottom Up stresses open communica-*
> *tion on strategic issues. If employees are well informed about strategy*
> *they will take up their responsibility, show initiative and come up with*
> *creative new ideas and solutions. Traditional labor relations do not permit*
> *employees or workers to take part in strategic decision making ...... It is*
> *argued that the turbulence in the business environment on the one hand,*
> *and important changes in norms and values on the other, demand institu-*
> *tional changes in terms of labor relations'*
> (Roobeek, 1996: 67).

Roobeek (2008) argues in favor of 'Knowledge-Based Network Organizations' (KBNO) as an organizational form. The essence of such a KNBO is:

> *'Removing command & control as a management principle and innova-*
> *tion-oriented strategic management by stimulation network connections*
> *to establish new knowledge combinations within and outside of the or-*
> *ganization. Leadership in a network organization is not just located at the*
> *top, but everywhere in the organization where people can initiate activi-*
> *ties that reinforce the strategic course'*
> (Roobeek, 2008: 5).

A Knowledge-Based Network Organization can be seen as a concrete organizational form that has open network at its core. An organizational form that, in its ideal form, can give expression to governance. However, at the same time, Roobeek indicates that that is not 'permitted' by traditional relationships in organizations.

2.5   No 'New Techniques' with limited ability to adapt

The comments above say something about organizational forms, but also about the ability of governments to solve social problems.

> *'Governance recognizes the capacity to get things done which does not rest on the power of government to command or use its authority. It sees government as able to use new techniques to steer and guide'*
> (Stoker, 1998: 120).

In this thesis, Stoker's (1998) *'New techniques to steer and guide'* are summarized as 'Open Multi-Stakeholder Policy Development (OMSPD)'. A wide range of workable open approaches has emerged. However, government has not yet managed to reduce its vertical orientation. One reason to carry on in the same old way is that a process that involves a smaller group of stakeholders/usual suspects who know each other is clearer and seems to me more 'manageable' (WRR, 2006).

Stoker (1998) argues that 'government' is proficient in utilizing (new) open methods and techniques *'to steer and guide'*. Goldsmith & Eggers (2004) have their doubts:

> *'Government has to come to rely far more on a vast complex of nongovernmental partners, but it has not yet figured out how to manage them well'*
> (Goldsmith & Eggers, 2004: VIII).

The question is whether public administration will change. Frissen (1999: 71) remarked 16 years ago:

> *'Common opinion appears to be that public administration will also not change essentially. That is confirmed by a top civil servant from the Hague and a professor of business administration.'*

Frissen (2002) refers to a remark made by former secretary-general Roel Bekker, who questioned changes within government:

> *'Government has to ask itself whether it is still able to govern in a seriously changing society, when government itself has not changed essentially in 50 years'*
> (Frissen, 2002: 28).

The ability to adapt appears to be limited. At the same time, according to Frissen (2002: 105), Geelhoed notes:

> *'It is noted too little that the acceleration of dynamics and the increase in social variety as a result of developments in IT render the traditional policy instruments an decision-making processes completely obsolete.'*

2.6   Conclusions

The research question to be answered in this chapter was: 'Why does the approach to 'wicked problems' require openness in policy development?

In this chapter, that question was answered by looking at the new opacity, complexity and wicked problems in the network society, whereby, in addition to divisions by Van Heffen (1993) and Hisschemöller (1993), it can be determined when a problem is called 'wicked'. Wicked problems have a multiple rationality *and* cannot be comprehended by one individual person. 'Wicked' transcends rationality.

The consensus appears to be that the number of 'wicked problems' is growing and that they require openness in policy development. It seems logical for government to develop from a vertically functioning organization (government) into more horizontal chains and networks (governance). A comparable expectation exists in business.

The reasoning goes as follows: The issue is no longer known and understood. More parties have to contribute their tacit knowledge and competencies. This is the principle of multiple rationality, which is also discussed in literature. According to Roobeek (1996, 2008) and Houppermans (2011), 'unusual suspects' possess knowledge that offers a positive contribution to the quality of policy.

And yet, government, as a vertically functioning organization, is reluctant to change. Although the development from government to governance, from professional bureaucracy to network organization, may be a necessary one, it is by no means an easy transition. There is tension and there are doubts as to whether the government ('government') has the ability to embrace governance-like approaches.

Civil servants experience that tension on a daily basis, making research into that tension between internal approaches and the level of openness relevant. The next chapter takes a look at government, and in the following chapters, we examine what the internal world looks like. Our argument will be that hard unwritten rules are crucial.

Chapter 3

Openness and (new) policy roles

Chapter 3   Openness and (new) policy roles

In the following three chapters, the three central variables are explored that play a role in all research questions: openness, (hard) unwritten rules and coping strategies.

This chapter takes a look at 'openness', beginning with the connection between 'interactive policy' and 'openness'. Next, 'openness' is made concrete to enable (ordinal) measurement and 'Open Multi Stakeholder Policy Development' (OMSPD) is introduced to interpret policy processes. We examine different expressions of OMSPD, compared to traditional forms of policy development. The research questions that are answered in this chapter are:

- *What is openness?*
- *What are levels of openness?*
- *How can openness be measured?*

3.1 Interactive policy

There is a growing interest in interactive policy. According to De Graaf (2007: 1), interactive policy was put on the map in the Netherlands by authors like Pröpper and Steenbeek, Edelenbos, Monnikhof, Hendriks and Tops. They use synonyms like 'interactive policy' (Pröpper and Steenbeek, 1998), interactive policy formation (Edelenbos, 2000: 391; De Jong and Mulder, 2000) and interactive management (Boogers and Hendriks, 2000). Pröpper and Steenbeek (1998: 293) describe interactive policy development as:

> 'A policy process in which citizens, social organizations, businesses and/or other governments are involved at as early a stage as possible to prepare, determine, implement and/or evaluate policy in an open exchange and/or collaboration with them.'

Edelenbos, Domingo, Klok and Van Tatenhove (2006: 25) describe interactive policy development as:

> 'A form of policy in which governments involve other public and private actors at as early a stage as possible to develop and execute policy together.'

At the core of these descriptions are early involvement and joint policy development with a diversity of stakeholders. They express the idea of governance. De Bruijn, Ten Heuvelhof and In 't Veld (2002) draw a distinction between (closed) process management and (open) interactive policy development. Process management is focused on actors who work together in administrative management processes. The number of actors involved is limited and they know each other. In that sense, process management represents a more closed network.

In the case of interactive policy development, an organization that is authorized to make certain decisions involves other actors, in addition to the usual suspects, in the decision-making process, including citizens, businesses and interest groups. In the case of process management, the actors involved can have a far-reaching collaboration, but in a closed circle. The circle is wider in the case of interactive policy development.

3.2   Features of openness

Various authors use the term openness in relation to interactive policy development. According to Pröpper & Steenbeek (2013: 63. 67), openness has three dimensions:

- *Substantive openness*
  The room for new ideas, plans and actions (formulation of problem and of policy) and the room to deviate from the opinions, intentions and operational frameworks of the administration.
- *Openness for outside participation*
  Accessibility to citizens, social organizations and business to take part in policy development (how large is the arena?).
- *Openness of the process*
  Transparent policy processes; to what extent is it clear to everybody who is involved, what the (decision-making) procedures are, what roles the administration and participants play, what will happen with the results of the interactive process and how decisions are ultimately reached.

Edelenbos, Klok, Domingo & Van Tatenhove (2006: 24, 72, 75) distinguish:

- *Substantive openness:* the extent to which new ideas, problem definitions and solution directions are legitimate and can play a role in the policy process.
- *Actor openness:* to what extent are actors denied access to the process or phases in the process?
- *Transparency of the interactive process or some of its phases:* is it clear and transparent enough to participants what happens at certain moments in the interactive process?
- *Openness of information and knowledge:* to what extent is information accessible to participants and is it shared deliberately? At the same time, it is about providing knowledge to give citizens an equal starting position or remain up-to-date about developments that occur during the interactive process, for instance insights that are obtained via (economic, technical) research or administrative consultation.

In addition, Edelenbos & Klijn (2005a) speak of width and depth:
- *Width:* extent to which various actors have the opportunity to be involved in each of the phases in an interactive process. The number of (different) actors involved in the interactive process determines the width of participation.
- *Depth:* extent to which actors can determine the ultimate outcome. (Edelenbos & Klijn, 2005a, 428).

Openness: two main characteristics

The dimensions of openness listed above can be ordered based on 'who' is involved in policy development and 'how' that happens.

Who? Openness to the process: <u>who</u> is involved in policy development?

In essence, it is about who is included/excluded and the number of stake-holders. A large diverse group participating is different from a limited, more homogenous group of stakeholders. Policy is often developed with a small group of authoritative actors (usual suspects) who have great influence. It is possible to aim for a higher level of inclusivity. Fung (2006: 66) distinguishes 'More exclusive' ('Invite only elite stakeholders') and 'More Inclusive' ('Open to all'):

> *'Some participatory processes are open to all who wish to engage where-as others invite only elite stakeholders such as interest groups.'*

Between the extremes, there are gradations. Some parties play a bigger part in policy development than others: they belong to the inner circle. That is why Fung's scale has been extended with 'professional stakeholders, not part of the usual suspects'. In the case of elected representatives (level 5), the emphasis is placed on administrators of small municipalities. Large municipalities are usual suspects that are always included. The order of the types of participants has been modified to match the policy development of the Ministries under examination. In the case of elected representatives, the emphasis is on small municipalities (level 5).

How? Substantive openness: level of <u>participation</u>

Substantive openness is related to the ability to introduce new ideas, problem definitions, solution directions, plans and actions and whether they are discussed respectfully in the policy development towards a possible ultimate outcome. Is all the relevant information shared with the stakeholders involved and does it affect the ultimate outcome? I consider the 'transparency' of the process, mentioned by the authors, to be an element of substantive openness. It creates a situation in which it is clear to all the stakeholders involved who is involved when and in which phase of the policy process, and what their contribution is.

To make substantive openness measurable, participation ladders are useful. The comparison of the participation ladders proposed by Arnstein (1969), Schiphorst (Veen, 2005) & Edelenbos (2005b) in Appendix 4 has resulted in an overall participation ladder (Table 7).

TABLE 7: OVERALL PARTICIPATION LADDER: PARTICIPATION LEVELS AND DESCRIPTIONS

Participation level		Descriptions
1	Informing	Politicians and government set the decision-making agenda and inform the parties involved. No further communication.
2	Formal input	At the end of the policy process, stakeholders can respond to proposed policy decisions. Decision-makers display try to 'convert'.
3	Research	Especially through questionnaires, neighborhood/actor meetings and public hearings.
4	Consultation	Politicians and government set policy agenda, but consult parties involved in policy development. Politicians are not committed to outcomes talks.
5	Advice	Politicians and government in principle determine policy agenda, but allow parties involved to point out problems and formulate policy solutions. Politicians are in principle committed to results of the policy development, but can deviate when making decisions.
6	Partnership	Actors and civil servants shape part of or overall policy together. Actors are part of program councils, planning committees and processes. Ground rules are laid out and observed.
7	Delegated power	Actors involved hold the main cards to make the policy program successful. In case of disagreements, politicians and government start a negotiation process.
8	Joint production	Within a framework, the policy-maker gives responsibility for both the development process and the content of policy/plans to external stakeholders.
9	Joint decisions	Politicians and government leave policy development and decision-making to stakeholders. Politicians accept proposed policy solutions as binding.
10	Free market	No intervention from government.

TABLE 8: EXCLUSIVE-INCLUSIVE (AFTER FUNG, 2006).

Exclusive Inclusive	Who to involve in policy development?
More exclusive	1. Fellow civil servants of one's own Ministry.
	2. Experts from other ministries.
	3. Professional stakeholders I: *Usual suspects (officially recognized stakeholders).*
	4. Professional stakeholders II: *Experts who are not aiming the ministries' usual suspects.*
	5. Elected representatives: *Political representatives of province and small municipalities.*
	6. Lay stakeholders: *Unpaid citizens with a deep interest in a certain policy area.*
	7. Random selection of participants.
	8. Open, focused selection: *Focused selection, including subgroups who have a lower tendency to participate.*
	9. Open self-selection: *Open to anyone who wants to take part in the participation process.*
More inclusive	10. Diffuse public space: *mass media, organizations not directly involved in policy, informal meetings.*

3.3   Open Multi Stakeholder Policy Development (OMSPD)

In the case of OMSPD, policy is development in collaboration and interaction with citizens, social organizations, businesses and/or other governments. On the participation ladder, that is the case from the consultation level on (Table 7). With regard to exclusivity/inclusivity, it starts at level 4 (Table 8). In terms of time, OMSPD focuses on involving stakeholders early (Pröpper & Steenbeek, 1998; Boedeltje & De Graaf, 2004) and preventing one-sided lobbies.

SCHEME 2: OPEN MULTI STAKEHOLDER BELEIDSONTWIKKELING (OMSBO)

Level of exclusion-inclusion	Participation level						
	Formal input	Research	Consulting	Advising	Partnership	Delegated Power	Producing together
1. Fellow civil servants own Ministry				Powerful usual suspect are part of tripartite systems, program councils, etc.			
2. Expert civil servants other ministries	Closed Policy Development						
3. Professional stakeholders I: Experts, Usual Suspects							
4. Professional stakeholders II: Experts, **UN**usual supects	Grey area						
5. Chosen administrators (e.g. small municipalities)							
6. Deliberately inviting interested stakeholders who are laymen (amateurs)			Open Multi Stakeholder Policy Development (OMSPD)				
7. Deliberate random selection in target group							
8. Open but focused selection in target group							
9. Open self-selection (anyone interested can participate							
10. Diffuse public space							

3.4 Expressions of openness (and closedness)

Three practical forms of closed policy process have been identified, an in-termediate version and three practical forms of open policy development (OMSPD) that are discussed. Parallels can be drawn to Meuleman, who, in 2006 and in 2008, addresses 'meta-governance' via hierarchy, markets and networks:

> 'The three ideal-typical modes differ in several relational aspects, like the dependency of actors, the type of societal interactions and the type of coordination mechanism. In terms of the relative dependency of actors, Kickert (2003: 127) observes the following differences:
> • Hierarchical governance puts public administration in a central role: other actors are dependent;

- *Market governance is the opposite: societal actors are in principle in-dependent, autonomous;*
- *In network governance, actors are interdependent'*
(Meuleman, 2006: 3).

Meuleman (2006: 7) provides descriptions of these levels:

- Hierarchy: government governs society
- Market: government delivers products to society
- Network: government is a partner to other parties.

The approaches we found help make hierarchy, market and network con-crete in an entirely different way. For the sake of clarity, the levels of exclusivi-ty/inclusivity (who to involve) have been reduced to three levels:

- The interdepartmental circuits + usual suspects.
- Experts who are not usual suspects.
- Oher unusual suspects.

With regard to the 'how', we did the same thing with the participation levels, based on the following reasons.
With the levels 'consultation' and 'advice', government still makes the deci-sions. Although actors, in the case of 'advice', are able to introduce problems and think about possible solutions, it is government that makes the ultimate decisions.

The participation levels 'partnership', 'delegated authority' and 'producing to-gether' have been merged into 'co-creation', where there I equality between actors.

- Consultation: government decides.
- Co-creation: equality.

These merged categories, together with the levels proposed by Meuleman (2006) provide an order for the additional insights from phase two of the re-search.

Meta-governance level: hierarchy

This is a level where government (sometimes together with authoritative usual suspects) pulls the strings. Four kinds of policy process can be distin-guished.

1. *'Classic' closed policy consultation/advice – process*
   Policy is developed with the usual suspects and science. Civil servants from other Ministries and usual suspects are approached bilaterally. The Ministry itself decides.
2. *Closed policy consultation/advice – process by invitation*
   Usual suspects in a closed network are brought together to explore an item. Sometimes, that network is expanded with experts from the field. The civil servant selects and invites the participants. The Ministry itself decides.
3. *The 'classic' closed policy – co-creation – process*
   Both the exploration and solutions occur in a closed network. In some interviews, this was indicated as 'work form' with powerful stakeholders, which include civil servants from Ministries and usual suspects, and there is equality between the actors. According to Mak (2012), such a closed network was common in the Netherlands in the 1950's:

> *'The then Minister for Economic Affairs told me that, in those years, economic policy was largely determined during a weekly get-together of the main policy-makers in the business community, employees, employers, government and the political parties in a living room in the cozy Jan Luyckenstraat in Amsterdam-Zuid. We essentially were always in agreement. If the directors of the Central Planning Agency and the Dutch National Bank told us we should head in a certain direction, that's where we would head. The leaders of the employers and employees would then sell it to their supporters'*
> (Mak, 2012: 29).

In these three processes, 'government thinking' is dominant, expressed in hierarchy, top-down thinking/acting and closed networks. That changes when a civil servant starts to think and act more like an entrepreneur.

Meta-governance level: market

A (societal) market where, among others, government delivers products, can be seen as a place where (social) problems and products, as solutions to those problems, find each other (Herold, 2008a). This is a different approach to a government market than the one described by Meuleman:

> *'In a market approach, governments may be looking for societal parties that can take over a specific public task. Communication may be used as a policy instrument: communication as policy, for example a PR campaign in order to stimulate self-organization of society'*
> (Meuleman, 2006: 18).

Looking at society as a (social) market allows policy entrepreneurship to flourish optimally. The policy entrepreneur monitors the field looking for problems, solutions to problems and opportunities. That brings a new level of closedness-openness to the fore when looking at its approach.

4. One step further, we found civil servants who were frequently out in the field looking for signals among usual suspects *and* unusual suspects. Their actions are a structural form of 'taking the pulse'. If these civil servants came across an interesting signal, the signal was translated into a question to be investigated and its validity was examined, for instance through a small expert session. If there was a high level of validity, the signal in question was transferred to a fellow civil servant/policy department with the subject in question in the portfolio. This approach can be seen as 'horizontal marketing' in the Ministries' policy areas.

    At the same time, these policy entrepreneurs bring parties or individuals together who previously had little or no contact with each other (Bekker & Veerman, 2009: 28). That led to new insights, new combination and subsequent opportunities to encourage innovation; a continuous flow of policy-practice-initiatives. This can be seen as a <u>half closed, half open</u> process. Incidental networks are formed around signals, with the Ministry ultimately deciding what to tackle.

    Finally, this approach also works with policy entrepreneurship translated into policy processes that deliver a <u>concrete practical product</u> as a final outcome for a specific target group.

In the process of signaling and design, the civil servant <u>himself</u> plays an entrepreneurial role. He explores the (social) market and ensures that solutions are designed to the problems that have been identified. For instance, once civil servant at the Ministry for Education, Culture and Science was able to assume an independent position between Ministry and field. When colleagues at the Ministry said A, and parties in the field said B, this civil servant was able to maintain his independence and keep focused on the question: 'Who is right?', and then, together with internal and external actors, examine 'what is true' and from there look for solutions to an issue. The policy entrepreneur described his approach as a pilgrimage in which he was at the same time a social worker. He played an independent, inquisitive and at the same time facilitating role.

Metagovernance-level: netwerks

Types five through seven do justice to openness from the outset. At least consulting AND allowing and utilizing <u>un</u>usual suspects. Typically <u>open</u> processes were represented in three ways by the interviewees. Level 7 is a practical experience of the researcher himself.

5. *Open consultation/advice process*
    Here, unusual suspects are openly invited. There are variations where parties themselves can join the consultation-discussion about a policy theme. The Ministry ultimately makes the decision about what is done with the resulting insights. On the other hand, the Ministry has to have very good reasons for going against collectively produced insights.
6. *Open co-creating knowledge (sharing) process, for instance of best practices*
    Here, parties share knowledge that contributes to solutions, for instance, in addition to scientific knowledge, practical knowledge in the form of best practices that help solve a problem. In other words, in terms of knowledge, there is equality between scientific knowledge and practical knowledge, among other things because, with co-creation, all individual perspectives are treated as equally important.
7. *Open co-creating vision process*
    Finally, it is possible to let the network itself develop and implement a vision. Although this version did not emerge during the interviews, the researcher has supervised network meetings with a similar approach.

Levels 5, 6 and 7 can be implemented methodologically in policy practice in the following way:

*   Application of more or less recognized consultation and co-creation standard methods, like the Klinker Method, Appreciative Inquiry and Future Search.
*   A combination of (parts of) recognized methods.
*   New methods that are developed by civil servants (or third parties) in which policy is developed in phases and in an open way.
    These practice-policy development levels provide insight into possible functional descriptions with which OMSPD can be embedded systematically in the government organization.

TABLE 7: POLICY DEVELOPMENT TYPOLOGY ORDERED BY THE LEVEL OF OPEN-NESS/CLOSEDNESS

Level of closedness – openness	Type policy process	Short Description
Closed	The 'classic' closed policy consultation process	Top-down policy primarily with usual suspects and science. Politicians and government decide.
	Closed policy consultation process by invitation	Usual suspect and experts who are not usual suspects are invited bilaterally in small-scale, manageable meeting. Politicians and government decide.
	Closed co-creating process	Closed network of usual suspects and civil servants who determine and decide together.
Open	Practical signaling and design process (Policy entrepreneurship: half open/half closed)	· Exploring the field for signals, 'test' those signals and introduce them to colleagues. · Bringing parties/individuals together. Help create new insights. · Seeing policy as a product design process, with a concrete practical product as a result
	Open consultation process	Explore together with usual and unusual suspects. Politicians and government decide.
	Open co-creating knowledge (sharing)process	Facilitating network actors to share knowledge/practical solutions that contribute to a common goal.
	Open co-creating vision process	Facilitating network to develop and implement a vision itself.

The design of an open policy process in policy practice is often not limited to one of the levels outlined above. There are combinations of both more open and more closed approaches. In the Table presented below, the open policy process is shown as it took place at the Ministry for Economic Affairs. Because there were stalemates between important stakeholders, it was decided to start with a closed approach with the parties involved, with the aim of re-ducing resistance, generating acceptance for OSMPD and jointly determine the scope of the policy theme. The method that was chosen turned out to be effective.

It is also important to realize that the concrete outcomes of a phase in OS-MPD are not known in advance. In that respect, OSMPD is different from traditional project management, where the final and intermediate results (and phases) are defined in advance in a SMART way (Grit, 2005): specific, measurable, agreed, realistic and timely. In OSMPD practice, the next phase does not take shape until the results of a previous phase are known. Or when a new phase has to be inserted in an existing OSMPD process.

TABLE 8: COMBINATION DIFFERENT LEVELS OPENNESS AT EA POLICY TRAJECTORY

Phase	Type of policy process	Who to invite?	Selected methods
Start of the policy trajectory	Closed consultation/advice process by invitation (determining scope)	1. Expert civil servants from other Ministries 2. Professional stakeholders I: usual suspects	Small-scale manageable Group Decision Room meeting
Phase 1: The future	Co-creating open vision process	1. Expert civil servants from other Ministries 2. Professional stakeholders I 3. Professional stakeholders II: Experts who are not among the usual suspects of Ministries	Appreciative Inquiry
Phase 2: Product design and feedback (via mail)	Open creating knowledge-sharing process	Professional stakeholders I (they did the work)	Open sharing of insights via mail and asking for feedback
Phase 3: Large-scale feedback-meeting	Open consultation AND open vision formation aimed at the core product from the previous step	1. Expert civil servants from other Ministries 2. Professional stakeholders I 3. Professional stakeholders II: Experts who are not among the usual suspects of Ministries	Combination World Café and Group Decision Room
Phase 4: Working out product for practice	Open creating knowledge-sharing process	Professional stakeholders I	No specific method but concluding meetings

3.5   Openness: job descriptions and roles

In an organizational sense, the seven types of policy processes can be translated into job descriptions with which a targeted match can be made with
issues that are more, or less, structured ('wicked'):

1.   *The traditional civil servant*
     Matches the more closed forms of policy development; works predomi-
     nantly with usual suspects and science.
2.   *Policy entrepreneur in two types*
     Matches the more open forms of policy development.
     o   The policy marketer who walks around in the field, picking up and
         testing signals.
     o   The policy entrepreneur who tackles policy processes in such a way
         that the end result is a product for a problem in a target group.
3.   *The OMSPD civil servant*
     Is an expert in applying open consultation and co-creation methods in
     policy processes.

Where the research results provide a connection to the new job descriptions,
Van der Arend (2007: 175) distinguishes three roles for civil servant within
what she calls 'participation trajectories': the facilitator, the process manager
or the network prompter.

A facilitator supervises individual meetings, for instance in a Group Decision
Room, of which Van der Arend (2007) says:

> *'The result of the session – the insight, expressed emotions, decision, plan
> – comes from the group'*
> (Van der Arend, 2007: 173).

The process manager manages and carries out an OMSPD trajectory that
is divided into different phases and involves an open and equal process of
policy development together with stakeholders. The process manager and
process designer can be one and the same person:

> *'The design, organize and supervise processes, usually for longer and less
> predefined periods of time'*
> (Van der Arend, 2007: 170).

This role matches the job description of OSMPD civil servant. A third role is
that of network prompter. Within the policy development context, this is a
civil servant who influences a network with a predefined plan that is unknown

to others. For instance by getting people in touch with each other. Network prompters advise actors and

'intervene in the knowledge and knowledge circle of others'
(Van der Arend, 2007: 177).

A presupposition is that the facilitator and network prompter are accepted roles within government. The idea is that the facilitator operates in usually low-key small-scale meetings that, because they are small-scale, involve a limited risk (level 2: Closed policy consultation/advice – process by invitation). As far the network prompter is concerned, his approach is not immediately visible and is not put on paper. Because it happens in a low-key manner, no serious risk is experienced/perceived.

That is different with regard to the role of process manager; a role with a more horizontal, phase-oriented and visible nature. Such a role can be a problem for the more vertically organized, hierarchical 'command and control' systems.

When a policy development method fits the OMSPD framework, the assumption is that a role as process manager is desired. The process manager can be positioned within the hierarchical lines with policy management, or alternatively, outside policy management, but within the Ministry. Finally, the process manager can operate outside the official hierarchy of the Ministry, for instance in the form of a taskforce.

The job descriptions and roles discussed above can be used to specify the target group on which this research is focused. Who will benefit from the end results of this study?

Focus on internal civil servant as process manager

In addition to the positioning of policy development, within our outside the hierarchy, within or outside a Ministry, whether or not the process manager is on the payroll or the policy development process has been outsourced to an external party also plays a role.

The general assumption of the researcher is that, the further the process is removed from the hierarchical line in an organizational sense, the more freely and quickly the process manager will be able to operate. It is also assumed that the inability to create openness, given certain unwritten rules, is especially prevalent among civil servants 'in the vertical line' with many layers above them. This assumption is in line with insights into the organization of innovation processes. Quinn (1985) talks about 'controlled chaos', whereby the people who are innovating and learning collectively should not be bothered too much by the regular organization barriers. Analogous to this analysis by Quinn (1985) is the thought: the more hierarchy, the greater the number of barriers to methods that fit into the OMSPD framework. When it comes to hiring an external party, the assumption is that outsourcing means that that external party may have greater freedom than an internal party working in the line.

In terms of OMSPD, this study focuses on the role of an internal civil servant wanting to coordinate and supervise an open development process, as process manager, and at the same time is on the payroll of policy management. In that position, he is subject to the tension between the vertical and horizontal traditions discussed earlier. In the Table below, that is number 6; the focus in this study will be on that position.

TABLE 9: POSITION OF THE PROCESS MANAGER

Salary position	Position OMSBO process manager in the organizational structure		
	Outside the Ministry	Within the Ministry, outside the hierarchical line (policy management)	Within the Ministry, within the hierarchical line (policy management)
External process manager	1	2	3
Process manager on payroll	4	5	6

In short, if a civil servant wants to function as a process manager who applies method that fall within the OMSPD framework, that civil servant has to deal with (hard) unwritten rules. Rules that may hinder the application of open methods, even when the issue requires methods that are 'OMSPD-proof'. It is possible that the civil servant will have trouble with the internal unwritten rules, which is an issue to which this study wants to contribute.

3.6   Conclusion

In this chapter, three research questions have been answered:

- What is openness?
- What are the levels of openness?
- How can that openness be measured?

There appears to be some convergence in the <u>thinking</u> about policy development. Support, sense-making and taking into account contextual circumstances become more important (Bekkers, 2007). Existing literature is unclear about whether or not this practice is indeed reflected systematically and permanently among national governments.

It is noteworthy that literature offers no precise definition that indicates in concrete terms when openness of closedness occurs in policy development, both in terms of the participation level and the level of inclusion. This study orders open processes via participation level and inclusion. Open Multi Stakeholder Policy Development (OMSPD) develops policy in collaboration and open interaction with citizens, social organizations, business and/or other governments. On the participation ladder, that is at least level 4 (consultation). On the inclusion scale, it is also at least level 4 (professional stakeholders, Unusual suspects).

Furthermore, this chapter shows that there is no single method, but a variety of methods that can be combined within a practical situation to arrive at a fitting OMSPD. The criteria indicate the minimum conditions that a policy process has to meet to be classified as an OMSPD.
When we make OMSPD concrete, analogous to Meuleman's hierarchy – market – network, we see an ordering of policy roles. In addition to the traditional civil servant, there is room for policy entrepreneurs and OMSPD civil servants. This job typology is not included in the national government's job structure, but embedding may give OMSPD a stronger position within the organizational structure.

Chapter 4

Unwritten rules

Chapter 4   Unwritten rules

The second central variable that returns in all research questions is 'unwritten rules'. The research questions that are answered in this chapter, as part of the theoretical framework, are:

- *What are (hard) unwritten rules?*
- *How do you find (hard) unwritten rules?*

One of the goals of this study is to provide insight into the internal reality of government organizations, the 'this is how we do things here', based on the existing rules. A distinction is made between 'written' and 'unwritten rules', after which the core concept of 'hard unwritten rules' is introduced. They tell us something about the 'deep structure' of organizations and offer a mental programming of civil servants.

4.1   The purpose of rules

'In every realm of our lives, whether we're at work or play, there are Rules of the Game. And these rules always come in two forms – written rules and unwritten rules'
Peter Scott-Morgan (1993: 5).

The government, as an organization, to a large degree functions through rules, for instance mandate rules, organizational decisions, function and procedure descriptions and other forms of instructions. Those rules tell civil servants how to deal with situations that occur. They can help prevent problems, or solve them. On the back of their book 'The dynamics of rules', March, Schulz & Zhou (2000) write:

'Organizations respond to problems and react to internal or external pressures by focusing attention on existing and potential rules. The creation, modification, or elimination of a rule is a response to events in the outside environment (such as new government regulations) or to events within the organization (such as alterations in internal government structures)'
(March, Schulz & Zhou, 2000; back of their book).

North (1990) typifies rules as:

'A framework of formal (i.e. laws, regulations) and informal constraints (i.e. customs, taboos); the 'rules of the game', that shape social, political and economic aspects of human interactions. The constraints give rise to a set of opportunities and provide incentives for individuals and organizations; the 'players in the game', to engage in economic activities'
(North, 1990: 24).

So North (1990) sees forma land informal rules as constraints. They create stability in the way in which activities in an organization take place and bring clarity to mutual relationships between people. Rules rationalize (production) processes.

Not all rules come from the desire to solve problems. In addition to creating stability and solving problems, March, Shulz & Zhou (2000) argue, rules are the result of political fights within an organization. They show who has won, or lost, something in the competition that exists.
Ledeneva (2001: 5) draws attention to a specific term in the description by North (1990): 'rules of the game'. That is a competitive image that is often taken for granted, but at the same time say something about the way employees function within and outside of the organization. As though the functioning

of employees were a competitive sports match with winners and losers. The same is true at an institutional level. Ledeneva (2000: 5) refers to North (1990), who sees institutions as:

> 'The _rules of the game_ in a society or, more formally, humanly devised _constraints_ that shape human interaction'
> (Ledeneva, 2005: 5; North, 1990: 1).

The rules they issue mark the boundary within which interaction takes place. Scott-Morgan (1995), in his classic book, talks about 'the unwritten rules of the _game_'. Barker (1992) compares rule to paradigms:

> 'The written and unwritten rules that establish or define _boundaries_ and explain how to behave in order to be _successful_ within these boundaries'
> (Barker, 1992: 32).

In order to be successful, it is necessary to understand the 'rules of the game'. They impose boundaries, but also allow people to take part in the game. Not playing according to the rules, not conforming and being unconventional, can lead to a situation where an employee is told to adapt or leave. If that happens a lot, courage, imagination and initiative disappear from the organization.

4.2   Rules as inert 'deep structure'

Many authors are aware that rules can promote rigidity (March, Schulz & Zhou, 2000: 4, 9). Sometimes, rigidity is reinforced from a tendency to lay down every exception that occurs in a procedure or work instruction, resulting in too many rules (Appendix 2 discusses ways to solve problems in relation to changing contexts). Rules and subsequent task differentiation can or cannot encourage employees to work together and find creative solutions outside the beaten path. They can slow down compartmentalization and mutual policy competition, or encourage them (Dynamics, 2008). Schillemans (2008: 144) lists six consequences of compartmentalization:

- Working past each other.
- Carry out opposing interventions or making conflicting demands.
- 'Blindness' to other aspects and an exclusive focus on certain aspects of problems.
- Failure to communicate.
- Serving conflicting goals.
- Social dramas, because governments fail to recognize, through a lack of communication, how alarming the information is about a situation in which they are active together.

These problems are persistent, in part because the rules are persistent on a deeper level. Certain rules in the *'framework of formal and information constraints'* (North, 1990) turn out to be impossible to change. They can create a fundamental blockade to new approaches. That is an insight on which we build here.

Zuboff & Maxmin (2002: 19) use the term 'deep structure' and refer to Gersick (1991: 16), who sees 'deep structure' as *'the design of the playing field and the rules of the game'.* With regard to the design of the playing field (i.e. of the organization) they remark the following:

> *'It is a highly durable order that expresses its internal organization as well as the basic activities that define its existence and governs its interaction with the environment ...... It is the deep structure that helps an organization to persist and to limit change. As Gersick notes 'It generates a strong inertia, first to prevent the system from generating alternatives outside its own boundaries, then to pull any deviations that do occur back into line'* (Zuboff & Maxim, 2002: 19; Gersick, 1991: 19).

That inertia is also observed by Mintzberg (2010). In organizations, a lot has remained the same over the decades.

> *'The more the things change, the more they stay the same'* (Mintzberg, 2010: 208).

Mintzberg points to the introduction of the Internet. Although changes occurred at the surface, things stayed the same at a deeper level. The same is true about management within 'design' and the 'rules of the game'.

> *'Internet does not change the practice of management fundamentally, but it establishes the characteristics which exists for decades'* (Mintzberg, 2010: 208).

The organizational design translated into rules determines the boundaries of what player are and are not allowed to do and how they can or cannot be successful. At the same time, a deeper pattern can be observed: a 'deep structure'. Changing that deeper pattern is not easy. There is 'inertia' that can be obstructive to OMSPD. A follow-up question involves the elements of an organization design. What can we learn from them about inertia?

Organizational design: general elements

Mintzberg (2006), in his classic book 'Organizational structures', provides an overview of the designs and structures of organizations. He states that every organized activity has to meet two fundamental and opposing conditions: division of labor and coordination (Mintzberg, 2006: 3). He distinguishes five structural elements: strategic top, operational core (those who carry out the primary process), line management, technical staff (those who prescribe the guidelines, plan and budget the work, etc.) and service staff (which advises and, on request, provides support). Mintzberg (2006) distinguishes seven coordination mechanisms:

1. Direct supervision: someone gives instructions for the work of others.
2. Standardization of activities.
3. Standardization of skills.
4. Standardization of the output.
5. Mutual consultation (adjustment on the basis of mutual arguments).
6. Centralization of values (sharing the same system of convictions).
7. The pay for (informal) power.

Kor, Wijnen and Weggeman (2007: 61) list six design variables, based on McKinsey's 7-S model:

- Structure: division of tasks, responsibility and authority.
- Systems: rules and procedures that govern everyday life.
- Management style: the characteristics and behavioral patterns of man-agement.
- Personnel: characteristics and skills of the employees.
- Culture: shared standards and values of people and the resulting way of doing things.
- Strategy: way in which and means with which goals are realized.

Themes like standardization, procedures and systems refer to a constant in organizational designs: bureaucracy. Diefenbach & Todnem (2012) point to the continuity of bureaucratic characteristics in organizations:

'Despite the constant introduction and re-introduction of 'new' business concepts and change rhetorics, key principles and mechanisms of management and organization do not change: the <u>hierarchical order of social relationships,</u> the dominance of superiors, their prerogatives and privileges as well as the well-functioning, obedience and tight control of subordinates via <u>all sorts of fysical and virtual bureaucratic means</u> continue whatever the actual change initiative (seemingly) suggests' (Diefenbach & Todnem, 2012: 4).

In line with the comments by Mintzberg (2010) about organizational inertia, there is a *'history of no change'* (Diefenbach & Todnem, 2012: 5). While a society changes, much about government stays the same, especially with regard to rules and bureaucracy. Graves (1974, 1981) shows that attempts to solve problems purely on the basis of rules and bureaucracy fail to deal responsibly with 'wicked problems' (see Appendix 2, Table 30), resulting in a discrepancy *'between an increasing demand for "good governance" and the ability on the part of governments to deliver it'* (Kupchan, 2012: 62).

Bureaucracy is a constant and that entails generic patterns of bureaucratic standardization. Rainey (2009) characterizes a developed bureaucracy as:

- Demarcated (legal) task areas through rules that officially lay down regular activities and requirements, and divide them among fixed positions and departments.
- There is an authoritative hierarchy with lower ranks being supervised by higher ranks.
- Positions in a bureaucracy require an expert training and the full work capacity of the civil servant.
- A management position is a full-time calling, or career, for the civil servant.
(Rainey, 2009: 29).

The characteristics listed above reoccur in every organizational design and, whether or not under pressure from experts in administrative organization and compliance, are translated into structures like mandate rules, organizational decisions and task descriptions, which regulate responsibilities, authorities, required qualifications and manner of execution. Higher levels of government management go hand in hand with higher levels of formalization, standardization of personal procedures and centralization (Holdaway, Newberry, Hickson & Heron, 1975; Rainey, 2009: 225). Fiol and Lyles (1985) indicate that it is not innovation, but past behavior, that is perpetuated and reinforced:

> '*A centralized, mechanistic structure tends to reinforce past behaviors, whereas an organic, more decentralized structure tends to allow shifts of beliefs and actions*'
> (Fiol & Lyles, 1985: 805).

Diefenbach & Todnem (2012: 2) emphasize the distinction between hierarchy and bureaucracy. They describe hierarchy as '*A vertical organization of tasks*' and bureaucracy as '*Rule-bound execution of tasks*'. Hales (2002) states that, when bureaucracies change, two characteristics remain the same: a) hierarchical control and b) rules that can be imposed from a central point (bureaucracy). As a result, the characteristics 'vertical accountability' and 'individual management responsibility' are unaffected. The two characteristics Hales (2002) mentions are also mentioned by Redder & Woolcock (2004) when they discuss governments and focus on accountability systems. They state that these have been designed based on hierarchical 'command and control' assumptions.

'Command and control' comes with demarcated task areas, the rule that a superior can appoint a subordinate and that management is allowed to issue rules (Sharitz & Hyde, 2012; Weber, 1922). Civil servants, for example, are accountable to the next higher level in the line, who in turn is accountable to their Minister, who in turn is accountable to Parliament. March (2010) argues that rules are more indicative of tasks and obligations than helping employees anticipate situations and making decisions for themselves.

A hard (structure) and soft (culture) aspect

When comparing the authors, a structural component of rules can be distinguished, to be translated into explicit rules that express hierarchy (vertical organization of task) as well as bureaucracy (rule-bound execution of tasks). On the other hand, a cultural aspect is recognized, expressed in informal, unwritten rules that steer behavior. Table 12 shows both the structural and cultural components.

TABLE 10: HIERARCHY, BUREAUCRACY AND CULTURE

Who?	Structural aspects of organizations expressed in a (written) organizational design (Diefenbach & Sillince, 2011)		Cultural aspects of an organization
	Hierarchy	Bureaucracy	
Weber (1922) according to Rainey (2009)	Authoritative hierarchy/top-down supervision with authority to discharge activities.	Demarcated task areas through rules; Management position is full-time calling/career; Positions require expert training and full work capacity.	
Mintzberg (2006)	Coordination as a basic condition. Elements are: * Strategic top. * Line management. Direct supervision: Someone gives work instructions to others.	Labor division as a basic condition. Structural elements: * Operational core. * Technical staff. * Service staff. Standardization of: *Activities. *Skills. *Output.	Mutual consultation via exchange of arguments Centralization of values (sharing the same system of convictions). Play for (informal) power.
Kor, Wijnen & Weggeman (2007)	Structure I: The hierarchical division of tasks and authority.	Structure II: Rule-bound division of tasks and authority. Systems: Rules and procedures that steer daily activities.	Management style: Characteristics and behavioral patterns of management. Personnel: Characteristics and skills of employees. Culture: Shared standards and values and resulting way of doing things. Strategy: Way in which and means with which goals are realized.
Hales (2002)	Hierarchical control. Rules imposed from a central point; individual management responsibility. Vertical accountability.		

Via this analysis of deep structure in relation to organizational design, two types of rules have been identified with which employees have to deal:

1. Rules expressed in the words formal and bureaucracy
2. Rules associated with the words informal and unwritten.

4.3 Connection between written and unwritten rules

The question is how the written and unwritten rules are connected. To understand that, Gilsdorf (1998) offers clues when she describes rules as:

> 'The assumptions organizational members make about the _right way_ to communicate in given situations in their particular organization' (Gilsdorf, 1998: 174).

Although her description focuses on communication, they can also be applied to the practical actions of employees in organizations. Rules are assumptions of members of an organization about the 'correct' way to act in given situations in their organizations. Gilsdorf (1998) also states that rules:

'Can be formal and informal, written or oral, implicit or explicit, organization-wide or organization-specific'
(Gilsdorf, 1998: 175).

There is a distinction between rule and policy measure. A policy measure gives a conviction and/or course of action with regard to an important organizational theme. Various rules can be seen as policy measures, but other rules fall outside policy measures (Gilsdorf, 1998: 175).
Gilsdorf (1998: 175) distinguishes four categories of written and unwritten rules:

1. Written, recognized rules, which have been communicated explicitly and are observed and are in accordance with organizational objectives.
2. Written, non-recognized rules, that exist but are outdated and are no longer observed. They are not in accordance with organizational objectives.
3. Unwritten rules that are recognized because they are in accordance with organizational objectives
   (example: of you have a contract for three days a week, you are expected to be available 24 hours a day to the top of the organization).
4. Unwritten rules that not recognized because they are not in accordance with organizational objectives (example: employees can show up 20 minutes late without calling their boss).

The table presented below summarizes the insights from Gilsdorf (1998):

TABLE 11: GENERAL ORDERING OF RULES (AFTER GILSDORF, 1998)

Rules: Assumptions about right way of acting in given organizational situations			
Formal/Explicit/Written		**Informal/Implicit/Unwritten/Oral**	
Organization-wide:	*Organization-specific:*	*Organization-wide:*	*Organization-specific:*
• Recognized rule • Non-recognized rule	• Recognized rule • Non- Recognized rule	• Recognized unwritten rule • Non-recognize unwritten rule	• Recognized unwritten rule • Non-recognize unwritten rule

This results in a demarcation of types of unwritten rules. This study focuses on informal recognized unwritten rules that belong to the 'deep structure'. March (2010) describes the connection between formal rules and informal rules as follows:

> 'Routines, procedures, conventions, roles, strategies, organizational forms, and technologies around which political activity is constructed. We also mean the believes, codes, paradigms, cultures, and knowledge that surround, support, elaborate and contradicts those roles and routines ...... Rules are codified to some extent but the codification is often incomplete. Inconsistencies are common. As a result, compliance with any specific rule is not automatic'
> (March, 2010: 22).

The written ('codified') rules are usually incomplete and inconsistent, and a core around which political activity is constructed. Scott-Morgan (1995) gives the following definition of written rules:

> 'All formal and understood aspects of an organization. It includes a wide range of aspects, such as the vision of the enterprise, the organizational structure and policy, as well as the specific aspects of strategy, procedures, process descriptions and reward systems'
> (Scott-Morgan, 1995: 30).

Written rules are what is on paper, which has meaning within an organization. Unwritten rules involve the internal politics within an organization and

105

often start with the leadership: the way it behaves. Unwritten rules can be seen as a result of written rules *and* the way leadership behaves. The result is expressed in the way written rules that are issued by a leadership are interpreted and given shape my employees in everyday practice (Scott-Morgan, 1995: 30). Unwritten rules can have positive and negative effects in and for organizations (Scott-Morgan, 1995: 37). The origin of unwritten rules is that a variety of factors affect written rules that cannot be measured or managed by management, for instance the effect of a local culture. As Scott-Morgan (1995) argues, written rules are undermined, reinforced or changed, resulting in hidden or unwritten rules that determine the actual behavior of employees. Ledeneva (2001: 5) supports the idea that unwritten rules determine the actual behavior of employees: *'The informal order balances the formal one'.* Informal rules take the rough edges off written rules and make them workable. In practice, it is especially informal rules that determine what people do.

> *'Informal constraints are defined by codes of conduct, norms of behavior and conventions. Underlying these informal constraints are formal rules, but these are seldom an obvious and immediate source of choice in daily interactions. Formal rules include political (and judicial) rules, economic rules and contracts, and they determine formal constraints'*
> (Ledeneva, 2001: 5; North, 1990: 3).

The common idea with March, Scott-Morgan and Ledeneva is that unwritten rules emerge to make written rules workable.

4.4 Detecting unwritten rules via Scott-Morgan

Scot-Morgan (1995) uses three perspectives, with associated questions, to identify unwritten rules:

1. *Motivators* (Scott-Morgan, 2005: 39/71)
   These are elements that are important to the employees in question. Unwritten rules can be identified through motivators by the following questions:
   o What motivates employees in this organization and how do they behave as a result?
   o What is the reason they get out of bed in the morning and how do they behave as a result?
   o What do they consider a reward and how do they behave as a result?
   o What do they want to avoid? What do they consider punishment and how do they behave as a result?

2. *Power generators* (Scott-Morgan, 2005: 40/71)
    These are the people who enable people to get what they want. People who can hand out the rewards or punishments mentioned under motivators. Core question is: given the motivators, who is important to the people and how do they behave as a result?
3. *Levers* (Scott-Morgan, 2005: 41/71)
    Levers are conditions that people think should be created. They match the supposed performance criteria. These can be found through the question: given the motivators and power generators, how and for what are people assessed and how do they behave as a result?

Scott-Morgan (1995) distinguishes eight steps:

1. Discussing the central question.
2. Exploratory talks: subjects related to the central question.
3. First seven conversations: exploring subjects and associated unwritten rules in greater depth.
4. Initial evaluation and selection of important behaviors.
5. Second seven conversations: focus on insight in causes and connections.
6. Confirming or verifying the insights.
7. Concluding team workshop: classification unwritten rules.
8. Presentation to management.

Within the framework of this study, the method was adjusted to establish a connection between unwritten rules and openness, obtain explanations for the connections indicated by the interviewees. This adjustment is discussed in Chapter 5.

4.5   Individual versus collective interpretations

When examining unwritten rules, it is important to make a distinction between individual interpretations of written rules by employees and collective interpretations. It is in particular collective interpretations that offer insight into the unwritten modus operandi at an organizational level. But what do we mean by collective interpretations? Argyris and Schon (1978) indicate that employees in organizations and shared assumptions that protect the status quo. Weick and Roberts (1993: 357-358) talk of *'organizational mind'* and *'collective mental processes'*. Kim (1993), in line with Senge (1990), writes about *'mental models'*:

> *'Deeply held internal images of how the world works, which have a powerful influence on what we do because they also affect what we see'*

(Kim, 1993: 39; Senge, 1990).

'Even in the most bureaucratic of organizations, despite the preponderance of written SOP (standard operating procedures) and established protocols there is much more about the firm that is unwritten; it's essence is embodied more in the people than in the system. Comparatively little is put down on paper or stored in computer memories. The intangible and often invisible assets of an organization reside in individual models that collectively contribute to the shared mental models'
(Kim, 1993: 41).

Collective interpretations of written rules can be seen as a shared mental model of unwritten rules that gives the actions of employees direction. This study calls collectively shared unwritten rules **'hard unwritten rules'.** Hard unwritten rules are part of the 'shared mental models', a structured set of rules that determines the actions of employees, a 'programming' to realize certain organizational objectives.

They are implicit decision rules that employees follow collectively. Contrary to Scott-Morgan (1995), we argue that unwritten rules are not dependent on the organization's leadership. Because they part of the 'deep structure', they are hard to change.

TABLE 12: OVERVIEW OF IMPORTANT CONCEPTS

Concept	Description
The deep structure of an organization	A very persistent/hard to change order that is an expression of the internal organization and fundamental existential activities.
System inertia	Sticking to what/how things are done. Limiting change, bringing deviations back within existing lines.
(Continuity of) bureaucratic characteristics	Important principles and mechanisms organization and management: hierarchy with rights/privileges, obedience and tight control to continue old system.
Collective interpretations	Unwritten modus operandi at organizational level.
Informal rules	Behavioral codes, behavioral standards and conventions. Below them are formal rules, but they are rarely a clear and direct source of choice in daily interactions.
Shared mental models	Deeply rooted internal (collective) ideas about how the world is organized.
Unwritten rules	A result of written rules *and* the way leadership behaves. The result expresses itself in the way written rules issued by leadership are interpreted and giving shape by an employee in everyday practice.
Hard unwritten rules	Implicit decision rules that employees follow that do not depend on the type of managers and are therefore hard to change.

With the insights provided by Schein (2010) and Graves (Cowan & Todorovic, 2000), hard unwritten rules can be positioned as 'unwritten <u>deep</u> value system rules'. Schein (2010) describes cultural levels as follows:

> *'The degree to which the cultural phenomenon is visible to the observer*
> *...... these levels range from very tangible overt manifestations that one*
> *can see and feel to the deeply embedded, unconscious assumptions that*
> *I'm defining as the essence of culture'*
> (Schein, 2010: 23).

Schein (2010: 24) draws a distinction between 'artefacts', supporting convictions and basic assumptions. To explain the concept of 'basic assumptions', he establishes a connection to Argyris and Schon by stating:

> *'Basic assumptions, in this sense, are similar to what Argyris and Schon*
> *identified as 'theory in use' – the implicit assumptions that actually guide*
> *behavior, that tell group members how to perceive, think about and feel*
> *about things'*
> (Schein, 2010: 26).

His division can be compared to Graves. Cowan & Todorovic (2000) have worked out how Graves examined origin and patterns of 'deep values' that create world visions and determined organizational principles and 'mindsets', cast leader/follower relationships in certain molds, shape decision-making structures and 'define reality' (Cowan & Todorovic, 2004; Beck & Cowan, 1996). The comparison produces the following table. (Right)

Hard unwritten rules are embedded in the 'deep value systems' of organizations. They are self-evident, but, in a changing context, can put organizations in trouble. As Drucker (1994) describes it in 'The theory of business':

> *'But as it becomes successful, an organization tends increasingly to take*
> *its theory for granted, becoming less and less conscious of it ...... It be-*
> *gins to pursue what is expedient rather than what's right ...... It stops*
> *thinking. It stops questioning. It remembers the answers but has forgot-*
> *ten the questions. The theory of business becomes culture.'* And further
> *'some theories of the business are so powerful that they last for a long*
> *time. But eventually every theory becomes obsolete'*
> (Drucker, 1994: 101).

TABLE 13: A POSITIONING OF WRITTEN AND UNWRITTEN RULES IN SCHEIN'S 'LEVELS OF CULTURE' AND THE VALUE TYPES OF CLARE W. GRAVES

Schein (2010)		Graves / Cowan & Todorovic (2000)	Type of rules	Level of visibility
Artefacts	Organizational structures, procedures, etc.	Surface values	Written rules	Visible
Supporting, hidden convictions and values	Strategies, goals, philosophies (supporting 'why's')	Hidden values	Unwritten rules and 'coping strategies'	Less/not visible
Underlying (collective) basic assumptions	Subconsciously assumed convictions and perceptions, thoughts and feelings	Deep value systems	Hard unwritten rules	

4.6   Conclusions

One of the goals of this study is to provide insight into the internal reality of organizations, the 'that's how we do things here', on the basis of existing rules. Rules prescribe how civil servants should handle situations. They help prevent or solve problems, but also have a downside. They are rigid and compartmentalizing and extinguish imagination, courage and initiative.
This study focuses on <u>hard</u> unwritten rules and, in doing so, introduces a new concept in management literature. While the assumption is that unwritten rules can be influenced by leadership styles, this chapter shows that there are deeper unwritten rules that cannot be influenced by leadership. These rules can be considered hard to change. In line with Gilsdorf (1998), they are informal recognized rules that are part of the 'deep structure'. They are embedded in the collective mindset (Schein, Graves and Drucker).

Chapter 5

Coping strategies

Chapter 5   Coping strategies

In this chapter, we discuss the third central research variable: coping strate-gies. The central research questions in this chapter are:

- *What are coping strategies?*
- *How do you analyze coping strategies?*

Using an overview article by Tummers et al. (2015), we will position the way in which we look at coping strategies in this study to current insights. The ultimately selected description of the term 'coping strategies' the analytical approach down to the level of concrete instructions, for which a specific skill analysis method is use that is explained in this chapter.

This chapter yields clusters of coping strategies, with associated detailed descriptions of behaviors that can be transferred 'from professional to profes-sional' (i.e. from employee to employee).

5.1 Coping strategies, concept definition for this study

In 2015, Tummers, Bekker, Vink and Musheno published an exhaustive overview article about coping strategies, focusing in particular on public service deliveries where there is direct contact with customers. The term coping is related to stress. The authors see coping as a sensitizing concept and define it as:

> 'behavioral efforts frontline workers employ when interacting with clients, in order to master, tolerate or reduce external and internal demands and conflicts'
> (Tummers et al., 2015: 5).

Furthermore, the article describes clusters of coping strategies, like moving towards customers, moving away from customers and working past customers. Finally, it focuses on 'behavior coping, type 1 in Table presented below.

TABLE 14: EXAMPLES OF VARIOUS WAYS OF COPING OF FRONTLINE WORKERS. WE FOCUS ON TYPE 1. (TUMMERS ET AL.: 8)

	Behavioral coping	Cognitive coping
During client-worker interactions	1. Rule bending, rule breaking, aggression to clients, routinizing, rationing, using personal resources to help clients.	2. Client-oriented cynicism, compassion towards clients, emotional detachment from clients
Not during client-worker interactions	3. Social support from colleagues, complaining towards managers, turnover, substance abuse.	4. Cognitive restructuring, cynicism towards work, work alienation

While Tummers et al. (2015) focus on the 'frontline workers', in this study, the focus is on policy employees, with attention to the following issues:

1. Policy employees also use coping strategies in their daily activities.
2. The specific factor in the case of policy employees, the so-called stressor, that is central to this study is the tension between vertical and horizontal.
3. In the case of policy employees, the target group 'clients of public services' becomes 'usual suspects' and 'unusual suspects' from a horizontal perspective, and the 'hierarchical line' from a vertical perspective.
4. With regard to 'rules', which is the focus of Tummers et al. (2015), a distinction can be made between written and unwritten rules.

5. Many of the coping strategies that Tummers et al. (2015) vary in their degree of concreteness. The skill analysis method used in this study makes coping strategies concrete in such a way that they can easily be transferred 'from professional to professional'. This method in part determines the way coping strategies will ultimately be defined in this study.
6. Tummers et al. (2015) have described families of coping strategies for the target group 'frontline workers'. This study yields families (clusters) of coping strategies for civil servants wanting to realize openness in policy development with the stressor vertical-horizontal.

Ledeneva (2001) shows that people can deal with written and unwritten rules. Ledeneva (2001: 5-6) states that the unwritten rules can be used 'to play the game':

> *'To put it more bluntly, unwritten rules define the ways of circumventing constraints, both formal and informal, of manipulating their enforcement to one's own advantage, and of avoiding penalties by combining the elements of the rules of the game creatively.'*

There are 'coping strategies' for using the rules for a desired goal. In this thesis, that desired goal is openness in policy development within the tension between vertical and horizontal. Folkman & Moscowitz (2004: 745) describe the word 'coping' as:

> *'The thoughts and behaviors used to manage the internal and external demands of situations that are appraised as stressful'*
> (Folkman & Moskowitz, 2004: 745).

Looking ahead at the skill analysis method that is used in this study, 'thoughts' are seen as the principles on the basis of which people act, 'behaviors' as 'structured sets of actions' and 'internal and external demands of situations that are appraised as stressful' as 'problems that have to be dealt with or goals that have to be realized'. In particular, it involves strategies with which hard unwritten rules can be utilized (or circumvented) to realize more openness in policy development (shaded part in Table below).

In this study, a coping strategy is defined as:

'Principles from which people act (operational principles) and the related structured sets of actions, for the purpose of dealing with a problem or realizing a goal.'

TABLE 15: WRITTEN RULES /HARD UNWRITTEN RULES /WHAT TO DO WITH THEM?

Written rules	Hard unwritten rules: (shared collectively)	What to do with them?
		Follow
	XXXXXXXXXXXXXXXXXXXXXX	Utilize

5.2 Coping strategies: making implicit knowledge explicit

Mapping a coping strategy is called 'modeling'. According to Dilts (1994), modeling is:

'Breaking up a complex skill into smaller pieces that can be repeated or applied by someone else'
(Dilts, 1994: XXV).

A model is defined as:

'A description or analogy that is used to visualize something that cannot be observed directly'
(Dilts, 1998a: 28).

The aim of modeling is to describe a specific skill in the form of a model. The question is no whether the model is 'true', but whether it is usable (Dilts, 1998a: 26). A description is not reality itself:

'A useful and procedural abstraction of reality. It has a goal and is a procedural understanding of reality'
(Koohang, Harman & Britz, 2008: 67).

It is an abstraction from which people act in the world. All models are *'simplifications'* (Senge, 1990b: 176). Additionally, it is important that a model description that is made of a coping strategy provide insight into:

*   An end result that can be described in criteria that have been made concrete.
*   If necessary, specifies ways in which (intermediate) results can be compared to the desired situations (Miller, Galanter & Pribram, 1986: 31).

For modeling a 'coping strategy', the concept of Logical Levels offers a handle. Logical Levels originated in the work of anthropologist George Bateson (1979). Robert Dilts (1991) has converted them into a practical division of logical levels:

- Identity: Who am I?
- Convictions: What do I find important?
- Capacities/strategies: How do I do things?
- Behavior: What exactly do I do (visible behavior)?
- Environment: In what environment do I do what I do?

The logical levels enable us to bring structure to coping strategies. As Dilts (1991) states:

> 'The environment level involves the specific external conditions in which behavior takes place. Behaviors are those occurrences that can be seen, heard, felt etc. in the sensory world. Capability is the level at which one is able to select, alter and adapt a class of behaviors to a wider set of external situations. At the level of beliefs we may encourage, inhibit or generalize a particular strategy, plan or way of thinking. Identity consolidates whole systems of beliefs and values into a sense of self'
> (Dilts, 1991: 3).

Miller, Galanter & Pribam (1986) emphasize capacities, know-how (skills). They write:

> 'Skills are normally tacit, but by careful analysis and investigation we are often able to discover the _principles_ underlying them and to formulate _verbal instructions_ for communicating the skills to someone else'
> (Miller, Galanter & Pribam (1986: 143).

That makes it possible, analogous to Seymour (1993), based on the logical levels _and_ Miller, Galanter & Pribam (1986), to indicate what the characteristics of a coping strategy mean:

- Behavior: What a person does (specific instructions) for each key step.
- Strategies: What is the outline of important key steps a person has to do?
- Operational principles: When applying a strategy, what is essential?

In the logical levels of Dilts (1991), convictions are the 'operational principles' on the basis of which people act. Between the specific behavioral instructions and general principles in this description by Miller, Galanter & Pribam (1986), based on Dilts (1991) and Seymour (1993) an intermediate level is added: strategies. An analysis of a 'coping strategy' makes it possible to map the operational principles, key steps (strategy level) and more specific instructions (behavior level) and convert them into a transferable model. The methodological question is: 'How can implicit (tacit) knowledge be converted and "formalized" into an explicit, transferable form?' According to Ambrosini & Bowman (2001: 812-813) has four characteristics:

- Hard to write down, formalize.
- It is personal knowledge and has cognitive characteristics in the form of mental models that are embedded 'deep' in a person and are considered to be 'self-evident'. That makes this form of knowledge hard to express by the person possessing the knowledge.
- It is practical knowledge in the form of a 'process'. It is 'know-how'.
- It is contextual knowledge.

Because the knowledge is embedded 'deep' in the person and 'self-evident', it is hard to make tacit knowledge objective and transferable. Like unwritten rules, coping strategies are not written down. Literature provides no recognized method for finding the underlying principles of a certain 'skill' or how to translate that skill into verbal instructions. Relatively few attempts have been made to develop such a method. Ambrosini & Bowman (2001) refer to Nonake (1991) for an explanation:

> *'One of the main reasons why there have been very few attempts to empirically research tacit knowledge is that it is problematic. Research instruments such as surveys and structured interviews are likely to be inappropriate insofar as individuals cannot be asked to state what they cannot readily articulate. The main challenge that has to be faced, is finding way of expressing what is, or more correctly, what has not been up to now, expressible'*
> (Ambrosini, V., & Bowman, C., 2001: 815).

Over the years, the researcher himself has developed an published a method.

5.3 Coping strategies: steps in the model-learning-process

To analyze coping strategies, we use the approach published earlier (Herold, in Van Aken and Andriessen, 2012: 345-360). The approach allows us to make mental (implicit) models underlying coping strategies concrete, transferable and testable, by treating a coping strategy as a skill that can be divided into elements, which can be repeated or applied by other people.

The approach consists of the following seven steps:

1. Delineating the model.
2. Describing three or four conceptual metaphors for the model.
3. Generating additional associations with each metaphor.
4. Exploring the metaphorical expressions.
5. Translating the data that has been generated into a sequence of 'how' questions.
6. Describing a feedback loop for each 'how' question; T.O.T.E. (Test-Operate-Test-Exit).
7. Describing the 'Operating Principles'.

Step 1: Delineating the model
The aim is to formulate the skill to be modeled, while exploring the contexts in which the skill is applied. In a generic sense, it is a formulation with the following characteristics:
'How <verb> <what> <where>?' An example in line with the research question of this thesis:
How <verb: do you create> <what: openness in policy development> <where: in a policy context at a Ministry with prohibitive unwritten rules>?

Step 2: Describing three or four conceptual metaphors
Metaphors have two qualities (Ankersmit, 2008: 25-27). They form a semantic sieve and place some meanings in the foreground and others in the background. For instance, the metaphor 'the earth is a spaceship'. This metaphor focuses attention on the bio-system and our dependence on it. Abstract concepts can be understood through metaphors, whereby each metaphor emphasizes separate aspects of a concept (Lakoff & Johnson, 1980a).

'There are always "concepts" in people's experience through which that experience is structured metaphorically'
Lakoff & Johnson, 1980b: 475).

Secondly, a metaphor suggests a course of action. For instance, comparing the earth to a spaceship urges us to be careful with our planet. Metaphors teach us something about the people using them. They are 'mental models' with which people imagine something in the world (Ankersmit, 2008: 25-27). One way to express the essence of a metaphor is through the following comparison:

'Conceptual domain A (for instance the Earth) = conceptual domain B (here: spaceship)'
(Kövecses, 2010: 4).

Using metaphors proves to be a useful way of making people aware of their tacit knowledge. The respondent is asked to give three metaphors with which the skill can be compared. These three metaphors are seen as a form or tri-angulation within an interview. It increases the construct validity, because the model is examined from different angles.

Step 3: Generating additional associations for each metaphor
Next, each metaphor is complemented with additional associations, usually expressions that are close to the concrete experience (Kovecses, 2002: 4). The associations can be obtained by asking open questions like 'what are you thinking of with metaphor X' or 'can you tell me more about metaphor X'. To make the knowledge explicit of someone who is at designing a certain type of products, they are asked for a metaphor. That person compares de-signing with 'woodcarving' (conceptual metaphor).
Answers to the open questions can be:

- It is wrestling with your subconscious.
- You have to 'let something go'.
- You are looking for the essence of the product.
- You act a little 'crazy' to do it a little differently.

Step 4: Exploring the metaphorical expressions
The first three steps provide the contours of the model, but not enough to create a transferable protocol. That makes it important to know what exactly the interviewee means by the words he uses. What does he mean by 'wres-tling' or 'letting go' in the woodcarving example? Or other words that he uses?
To that end, the meta-model developed by Bandler and Grinder (1975) can be used. The model's underlying principle is Korzybsky's (1948: 59) idea that *'the map is not the terrain'.* Language can best be seen as a map. Words are not the objects, but representations of objects. In line with Korzybsky (1994: XVII), the following applies:

- No individual representation reflects the entire assumed terrain.
- Representations are self-reflective. We can map our own maps.
- Each representation is a map of the mapmaker himself.

So how can we use language to explore the *real* underlying terrain? Accord-ing to Chomsky's Transformational Grammar, all language can in essence be structured on three levels (Linden & Perutz, 1997: 226):

- Surface structure: refers to sentences and words people pronounce.
- Deep structure: provides details about who, what, where, when and how exactly.
- Reference structure: the sense-specific experience itself.

Language is seen as an abstract representation of actual experience. The words that are used are openings/gateways to the experience. It is important to realize that the opposite is also true. Language is used to make a 'map' of an experience, structuring it from a certain perspective. Language is a tool with which a stored experience can be transferred as an individual *'map of reality'* (Yeager & Sommer, 2009: 47).

There are three process to get from an actual experience to a linguistic expression at surface level (Bandler & Grinder, 1975: 33).

- Generalization: whereby parts of the person's model are separated from the experience and become representative for the category to which the experience belongs.
- Deletion: whereby selective attention is paid to certain aspects of the experience, while other aspects are left out (in the surface structure).
- Distortion: whereby relationships between parts of a model are represented differently from the relationships they are supposed to represent. One of the most common examples of distortion is a process represented as an event; this is called nominalization.

The function of the meta-model is to detect and analyze generalizations, deletions and distortions in order to obtain a representation of the deep structure (Zamfir, 2009: 69). The table presented below contains a simplified form of the meta-model.

TABLE 16: SIMPLIFIED REPRESENTATION OF THE META-MODEL (BANDLER & GRINDER, 1975)

Type of words	Challenge
Too much, too high, better, etc.	Compared to what?
Nouns and pronouns.	Who, what, where, when exactly?
Verbs.	How exactly?
Nominalization (non-tangible nouns).	How exactly?

Step 5: Make a sequence of 'how' questions from the obtained information
In step 5, an outline of a protocol is made. In the researcher's experience, this can be done via 'how' questions, which bring a person <u>in</u> the feeling of the

actions. The sequence of the 'how' questions becomes the cornerstone of the future model and can be seen as a schematic, generic modus operandi. The set of 'how' questions forms the connection between generating implicit data and creating specific instructions.

For both the interviewee and the interviewer, it is not always easy to determine the sequence of 'how' questions. Often, because of their education and profession, people are trained to answer 'how' questions and assuming a 'critical attitude', which is something that should not be done during the modeling interview. The aim is to determine a sequence of 'how' questions from the perception of the person being interviewed.

Step 6: Describing the T.O.T.E. for every 'how' question
The answer to every 'how' question needs to me a modus operandi. That is a concrete set of instructions with which the 'how' question is answered or addressed. Ackof, according to Allio & Russel (2003), states:

> *'Knowledge is transmitted through instructions, which are the answers to how-to questions. Understanding is transmitted through explanations, which answer the why questions. Herein lies a very fundamental difference'*
> (Allio & Russel, 2003: 21).

If these instructions are structured in the form of a T.O.T.E., they become transferable and testable. T.O.T.E. stands for *Test-Operate-Test-Exit*, and is a feedback loop (Miller, Galanter & Pribram, 1986: 31). According to T.O.T.E., to reach an objective, it has to be tested continuously what the position or state is in relation to the desired objective. For the test phase, it has to be indicated what information is needed to compare the current state (feedback) to the instructions that indicate what you can do on the basis of that information (Miller, Galanter & Pribram, 1986: 31). This involves questions like:

- What is your starting point?
- What do you do exactly?
- What is your endpoint?
- How do you know you are on the right path?

DIAGRAM 3: THE T.O.T.E. FEEDBACK LOOP (DILTS, 1994)

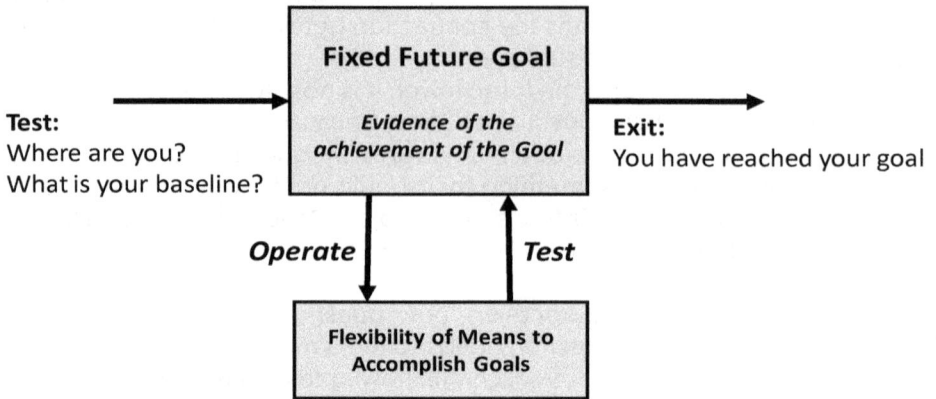

Fixed Future Goal

Test:
Where are you?
What is your baseline?

Evidence of the
achievement of the Goal

Exit:
You have reached your goal

Operate   *Test*

Flexibility of Means to
Accomplish Goals

It is important for a T.O.T.E. to take place in a context, which means that not only the objective itself, but also aspects of the environment are part of the feedback loops. Another issue is that resources and means are part of the T.O.T.E., as is how to gain access to them and how they are used.
To describe a T.O.T.E., the following questions are posed:

1. Can you indicate to which (concrete) result the answer to this 'how' question leads? When are you satisfied?
2. What is your starting point? What is present, what is absent, what is going on?
3. What do you do exactly in terms of behavior to answer this question?
4. What means of resources do you use? (And possibly: how do you use them?)
5. How do you know you are on the right path?

It is important that the result has to consist of concrete, specific instructions that the interviewer personally has to understand. During this step, the meta-model can help make the information being provided more concrete.

Step 7: Describing the main Operating Principles
After the 'how' questions have been made instructive and testable through the T.O.T.E's, it is time to describe the main operational principles. These are principles, often crucial do's and don'ts, that are considered to be important for working with the model.
Whereas, in the previous steps, the subject was interviewed in a way that helped him be in the actions, at this stage, it is important to step back and look at the model in its entirety.

5.4   Conclusions

'Coping strategy' is the third central variable in this research. As part of the theoretical framework, two research questions have been answered in this chapter:

- What are coping strategies?
- How do you analyze coping strategies?

While existing literature tends to focus on coping strategies for 'front-office workers', in this study, we argue that civil servants also use coping strategies in their daily activities. The specific factor with regard to civil servants, the so-called stressor, that is central to this research is the tension between vertical and horizontal. The target group 'customers of public services' in the case of civil servants involved in policy development becomes 'usual suspects' and 'unusual suspects' from a horizontal perspective, and the hierarchical line (politics) from a vertical perspective.

When talking about 'rules', which is the focus of Tummers et al. (2015), a distinction can be made between written and unwritten rules, a distinction that is not made explicitly by Tummers et al. (2015).

The skill analysis method used in this study makes coping strategies concrete in such a way that they can be easily transferred 'from professional to professional' in the form of practical knowledge management. The form of this skill analysis method in part determines the ultimate definition of coping strategies used in this study.

Ledeneva (2001) shows that hard unwritten rules can be followed, but also used creatively. This study focuses on the coping strategies that civil servants use to realize open policy development by using hard unwritten rules in a smart way.

A coping strategy is defined as principles on the basis of which people act (operational principles) and the associated set of structured actions. Those coping strategies can be analyzed, as skill-related knowledge, from a labor-analytical, managerial perspective. The steps include:

1. Delineating the model.
2. Describing three or four conceptual metaphors for the model.
3. Generating additional associations with each metaphor.
4. Exploring the metaphorical expressions.
5. Translating the data that has been generated into a sequence of 'how' questions.
6. Describing a feedback loop for each 'how' question; T.O.T.E. (Test-Operate-Test-Exit).
7. Describing the 'Operating Principles'.

Tummers et al. (2015) have described clusters of coping strategies for the target group 'front-office workers'. This study provides clusters of coping strategies for civil servants involved in policy development wanting to realize open policy development with a given stressor vertical-horizontal.

Chapter 6

Research structure and justification

Chapter 6 Research structure and justification

In the previous three chapters, the three central research questions were discussed and defined that are the theoretical framework of this research. The following questions were answered:

- *What is openness?*
- *What are levels of openness?*
- *How can openness be measured?*
- *What are (hard) unwritten rules?*
- *How do you find (hard) unwritten rules?*
- *What are coping strategies?*
- *How do you analyze coping strategies?*

For the research itself, three sub-questions and one central research question were determined:

1. *Why does the approach to 'wicked problems' require <u>openness</u> in policy development?*
2. *What are the <u>hard unwritten rules</u> civil servants are expected to observe in their own organization?*
3. *What discrepancy is there between the required openness in policy development and the internal hard unwritten rules?*

The central research question is:
  What <u>coping strategies</u> are available to civil servants to deal with certain hard unwritten rules and enable openness in policy development?

In this chapter, we discuss how the answers to these questions were translated into a research structure.

6.1   Research structure: two phases

In this chapter, we discuss the research structure and justification. Table 19 shows the research structure. The research took place in two phases, the first of which focused on finding hard unwritten rules and their effects on openness.
In the second phase, the coping strategies were reconstructed of civil servants who know how to realize openness in policy development.
Three sub-questions and a central research question were formulated:

Both the questions regarding the theoretical framework and the research questions have been put in a logical order and translated into a planned research structure, as shown in the table below.

TABLE 17: RESEARCH STRUCTURE

Research question	Data collection method	Data analysis method
What are 'wicked problems?	Exploratory literature study	Comparison definitions, concepts, conclusions
Why is there attention for 'wicked problems'?		Comparison definitions, concepts, conclusions
What is openness?	Exploratory literature study	Comparison definitions, concepts, conclusions
Why does the approach to 'wicked problems' require openness in policy development?	Exploratory literature study	Comparison definitions, concepts, conclusions
What are (hard) unwritten rules?	Exploratory literature study	Comparison definitions, concepts, conclusions
How do you find (hard) unwritten rules?	Exploratory literature study	Comparison definitions, concepts, conclusions + oefenen in interview-methode
What are levels of openness?	Exploratory literature study	Comparison definitions, concepts, conclusions
How can openness be measured gemeten?		
Phase I: *What discrepancy is there between the required openness in policy development and the internal hard unwritten rules?*	1. Selection of three Directorates General at three different Ministries. 2. Interview rounds (semi-structured) at the different Directorates General (DG) of three different Ministries, looking for hard unwritten rules, their effect on openness, explanations and initial insights into coping strategies. Six respondents per DG.	**See interview schedule Appendix 9.** Coding the results via Maxqda software package. Looking for differences and similarities.
	3. 'Member check', respondent validation, (semi-strucured) of the unwritten rules found in round 1 in a second round of interviews at the different Directorates General. Four respondents per DG.	

TABLE 17: RESEARCH STRUCTURE (CONTINUED)

Research question	Data collection method	Data analysis method
What are coping strategies?	Exploratory literature study	Comparison definitions, concepts, conclusions
How do you analyze coping strategies?	Exploratory literature study	Comparison definitions, concepts, conclusions + oefenen interviewmethode
Phase II: *What coping strategies are available to civil servants to deal with certain hard unwritten rules and enable openness in policy development?*	Detecting and analyzing coping strategies of employees who manage to realize a greater level of openness.	Analyzing coping strategies using modeling/ skill analysis technique. **See protocol described in chapter 5** Coding the results
	'Member check' of results via four presentations at the Ministries to which the Directorates General in question belong.	Ibid: looking for difference and similarities.

Phase I consists of two rounds. In the first round, the unwritten rules were collected and, in the second round of Phase I, they were presented to civil servants. At least two interviews per interviewee took place to find unwritten rules and explore the relationship to openness. More concretely: in the first interview, the focus was on finding unwritten rules and, in the second interview, the relationship between the hard unwritten rules and openness was explored. In round 2 of Phase I, the check of the interviews from round 1 involving specific dossiers, one interview per interviewee turned out to be sufficient.

In terms of research functions, adopting the categorization by Oost & Markenhof (2002), phase I can be characterized as an explorative explanatory research. On the one, it involved looking at the <u>effect</u> of hard unwritten rules on the level of openness, on the other hand, the interviewees were asked <u>why</u> the effect of certain hard unwritten rules on the level of openness was as they described.

In phase II, for the sake of modeling, at least two interviews per interviewee were conducted, to make (implicit) coping strategies explicit. In terms of the research functions categorized by Oost & Markenhof (2002), phase II can be characterized as **explorative** designing research. According to the Handbook Design-oriented Scientific Research (Van Aken & Andriessen, 2012), design science is:

> *'focused on developing and testing solutions for field problems, which means it is not only concerned with describing and analyzing said field problems'*
> (Van Aken, 2012: 13).

A result of design research is a design statement:

> *'in which that generic intervention is described to deal with the type of field problems, together with the outcomes one can expect and preferably an explanation as to why that intervention will generate that outcome in the context described'*
> (Van Aken, 2012: 3).

Solutions can also have underlying design principles:

> *'Design principles also often have a broader application domain than design statements .... An example of a well-known design principle in the area of designing itself is: "Never marry your first design idea".'*
> (Van Aken, 2012: 11).

The research into coping strategies via the skill analysis method provides both design statements (concrete interventions) and underlying principles (operating principles). Coping strategies are analyzed and described as they are represented by the civil servants. They have not been formally tested in the organization by a group of 'developers' (alpha tests), or via beta tests. In the latter case, users conduct the tests in everyday life (Magnée, Cox & Teunisse, 2015). The coping strategies that were found were presented to and discussed with civil servants in the Masterclass "From the Outside In", which was organized by the Learning and Development Square of ECS/SAW/HWS, which is why this research is described as 'explorative design research'.

Paragraphs 6.2 – 6.5 address important aspects for both research phases. Paragraph 6.6 addresses the research structure, validity, reliability and generalizability of the results of phase I, and paragraph 6.7 looks at the research structure, validity, reliability and generalizability of the results of phase II.

TABLE 18: NUMBER OF INTERVIEWEES PER PHASE

Where	Phase I		Phase II
	Round 1	Ronde 2	Round 3
	Target: 18	Target: 12	Target: 6
HWS	6	5	4
EA	6	4	3
ECS	6	4	2

6.2 Accessibility contacts

In the case of research into unwritten rules, networks and existing contacts turn out to be useful when it comes for arranging initial appointments with civil servants within Ministries. There were plenty of these contacts within the Ministries of HWS and ECS. At ECS, in part as a result of a contribution there to a study into unwritten rules in connection with the quality of policy. Within the Ministry for Economic Affairs, there were also many contacts available, because a number of the Ministry's employees had taken part in the Open Masterclass From the Outside in, mentioned in Chapter 1. As a result, the researcher had access to a wide pool of potential interviewees.

In phase I, the participants were selected 'from the phonebook' of the Ministries in question, and an attempt was made to get both 'employees' and 'senior employees' to take part.

To find civil servants who are able to realize openness in policy development for phase II, we asked the people we interviewed earlier. In addition, the research was able to approach his own network.

6.3 Not) recording interviews

Prior to conducting the interviews, the question was whether or not to record the interviews digitally. Yin (2009) says the following about that:

> 'A common question about doing interviews is whether to record them. Using recording devices is a matter of personal preference. Audiotapes certainly produce a more accurate rendition of any interview than any other method. However, a recording device should not be used when (a) an interviewee refuses permission or appears uncomfortable in its presence, (b) there is no plan for transcribing or systematically listening to the contents of the electronic records – a process that takes enormous time and energy, (c) the investigator is clumsy enough with mechanical devices that the recording creates distractions during the interview itself, or (d) the investigator thinks that the record device is a substitute for "listening" closely throughout the course of an interview'
> (Yin, 2009: 109).

We decided against recording the interviews. On the one hand, during the test interviews it became clear that not everybody liked being recorded. They were talking about 'sensitive information'. On the other hand the focus was on finding unwritten rules.

During a first interview, they were written down and, during a second interview, they were presented to the interviewees for additions and/or corrections.

6.4   Interviewers and authenticity data

Although the researcher conducted most of the interviews, some of the interviews in phase I were conducted by other interviewers. They were familiar with the concept of unwritten rules. The researchers discussed and practiced the interview protocol with them. This turned out not to be possible in phase II. Even though two of the three interviewers had taken a course in 'modeling', their work situation did not allow them to practice, which is who the researcher conducted all the modeling interviews in phase II himself.

To safeguard the authenticity of the data gathered during the interviews, all the interviewees were asked to send the interview report to an independent scientific supervisor of the research themselves, which happened in all cases.

6.5   Influencing factors selection research methods

There are three factors that influence the choice of research method.

- Experiences of the researcher
- Exploration of research methods.
- Conversations with research coaches.

Experiences researcher

In 2006, the researcher conducted a study at the Ministry of SAE into the management culture using Scott-Morgan's method. The study led to a presentation to the board's management team. It appeared to be desirable to change the existing culture, but that was prohibited by the unwritten rules. Later, the researcher assisted in a study at the Ministry of ECS into unwritten rules that affect the quality of policy. In addition to assisting in the structure of the study, this meant conducting interviews, including group interviews using the so-called Group Decision Room, and assisting in the analysis of the results. Various test interviews were conducted at the Ministry of SAW to get a better idea as to whether, and how, to use Scott-Morgan's method to determine how unwritten rules affect the level of openness in policy development. In addition, it is noteworthy that, each year, in the Open Masterclass From the Outside In, organized by the then ECS/SAE/HWS Academy (now the

Learning and Development Square ECS/SAE/HWS), together with groups
of participants, unwritten rules were explored using Scott-Morgan's method,
including discussions on the influence of those unwritten rules on the application of methods with an OMSPD nature. Finally, to examine and analyze
coping strategies, the structure was used from the handbook 'Design-oriented Scientific Research' (Herold, in Van Aken and Andriessen, 2012: 345-360).

Exploration research methods

Explorative literature research was conducted into qualitative research methods such as case studies (Yin, 2009), grounded theory (Goulding, 2002;
Glaser & Strauss, 2009), Naturalist Inquiry (Erlandson, 1993) and Qualitative
Data Analysis by Miles & Huberman (1994), on the basis of which the notion
emerged that an analysis of unwritten rules can be seen as a kind of 'grounded theory'. Principles from 'Naturalist Inquiry', mentioned by Erlandson et al.
(1993: 16), with reference to Guba (1981), provided a basis for the creation of
a research design:

1. *Go for in-depth interviews*
    In-depth interviews provide 'thick descriptions' that express the relation-
    ship with the organizational context, in terms of unwritten rules and cop-
    ing strategies, from the point of view of the interviewees.
2. *Go for relevance in the form of applicable knowledge*
    Knowledge that helps civil servants to enable openness in policy devel-
    opment.
3. *Fit with the context*
    To that end, the research results have to have a 'fit with the context' and
    'everyday realities'.
4. *Interview people in their own context*
    Talk to people in their own context, where unwritten rules are experience
    and coping strategies applied.
5. *Civil servants who use coping strategies possess 'tacit knowledge'*
    The challenge is to transform 'tacit knowledge' into 'propositional knowl-
    edge', explicit knowledge that can be applied.

Conversations with 'research coaches'

Conversations with research coaches, like Prof. Dr. Geert Teisman, Prof. Dr.
Mathieu Wegeman, Prof. Dr. Peter van Hoesel, Prof. Dr. Mirko Noordegraaf,
Prof. Dr. Annemieke Roobeek and Dr. Daan Andriessen, have helped focus
the research and the research method, in particular for phase I of the research.

Choice of generic research method

Based on the conversations with the research coaches, literature studies and personal experiences, it was decided to opt in favor of in-depth interviews and 'replication logic'. In this study, the latter was applied to the in-depth interviews. Yin writes about replication logic:

> *'A common question about doing interviews is whether to record them. Using recording devices is a matter of personal preference. Audiotapes certainly produce a more accurate rendition of any interview than any other method. However, a recording device should not be used when (a) an interviewee refuses permission or appears uncomfortable in its presence, (b) there is no plan for transcribing or systematically listening to the contents of the electronic records - a process that takes enormous time and energy, (c) the investigator is clumsy enough with mechanical devices that the recording creates distractions during the interview itself, or (d) the investigator thinks that the record device is a substitute for "listening" closely throughout the course of an interview'* (Yin, 2009: 109).

In-depth interviews are necessary to gain insight into the relationship between unwritten rules and openness and why that relationship is as it is in the perception of the civil servant. In part II of the study, in-depth interviews make the tacit knowledge explicit (coping strategies).

6.6   Phase I: Research structure and justification

Next, the target group for phase I was demarcated and it was determined how to collect and analyze the data. Inaddition, the validity, reliability and generalizability (external validity) of the results of this phase are discussed.

Demarcation target group

In the choice of which Ministries to include in the research, two criteria were applied:

1. Uniform characteristics type of Ministry/position.
2. Civil service pay scales 11, 12 and 13 in policy boards at a Directorate General. Usually, these are the scales in which the employees do not occupy managerial positions. The assumption is that the inability to create openness in policy development in the presence of unwritten rules is particularly relevant among employees 'in the vertical line' with several layers above them.

Literature distinguishes between night watcher and non-night watcher Ministries (Heldeweg, 2006). In the night watcher mode, government focuses on core activities like peace, security and public order. Non-night watcher Ministries are part of the welfare state. After discussions with Dr. Jaap Uijlenbroej of the Ministry for Internal Affairs and Kingdom Relations (IAK) and Prof. Roel Bekker (former secretary general), the idea emerged that non-night watcher Ministries have to prove themselves more than night watcher Ministries, and the decision was made to focus on the non-night watcher Ministries of Social Affairs and Employment (SAE), Economic Affairs (EA) and Education, Culture & Science (ECS).

The assumption was that, although night watcher Ministries may <u>not</u> have different accents in terms of 'wicked problems', they do have different accents when it comes to <u>unwritten rules</u>.
Within the three night watcher Ministries, attention focused on job scales 11, 12 and 13 of three Directorates General.

- Ministry of SAE: Directorate-General Work and boards Labor Market & Socio-Economic Affairs, Labor Relations, Work Health and Safety, International Affairs, Implementation Tasks Legislation Working Conditions, Project Management Learning and Working.
- Ministry of EA: Directorate-General Business and Innovation with the boards Industry and Services, Entrepreneurship, Innovation, Program Management Regulatory Pressure, Project Management Top Sectors, Program Bio-based Economy, ACTAL.
- Ministry of ECS: Directorate-General Primary and Secondary Education with the boards Childcare, Primary Education, Secondary Education, Labor Market and Personnel, Project Management School Drop-out and Youth, Education and Care (JOZ), Board of Education.
  We focused on policy boards in the regular line. These are:
- DG Work: Management Boards Labor Relations and Work Health and Safety.
- DG Business and Innovation: Management Boards Entrepreneurship, Innovation and Top Sectors.

- DG Primary and Secondary Education: Management Boards Childcare, Primary Education, Secondary Education, Labor Market and Personnel. (Note: In the course of this research, the Management Board Childcare was transferred to the Ministry of SAE)

The reason for focusing on employees in scales 11, 12 and 13 is that they have a hierarchy of three management layers 'above' them, before a product/ memo written by them reaches a Minister.

During the Masterclass 'From the Outside In', these employees often made comments like *great Open Multi Stakeholder Method, but my bosses will not allow it'.* So the tension is clearly tangible here.

Method data collection: adjustments method Scott-Morgan

We made four adjustments to the method proposed by Scott-Morgan:

1. *Hard unwritten rules*
   Scott-Morgan (1995) does not use the term 'hard unwritten rules'. For the interview protocol, that means that, after exploring with the interviewees which unwritten rules existed, the interviewees would indicate what they felt were the 'hard unwritten rules'.
2. *Finding deeper practical explanations*
   After the hard unwritten rules have been detected and the interviewee selects two or three hard unwritten rules, their effect on openness is explored through questions like *'To which participation level does the unwritten rule tend to move when looking at policy development from there? How far do you go?' 'Who do you involve in policy development, looking at it from the hard unwritten rule?'*
   An explanation is asked in relation to the hard unwritten rule: *'If this hard unwritten rule A leads to participation level P1 and an inclusive/exclusive level P2, what is the cause? Why is it like that?*
3. *Underlying written rules*
   The interviewee is asked which written rules underlie the hard unwritten rules being mentioned. (It turned out that this question was often hard to answer by the interviewees.)
4. *How to?*
   Questions that were asked here are: *'If you, as a civil servant, wanted to realize openness (applying an 'OMSPD-proof' method), how would you do that?'* This question was included to obtain preliminary insights into possible coping strategies.

Data analysis

In the data analysis, all the unwritten rules that were mentioned (hard and soft unwritten rules) were coded using the qualitative analytical program Maxqda, revealing the first common threads in the amount of unwritten rules.
Next, all hard unwritten rules were clustered and coded separately in Maxqda. They are rules that the interviewees see as collectively shared and recognized unwritten rules that are hard to change and that are not determined by the leadership style. For the sake of verification, all the hard unwritten rules were copied in Word and ordered a second time (Appendix 5), after which the most important unwritten rules were selected that can be seen as the 'essence' of all the rules that were mentioned.
The ordering criteria are:

• What respondents indicated in round 1 as being the most important hard unwritten rules.
• The number of times they were mentioned.
• Can the other hard unwritten rules be seen as being derived from the most important rules?
• Can they be seen as practical interpretations of important written rules of the democratic rule of law, such as political primacy, ministerial accountability, the rule of trust and official loyalty (Nieuwenkamp, 2001)?

We looked at what the interviewees said about the level of openness allowed by hard unwritten rules, taking into account explanations that provide insight into why a 'hard unwritten rule' allows a certain level of openness.

Ultimately, we were able to identify four hard unwritten rules that can be seen as a 'core construct' of 'collective mental programming' (Hofstede & Hofstede, 2005: 19). With the exception of the unwritten rule 'meet your deadline' (which was mentioned by 'only' 44% of the interviewees), these unwritten rules are broadly shared. However, the research decided to treat the deadline rule as a hard unwritten rule anyway, because failure to meet a deadline leads to a serious political problem.
Finally, in addition to round 2 of phase 1 (see Table 19), 'member checks' were conducted via lectures at the Ministries involved to present the core construct, the hard unwritten rules we identified.

Validity and reliability of the results

This research fits into the social-constructivist line: it is about mental images of respondents about their organizational context and the way they order and express that organizational context in unwritten rules. These are 'partial truths' (Denzin & Lincoln, 2011: 125).

According to Smaling (2010: 2), the social-constructivist is expressed in the old theorem: 'If men define situations as real, they are real in their consequences' (Thomas & Thomas, 1929: 572).

Smaling refers to Mortelmans (2007), who states that not every qualitative study falls under the header constructivism. Mortelmans did not consider some versions of 'grounded theory' constructivist, but post-positivistic (empirical-analytical), where social reality – the world of everyday signification – is a given. Via comparisons, concentration and reordering of categories, essential meanings, captured in core concepts, can be revealed. In that sense, in light of the depth of the interviews and the wealth of data, this study also has post-positivist characteristics.

In the constructivist corner, some authors object against the use of the word 'truth' in qualitative studies. Rolfe (2006) refers to Sandelowski (1993), who states that validity in qualitative studies should not be linked to 'truth', but to 'trustworthiness'. What is elicited are 'mental constructs' that are made 'credible' or 'plausible' because multiple persons share (part of) the mental construct. In that sense, Guba & Lincoln see 'member checks' as:

> *The single most critical technique for establishing credibility'*
> (Rolfe, 2006: 305; Guba & Lincoln, 1989: 239).

Guba & Lincoln describe reliability as a precondition for validity (here: credibility). They argue that it cannot be assumed that there is similarity between observation and reality if repeating the study yields different results (Erlandson, D.A. (Ed.), 1993: 34; Guba & Lincoln, 1989: 234-235).

Sandelowski (1993) nuances that notion and remarks that, if the reality in the qualitative paradigm is multiple and constructed, repeatability is not essential. She rejects reliability as a useful measure of the quality of qualitative research (Rolfe, 2006: 305; Sandelowski, 1993: 3).

In this study, reliability means that it can be expected that repeating the research will yield comparable unwritten rules. These mental construct translate into the behavior of employees in a certain context to allow them to 'fit' into that context.

Research validity in phase I of the study is safeguarded as follows:

1. For the operationalization of the concept of 'openness' (participation level), existing scales have been compared to each other and translated into an improved scale (see Appendix 4). For the level of inclusion, an existing scale was used.
2. Existing knowledge about unwritten rules, and the way to examine them, was used for the content of the interviews; this can be seen as a form of

'content validity' (are all facets of the construct measured?).

3. Control of the interview reports by the respondents themselves, including their written statement about that, eliminates any vagueness, errors, misunderstandings, misinterpretations, etc., which is good for both reliability and validity. On the one hand, this can be seen as a way to measure reliability (as a kind of 'retesting') and, on the other hand, as an improvement of the 'construct validity' (do you measure what you want to measure?).

4. With regard to the unwritten rules that were identified, phase I of the study was deliberately divided into two sub-phases. In round 1, unwritten rules were collected, which were presented to the a different group of civil servants in round 2. Not only does this increase reliability (as a condition for validity), it also deepens the outcomes. This can also be seen as a form of 'construct validity'.

5. In master classes From the Outside In, organized by the Learning and Development Square ECS/SAE/TWM, both the unwritten rules and the coping strategies were discussed. Discussion of the results with groups of civil servants can be seen as a test of the results, a form of 'construct validity', which boils down to an alternative measurement that shows whether a previous measurement is a match.

6. A further indication for the validity and reliability of the research results are the 'member checks' via many lectures in the past years at the Ministries we examined, presenting the core construct, the unwritten rules we identified. They yield agreement.

Box: tweets about the lectures
A tweet during a lecture on February 13, 2017, at the Ministry of Economic Affairs.
@mlborsje
Still a strong story: research @maxherold about unwritten rules.
#mustread for civil servants
http://twitter.com/mlborsje/status/831148084889526274?2=04

Generalizability (external validity) of the results

For the generalizability of the research results, we also looked at Lincoln & Guba (1985). Referring to Kaplan (1964), they state:

> 'The generalization must be truly universal, unrestricted as to time and space. It must formulate what is always and everywhere the case, provided only that the appropriate conditions are satisfied ...... Generalizations are assertions of enduring value that are context free.' Met als aanvulling: 'The only generalization, there is no generalization'
> (Lincoln & Guba, 1985: 110; Kaplan, 1964: 91).

In principle, the research results apply to the examined domain of civil servants in the three non-night watcher Ministries. For other contexts that match those in a political, hierarchical and bureaucratic sense, analytical generalizability can be assumed.

6.7   Phase II: Research structure and accountability

Phase II reconstructs coping strategies of civil servants who manage to realize openness in policy development. A coping strategy is characterized by its operating principles, on the basis of which actions are carried out, *and* a structured set of actions to deal with a problem or realize a goal. To that end, tacit knowledge has to be made explicit.

Delineation target group

The people who manage to realize openness were found via the interviewees from phase I and via personal contacts. After explaining to them what we meant by 'hard unwritten rules', 'openness' and 'coping strategies', we asked them if they knew civil servants who managed to create openness in policy development. That led to a set of civil servants who were approached and whose coping strategies were analyzed. Occasionally, we let go of the focus on civil servants and examined employees who managed a project that was started in a policy board, but that had been transferred into a project outside of that policy board's responsibility, due to their large-scale nature and the level of freedom they required. In addition, people were interviewed (modeled) who managed open policy processes for policy boards, even though there were not employees of the policy boards.

Data collection method: Modeling

It turns out that coping strategies can be analyzed from a labor-analytical, management perspective. The skill analysis method that is used is called 'modeling'. It includes the following steps:

1. Delineating the skill.
2. Describing 3 or 4 conceptual metaphors for the model to be modeled.
3. Generating additional associations for each metaphor.
4. Exploring the metaphorical expressions.
5. Translating the generated data into a sequence of 'how' questions.
6. For each 'how' question, describing a feedback loop; the so-called T.O.T.E. (Test-Operate-Test-Exit).
7. Describing the 'Operating Principles.

For each interviewee, the collected data was transferred in phase II into a protocol that represents the though/action strategy of the civil servant.

Data analysis coping strategies

To analyze the 'How To's', the data collected in phase I was used. At the end of each interview, the interviewees were asked what they would do it they wanted to create openness in policy development. Phase II produced a protocol per interviewee with transferable instructions of their approach. On the basis of the data of phase I and II, we looked at similarities, additions and differences. The analysis of the coping strategies consisted of six steps:

1. *Open coding: dividing into small sets of instructions that can be repeated or applied by someone else.*
   Dilts (1994: XXV) describes modeling as *'dividing a complex skill into small parts that can be repeated or applied by someone else.'* This step yielded 62 coping strategies (see Appendix 6).
2. *Axial coding step 1; comparison of the 62 coping strategy clusters.*
   The 62 coping strategies were compared and clustered. In Tables 35-39, column 4 of Appendix 6, this leads to 'subdivision coping strategies general'.
3. *Axial coding step 2; ordering according to the four hard unwritten rules we identified.*
   If hard unwritten rules can be seen as (part of) the collective mental programming of employees in an organization and implicit rules that they follow collectively, the 'subdivision coping strategies general' can be ordered according to the four hard unwritten rules. Column 3, Tables 35-39, Appendix 6 shows that that is possible.
4. *Axial coding step 3; following or using unwritten rules.*
   The focus in this study is on the use of unwritten rules. The ranking of coping strategy clusters on the basis of this criterion is found in column 2 of Tables 35-39, Appendix 6. The grey shaded coping strategies are examples of 'uses'.

5. *Selective coding*
   Finally, core categories were assigned and, with regard to the information in columns 3 and 4, the question was asked again: 'Of which group
   are the clusters a part or expression?' This leads to the core categories in
   column 1, Tables 35-39, Appendix 6.

The coding and main categories, as in the analysis of the unwritten rules,
were arrived at via observation and information processing by the researcher.
During the interviews, the interviewees were also asked about operational
principles that are the basis of the coping strategies. With that, three ordering steps were carried out in the data analysis.

1. *Open coding*
   Categorizing/clustering the operational principles that were mentioned
   via the underlying question: *'What is this about?'*
2. *Axial coding*
   Comparing the categories/clusters to operational principles with the
   question: *'Of which more general category are these "operational principles", when I compare them to each other, a part or an expression? And
   'What do I call that?'*
3. *Selective coding*
   Ordering the operational principles based on the question: *'What is the
   core of this operational principle?'*

Validity and reliability of the results

In this study, validity is above all 'pragmatic validity' (Van Aken, 2013: 8), a
concept with a learning component.

> *'The issue is not to understand what has happened at one point in time in
> a given context, but what can be learned from similar experiences in sev-
> eral contexts that can be transferred to inform skillful and informed action
> in other contexts'*
> (Van Aken, 2013: 12).

When we analyze the coping strategies of civil servants who managed to
reconcile openness in policy development with hard unwritten rules in non-
night watcher Ministries via the seven steps discussed in the previous chapter, and compare them to each other, that yields operational knowledge that
can be applied in other, comparable government policy contexts.
Validity with regard to the analysis of coping strategies in phase II, using the
skill analysis method, is safeguarded as follows:

1. In recent years, the skill analysis method was taught and tested frequently in a multitude of situations and subjects.
2. Prior to this research, two scientists have conducted a test and demonstration.
3. The skill analysis method has been published and studied by scientists prior to publication.
4. In accordance with the discussion about validity regarding unwritten rules, the control by the interviewees themselves, including their written statement about it, eliminates vagueness, errors, misunderstandings, misinterpretations, etc., which is good for both reliability and validity.
5. The 62 coping strategies, and the associated coping strategies, have been discussed in the aforementioned Master Class From the Outside In. The participants recognized the strategies and associated principles as ways to enable OMSPD.

Generalizability (external validity) of the results

With regard to generalizability, we refer to our comments about the subject with regard to phase I (paragraph 6.5).

6.8   Discussion research methods phases I and II

The method proposed by Scott-Morgan was adjusted with regard to finding hard unwritten rules and exploring their effect on openness and the deeper explanation of that effect. The method proved to be applicable and yielded rich data. At the same time, some methodological comments can be made.

External validity: generalizability of unwritten rules and their effect on openness
The research results are valid for the domain under examination: three non-night watcher Ministries ECS, SAE and EA. It is indicated that, for other contexts that are similar to these Ministries in a political, hierarchical and bureaucratic sense, generalizability can be assumed. There may be differences in emphasis. For example, at the Ministry for Financial Affairs, where it seems to be less problematic when a Minister approach a specialist civil servant and bypasses the hierarchy, which could create a problem for the civil servant in question at the Ministries we examined, although we did not test that.

A second example involves the game 'via the band'. Whereas it was not done dot play something via the 'external band' at the night watcher Ministries, at the more technical Ministries (Finance/Instructure and Environment) that was seen differently. At least, that was what the researcher was told during informal conversations after completing the research. Content has a higher priority at the night watcher Ministries. These are differences between night watcher Ministries and other Ministries. It is realistic to assume that provinces and municipalities also differ, among other things because they operate closer to citizens, and at the same time further removed from the media.

The reliability of the (hard) unwritten rules that were identified
Reliability means that it is expected that, when the research is repeated, it will again yield similar mental constructs in language (i.e. unwritten rules). In addition, the assumption is that these mental constructs, in a given context, will translate in similar behavior of employees.
Some nuances with regard to reliability in relation to the unwritten rules that were identified are in order. Several persons conducted the interviews. The researcher has taken that into account when ordering and classifying the data. Where he believed there was a real risk, further talks took place with the people who conducted the interviews. During 'member checks', there was agreement with the results.
It cannot be ruled out that a different researcher would order the data differently and may formulate the outcomes differently. The researcher expects that that will not lead to hard unwritten rules with a different meaning.

Completeness of the (hard) unwritten rules that were identified
Have all the hard unwritten rules been uncovered? Again, a different researcher may use different phrasings or arrive at a different number of hard unwritten rules as a core construct. The aim was to find a core construct of hard unwritten rules. The research has yielded important hard unwritten rules that determine the everyday activities of civil servant.

Coping strategies: remarks regarding research method

The researcher has described steps to make tacit knowledge in Van Aken & Andriessen (2011). In this research, those steps yielded focused data regarding coping strategies. In addition, it yielded a 'bonus' that has been translated into an ordering of policy processes.
The coping strategies are an addition to the method proposed by Scott-Morgan. The unwritten rules provide a mixture of 'why you have to do something' and 'how you need to do something' at a more general level. Research into coping strategies deepens the insight into the question 'how exactly should (or can) you do something to realize a result in a certain organizational context?'. It is a way to map tacit knowledge and provides an image of the organizational culture.
As a formula: (Hard) unwritten rules + coping strategies = analyzing/describing a form of culture from the perception of a certain target group/goal. Some comments can be made here.

External validity: generalizability of the coping strategies that were found
Can the coping strategies be generalized to civil servants in other political-administrative organizations? The idea is that that is possible, based on
the argument that all organizations are formed on the basis of similar vertical structures. Underlying concepts like vertical policy marketing, strategic
selling and framing (Chapter 8) and their translation into coping strategies
will not sound alien to civil servants in other political-administrative organizations, although that assumption was not tested.

Reliability of the coping strategies that were found
Is it expected that repeating the study will yield similar coping strategies?
Chances are it will. After completing the research, the researcher noticed that
civil servants mentioned coping strategies in conversations for a different
purpose than OMSPD, but they did mention coping strategies that emerged
in this study.

Completeness of the coping strategies that were found
Finally a remark about the completeness of the coping strategies. Have ALL
coping strategies been mentioned? This research contains the coping strategies that were mentioned by the civil servants we interviewed. It is expected
that the most common coping strategies that civil servants can use to get
OMSPD accepted will have been mapped. At the same time, it can be assumed that the inventory is not complete. For instance, two unorthodox coping strategies were not mentioned:

1. Seduce the Secretary, Minister or Director-General
    For instance, the example a Secretary of a Ministry who became involved
    with one of his employees. Next, encourage him to accept OMSPD ap-
    proaches within the Ministry and/or in a specific policy area.
    *Note: This strategy is loosely translated from Helen Gurley Brown, who
    published the book 'Sex and the Single Girl' in 1962. She advised every
    secretary to give her boss whatever he needed. And although there is no
    need to actually sleep with him, she needs to care for all his needs and
    become his best friend (Landin, 2014; Gurley Brown, 1962).*
2. Keep working as a civil servant but make sure you become famous for
    something else, to the extent that the administrative and/or political top
    loves having their picture taken with you and can score in public opinion.
    That will give you more influence when it comes to implementing policy
    projects using an OMSPD approach.

6.9 Conclusions

In this chapter, we discussed the research structure and accountability. In addition to delineating the target group, a description was provided of the Directorates-General and policy boards involved of the Ministries involved. In phase I, we examined what unwritten rules are and what their effect is on the level of openness. To identify causal relationships between hard unwritten rules and openness and to explain them from the perspective of the interviewees, we adjusted Scott-Morgan's method, which allowed us to answer the question 'What discrepancy is there between the required openness and the internal hard unwritten rules?'.
In phase II, we looked for coping strategies that are helpful (in the eyes of civil servants) to realize openness in policy development, given the hard unwritten rules.
This research structure allowed us to answer the central research question:

> *What coping strategies are available to civil servants to deal with hard unwritten rules and enable openness in policy development?*

The seven core concepts were defined as follows:

- *Openness*
  All concepts to do with horizontality have been reduced to one theoretical variable in policy development itself, which needs to be made measurable: openness. Openness has been made operational via the participation level *and* the level of exclusion – inclusion.
- *Open Multi Stakeholder Policy Development (OMSPD)*
  Pursuant to that, policy development that contains a sufficient level of openness is called Open Multi Stakeholder Policy Development. OMSPD involves utilizing the collective knowledge/intelligence in a network or letting the network serve as network (Roobeek, 2014), in function of the quality of the policy.
- *Hard written rules*
  Fundamental formal aspects that determine the design of an organization. For instance, mandate regulations and procedures as a 'phenomenon'. These have generic (bureaucratic) characteristics. Mandate regulations, for instance, organize in a top-down, hierarchical layering with associated accountability.
- *Unwritten rules*
  A result of written rules and the way in which leadership behaves. The result is expressed in the way written rules are interpreted (from their motivators) and given shape by employees in everyday practice (Scott-Morgan, 1995: 30).

· *Hard unwritten rules*
Collectively shared and recognized unwritten rules in an organizational segment that are hard to change. They can be seen as interpretations, from the employees' motivators, of fundamental written rules which, unlike Scott-Morgan's definition of unwritten rules, are not determined by the style of leadership.
• *Coping strategy*
Principles on the basis of which people act (operating principles) *and* the associated set of actions designed to deal with a problem or realize an objective.

In this study, we chose to follow the definitions proposed by Scott-Morgan (1995), to which we added the descriptions of hard unwritten rules and coping strategies. The reason we adopted this approach is that, in principle, we could use the research method proposed by Scott-Morgan (1995) to identify unwritten rules and the skill analysis method developed by the researcher. Scott-Morgan's division into motivators, authorities, levers and the associated questions offer the interviewee the opportunity to detect and explicate unwritten rules. Adjusting Scott-Morgan's method made it possible to find hard unwritten rule and determine their effect on the variable 'openness' from the point of view of the civil servant being interviewed (see diagram 4). To examine coping strategies at a deeper level in phase II, a separate approach was used.

Appendix 9 contains the complete research protocol for phase I, round I. The concepts of motivators, authorities and levers have been discussed in paragraph 4.4.

DIAGRAM 4: RESEARCH DIAGRAM UNWRITTEN RULES– OPENNESS

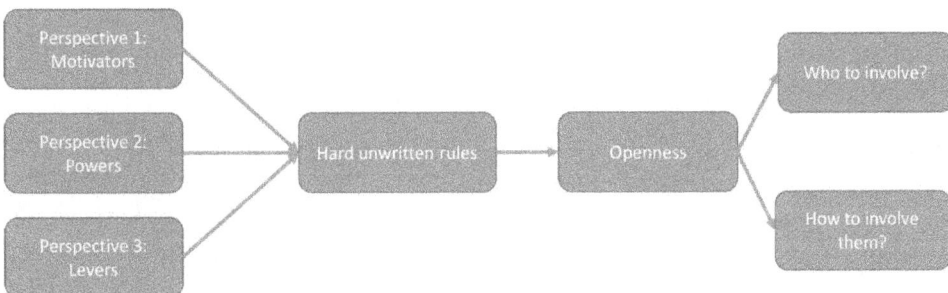

In the following chapter, the results of phase I of the research, the hard unwritten rules and their effect on openness, are discussed.

Chapter 7

Hard unwritten rules and openness

Chapter 7   Hard unwritten rules and openness

Chapter 6 provided a detailed description of how each research question was examined and conclusions were drawn. This chapter contains the results of phase I, which answers two of the sub-questions;

> *'What are the hard unwritten rules that civil servants are expected to observe in their own organization?'*

> *'What discrepancy is there between the required openness in policy development and the internal hard unwritten rules?'*

From the interviews that were conducted, four hard unwritten rules were reconstructed. Discrepancy between externally required openness in policy development and internal hard unwritten rules could be identified and explained from the perception of the respondents, using the scales that were used (participation levels and level of inclusion).

7.1   Four hard unwritten rules as core construct

In the first interviews in phase 1/round 1, with all 18 respondents, both unwritten rules and the relationship, in the perception of the interviewees,
between the hard unwritten rules they perceived and the level of openness
were explored.
Analysis of the results of those explorations and presenting the clustered results of round 1 in round 2 (12 respondents), yielded 112 models of hard unwritten rules. (Appendix 6 provides an overview of all the 112 hard unwritten
rules in question). These are clustered in four main rules, which together form
a core construct of the organizational culture. A core construct is a collective
mental model, an interpretation of hard _written_ rules by civil servants. The
core construct of this research can be summarized in three words: _calculat-
ed hierarchical subservience_. Every civil servant depends on approval 'from
above'. The underlying question is: 'How does what I do appear to those
above me?' Or: 'How do I get those above me to do what I want?' With the
Minister as the top layer. The core construct consists of four hard unwritten
rules:

1. Be aware, we serve the Minister here (via the line). _Closely observe
   the personality/character traits and interests of the Minister (and the
   hierarchy). How does he like to be served. Take those into account._
2. Be visible to the line.
3. Meet your deadline, especially with things that are politically important, because those in particular will be under a magnifying glass.
4. Cherish your network. Your network is crucial (especially with 'usual
   suspects').

The four rules illustrate that, in the functioning of the civil servants we examined, it is ultimately the Minister who (via the line) occupies the central position. As such, the 'quality assurance' of the production process 'developing
policy' is more vertical than it is horizontal.

In the following paragraphs, we discuss the four unwritten rules separately,
using the following format:

1. The unwritten rule itself and a detailed description.
2. The number of times the unwritten rule was mentioned in interviews in
   round 1.
3. Underlying written rules.

1. Hard unwritten rules and collectively shared, recognized unwritten rules that are hard to change. They are seen as interpretations, based on motivators (income, job security, recognition, career, social effect, etc.) of written rules. They are <u>not</u> determined by the style of leadership. The combination of hard written rules and motivators produces hard unwritten rules.

DIAGRAM 5: COMBINATION FUNDAMENTAL HARD WRITTEN RULES AND BASIC MOTIVATORS AS CAUSAL COMPLEX FOR HARD UNWRITTEN RULES

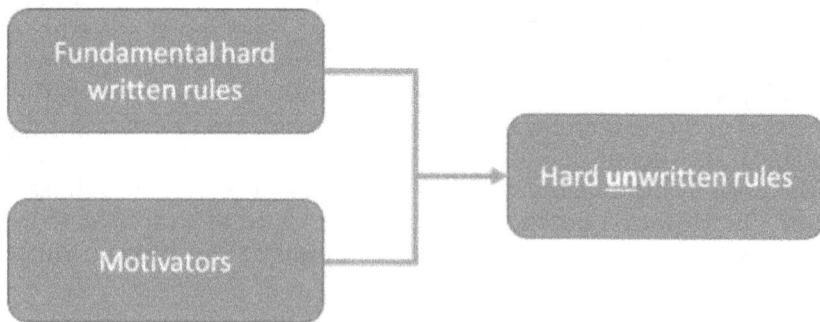

1. Similar formulations/practical interpretations that were mentioned. Formulations that are comparable to hard unwritten rules that are part of the core construct.
2. Effect on the level of openness.
    Both the effect on the level of exclusion – inclusion (who is involved in policy development and who is not) and the participation level (how actors are involved) are discussed.

7.1 Be aware, we serve the Minister here (via the line)

To define its effect in more precise terms, the hard unwritten rule 'Be aware, we serve the Minister here (via the line)' can be complemented with an unwritten rule that is derived from it: *'Closely observe the personality/character traits and interests of the Minister (and the hierarchy). How does he like to be served. Take those into account.'* This unwritten rules shows that attention focuses upward. A civil servants always has to realize that he is a representative of the Minister. The unwritten rule expresses obedience and hierarchical loyalty. A civil servant primarily does what he is told to do.
Based on that notion, information, in the form of memos, have to be sent to the Minister regularly. Before a civil servant can bring something to the Minister's attention, it will go through several hierarchical filters, each with their own perceptions. Looking at the personalities, character traits and interests

of the various hierarchical levels helps answer the question: 'How does it appear to those above me?'.

It is good to realize that civil servants, in line with the abovementioned rule, adapt to a large number of different political masters. *'Passing ships you have to serve'*, one civil servant characterized the situation in an informal conversation. Off the record, a high-ranking civil servant called it *'keeping amateurs in the saddle'*. 'Passing ships' are new Ministers, with their own wishes and a coalition to implement them.

In serving the Minister (via the line), there are three specific criteria that are important to a civil servant in terms of policy development:

- The political agreements that have been made.
- The quality of the policy content.
- Support (especial politically).

The political component was complimented by a civil servant, and by a Director-General, as follows:

- Negative publicity: when something appears in the media, that will lead to parliamentary questions.
- Is something risky? Or is there a perceived potential risk? The media are quick to make something of that too.
- Individual positioning politicians. Does a subject allow a politician to improve his profile?
- Difference substantive question/problem and political dimension:
  - o What is the problem in a substantive/technical sense?
  - o What is the political issue with regard to the problem?

Number of times mentioned in round 1
- *Be aware, we serve the Minister here (via the line)*
  Number of times mentioned by 18 civil servants: 18.
- *Closely observe the personality/character traits and interests of the Minister (and the hierarchy). How does he like to be served. Take those into account.*
  Number of times mentioned by 18 civil servants: 11 times.

Underlying written rules

The presence of the unwritten rule 'Be aware, we serve the Minister here (via the line) can easily be explained from hard written rules/laws, like ministerial responsibility, ministerial mandates, organizational decisions, functional structures and initialing procedures, in which that responsibility is delegated in a layered manner and refined down to the individual civil servant.

If the ministerial responsibility and the complementary layering are *the* structure that a civil servant experiences, it may be clear that, based on motivators like income and job security, career, recognition, etc., serving the Minister via the line is the top priority at a Ministry.

Other formulations

Other formulations of the unwritten rule 'Be aware, we serve the Minister here (via the line)' are:

- *Be aware, we serve the Minister here. Be loyal. Even if he is from a different party. You have to be able to work regardless of political preference.*
- *Make sure that the Minister makes a good impression, that he can score and, if necessary, protected.*
- *Ministers must not make a bad impression with respect to Parliament. They have to be able to score political points and show they have accomplished something. For a civil servant, this is more important that a positive effect in the field itself.*
- *Make sure that the Minister is able to accomplish something without being exposed to risks. That there are no obstacles, for instance from the social partners. How to pass something through Parliament in a smooth way?*
- *When something goes really wrong and the Minister is angry, he will vent to the people below him. Minister ⟶ Director-General ⟶ Director ⟶ Cluster leader ⟶ Civil servant.*
- *The work processes (policy development, memos, etc.) preferably yield information that the line itself can use and matches their direction (is in line with the political direction/coalition agreement/the Minister's wishes).*
- *Do not antagonize your superiors, because you need them to reach your goal.*

Effect on openness

Based on the rule, a civil servant has to pay attention to:

- What is going on in Parliament in relation to Ministers.
- What is going on in the field (especially usual suspects).
- What is going on in the media.
- Which developments there are outside the work field that may directly or indirectly affect the own dossier.

Solutions that are suggested by a civil servant are checked for two criteria:

- See what is possible politically.
- Check where the risks are for the Minister.

Based on those criteria, a civil servant formulates a certain solution, which is checked for the following criterion:
- See in what way Ministers can score with a certain solution.

In short, the focus of attention and checks is above all on the Minister and his political field, the media and usual suspects. With that, the unwritten rule 'Be aware, we are serving the Minister (via the line)' encourage the creation of a boundary that is 'More Exclusive'. In particular usual suspects with political influence that has to be taken into account are consulted. Based on this unwritten rule, openness often does not go beyond 'consulting'. Information is collected and the civil servants themselves decide what is done with the information. The following factors play a role in that:

- *Risk reduction and profiling opportunities*
  Avoid unexpected effects by involving too many parties too quickly.
  (Respondents: *'We don't want a Polish country fair, with lots of unwanted noises. Nor are you bothered with irrelevant sub-interests. Things are less chaotic'*).
- *Political parties and usual suspects*
  For the internal hierarchy, political parties and the political system with its usual suspects are the most important. The latter have political influence (Respondents: *'Other outside parties are not important to the internal line/hierarchy. Only political parties and the political system with its usual suspects are'*).
- *Control of the end result*
  The assumption is that there is less control of the end results when more other parties are involved. The Minister has to be able to explain the result in Parliament.
  (Respondent 1: *'The more others, the less control, and the Minister has to be able to explain it in Parliament. You need to stay in control and not present the Minister with a fait accompli. If you go further, you reduce the level of freedom for yourself and for the Minister.'*)
  (Respondent 2: *'Don't give room away to outsiders. That will cause problems for the internal hierarchy!'*).
  The hierarchical line has trouble receiving deviating, original products and taking them further. To prevent derailing, the creativity and room for maneuver of civil servants is restricted. There is management on details. Although the intention is to manage on broad outlines and give the policy development process room to grow, it goes against the unwritten rule.

The findings presented above are in line with the idea of policy as a *'plan ratified by politicians'* (Hoppe and Van der Graaf, 1996: 43). In this case, 'politicians' means 'Ministers'. An explanation provided by one of the interviewees not to go beyond consultation also shows how the written rule of ministerial responsibility works: *'Policy development is the responsibility of the Minister. Formally speaking as well! That is why we do not go beyond consultation.'* And Parliament, to which Ministers are accountable, plays a role, about which two of the interviewees state:

- *'The more quickly and strongly the position in Parliament, the fewer parties you will involve. After all, what would be the point?'*
- *'The more political an item is, the more it is closed off. If somethings becomes <u>really</u> political, it is taken out of the hands of the civil servant. The level of openness correlates with the sensitivity of a subject. If it is politically sensitive, you are told with whom to sit down. Decisions are made for you. If you go further, that is considered to be troublesome. In other words, preferably not.'*

7.2   Be visible to the line

Being visible to the line appears to be important to civil servants. If someone is invisible to the line, there may be doubts about what they are doing. And in particular about your added value to the people immediately above you in the line and ultimately the Minister. It has occurred regularly that civil servants solved a serious problem in the field without writing a memo about it. It turns out that that is not rewarded internally. One of the important things remains: 'Can the people immediately above you in the line use that solution to score visibly with their bosses'. If that is not the case, the solution to a problem is not interesting.

> Respondent: *'The common thread in the hierarchy: I can do well for you (higher up in the line), so that you can show that you are doing well. However, as a civil servant, you do not want a superior to score without him knowing about the glorious role you have played. And incidentally: if things go wrong, you, the civil servant, are to blame.'*

Number of times mentioned in round 1

'Be visible to the line'
Number of times mentioned in round 1 (18 civil servants): 10

Underlying written rules

The unwritten rule 'Be visible to the line' can be explained on the basis of written rules regarding ministerial responsibility, ministerial mandates, organizational decisions, functional structures and initialing procedures. Based on motivators like income and job security, career, recognition, etc., the people immediately above in the line are seen as 'legitimized' persons who can make or break a civil servant.

Other formulations/practical interpretations

Other formulations of the unwritten rule 'Be visible to the line' are:
* *That the work you have done is visible. What you have contributed.*
* *Make sure that your achievements and qualities are visible.*
* *Be careful towards the director. Do so by sending CC's at convenient moments, so what the work you have done and what you have contributed is visible.*
* *If you want to be appreciated by the managers/organization, make sure to work on high-priority dossiers.*
* *If you do things well, make sure they are visible, tell people about it (Be Good and Tell It). Primarily do things that are important* and *urgent.*
* *Show results. Make sure that the feedback about you overhead is positive. That you don't cause trouble.*
* *Create visibility in the (memo) productions with those who are considered important by the line and anyone who has even the slightest influence on the survival of the board.*

Effect on the level of openness

This unwritten line also encourages a 'More Exclusive' approach. Civil servants are expected to be in regular contact with usual suspects. They are supposed to know what goes on with those actors. A civil servant is visible in a positive way towards the hierarchy if he shows that the usual suspects have been consulted. There is a tendency only to <u>consult</u> powerful usual suspects with political influence. To maintain control of the end result. However, that is impossible. The usual suspects have political power that the Ministers (and hierarchy) have to take into account. As a result, the participation level moves up a few rungs on the ladder, to the level of partnerships. As one civil servant remarked:

> *'We have a number of contacts that we talk to regularly. This has been laid down at SAE in the tripartite system (employers, employees and government). If you want to go further in terms of involving parties, the question you get asked is "why?" Formally speaking, it is not our task to talk to those parties (i.e. <u>un</u>usual suspects). In discussions, the opinions of the usual are seen as the "truest", especially because they are connected to politics.'*

From that visibility, it is important for the civil servant to serve both the Minister and the line on time, which underlines the importance of the new hard unwritten rule: 'Meet your deadline'.

7.3   Meet your deadline!

Meeting deadlines is important. In particular in relation to the necessary internal and formal coordination. Deadlines are sacred, especially when they involve politically sensitive, officially controlled dossiers. Failing to meet a deadline, especially involving politically important dossiers, means losing momentum with which the civil servant can score visibly. Failing to maintain that momentum can land a Minister in political trouble. This reverberates back down the hierarchical line and ultimately to the civil servant in question. How important that is becomes clear from an additional unwritten rule that says that, for important dossiers, you have to be available 7 days a week, 24 for hours a day, regardless of whether you work part-time.

Number of times mentioned in round 1

'*Meet your deadline, especially involving cases that are politically important*' Number of times mentioned in round 1 (18 civil servants): 8

Underlying written rules

Here, too, especially ministerial responsibility, mandates and associated responsibilities, etc. play an important role. Failing to meet a deadline means that the ministerial responsibility in relation to Parliament can come under pressure. Based on motivators like income and job security, career, recognition, etc., failing to meet a deadline means negative visibility, through which a civil servant disadvantages himself.

Other formulations/practical interpretations

Other formulations of the unwritten rules '*Meet your deadline, especially involving cases that are politically important*' are:

- *Meet your deadline. It is sacred. Speedy delivery: deliver documents on time. A memo that is too late is not a memo. Loss of momentum. Do that ESPECIALLY with cases that are politically important. Be aware that they are put under a bigger magnifying glass. If you fail to meet your deadline, the Minister can get angry. Nobody likes that.*
- *When there are conflicting interests, we do not tend to be openly interac-*

tive. It is better to keep things small-scale, clear and closed. If you do not do that, you will usually be unable to meet your deadline.

- *If you do not know what the final product will be (in the case of open processes), that in no way matches the thinking in terms of deadlines, project goals and results, etc. Deadlines have to be met, which can be tricky in the case of projects where you want to adopt an outside-in (OMSPD) approach.*
- *The end date is sacred, but at the same time, you are increasingly dependent on complicated processes. You are dealing with administrative vestibules (sub-councils, ministerial vestibules, etc.), all with fixed dates when information has to be submitted.*
- *In short, all regular government circuits withdraw a lot of capacity and, combined with the 'sacred' end dates, that means you will not tend to involve many parties in policy development.*

Effect on level of openness

The unwritten rule focuses on the internal, administrative environment, rather than on the external environment. When there is time pressure, limiting oneself to consulting important parties is safe and responsible. The civil servants themselves can decide (quickly) what should be done with the outcomes of the consultation and thus control the lead time. Ministerial responsibility is safeguarded. The Minister can report to Parliament that authoritative parties have been consulted. The idea is that meeting deadlines is easier with closed networks.

Because of the unwritten rule, civil servants limit themselves to consulting the usual suspects. The assumption is that, the more quickly policy needs to be developed, the fewer parties will be involved. Openness takes a back seat. In addition, internal coordination takes a lot of time and it is hard to get everyone together with the increasing number of people working part-time. That is a problem for planning. Multiple people need to be in agreement in the initialing line.

Last but not least, to be able to serve the Minister and the line and to visibly serve the hierarchy in a positive way (and on time), ones network is crucial, especially the network of usual suspects.

7.4   Cherish your network

The discussion above shows that networks are crucial in the work of civil servants. The assumption is justified that a civil servant who is a poor networker cannot be a good civil servant. Civil servants depend on their network for relevant information if there is something they want to realize.

Number of times mentioned in round 1

'Cherish your network. Your network is crucial'
Number of times mentioned in round 1 (18 civil servants): 16

Underlying written rules

In this case, ministerial responsibility plays a role, with rules that govern the external communication and actions of civil servants. For instance, the rules of conduct regarding administrative integrity and the oath taken by every civil servant:

> *'I swear/promise that I will dutifully and conscientiously carry out the tasks that have been entrusted to me and that I will safeguard the confidentiality of matters that are entrusted to me in confidentiality by virtue of my position or of which I have to see the confidential nature to others than those I am officially obliged to inform; I swear/promise that I will behave as befits a good civil servant/good employee, that I will be careful, incorruptible and reliable and will do nothing that will damage the respect of the office'*
> (National Government, 2015).

As a result of this oath, civil servants are unable to communicate openly with third parties and regularly ask themselves questions like: 'What am I allowed to do? What can I say and what can I not say?' Based on motivators like income security, job security, career, recognition, etc., this makes civil servants cautious about who they interact with and how they handle their interactions. Not too much via e-mail and, especially when it involves sensitive issues, primarily exchange insights face-to-face.

Other formulations/practical interpretations

Other formulations of the unwritten rule *'Cherish your network. Your network is crucial'* are:

- *'Your network is crucial, so managing your network, especially with the usual suspect, is important. Without your network, you get nothing done. Also, things go a lot more quickly, for instance when you talk to recognized stakeholders.'*
- *'Through your network, you can also gauge how something will do politically in a broader sense. Make sure you know people of the usual suspects and that they know you. For that the 2nd and 3rd meeting moments are important, and will allow you to approach them informally with a question to explore themes, where there are real problems and what new insights or other types of solutions there are. Look at opinions/interests externally.'*
- *'You can only answer questions from above quickly and adequately when you have built a good and reliable network and you know who has what knowledge/abilities.'*
- *'Make sure you have a committed network that you can use when it turns out that an alternative road needs to be taken to realize a policy issue.'*
- *'Build a network around politically relevant themes so that, when necessary, you will be able to come up quickly with solutions that have support, or present interesting ideas.'*
- *'Be reachable, talk a lot with people inside and outside your network. That means signaling and where possible connecting. Compare initiatives from outside with the internal image and check internally for feasibility. Does it fit within how we work here, important themes and the coalition agreement. Look at what does and does not match the vision of the Minister/Secretary and whether it can be connected to that. Also look at opinions/interests externally.*

Effect on level of openness

Relationships with usual suspects are considered extremely important. Bad relationships, or insufficient coordination in that network, can create political risks for Ministers, especially if usual suspects have relationships with MPs and/or the media.

At the same time, as a result of this hard unwritten rule, in addition to usual suspects, also experts who do not belong to authoritative parties become important. These 'ordinary' professionals in the field are only consulted (there is no collaboration 'as equals') and have less influence. They do, however, allow the civil servant to hear 'something new'.

Three reasons are given for contacting experts who do not belong to the usual suspects:

- Keeping in touch with the field that the policy affects in practice.
- Obtaining input and new insights other than regular contacts.

- If a civil servant doubts the reliability of the input provided by usual suspects, which means there is a risk that the Minister is informed incorrectly.

Usual suspects do not always appreciate it when other parties in the field are contacted in connection with policy development behind their back. Because they want to maintain good relationships with usual suspects, civil servants are very cautious about this. If you do involve others, you will have to explain that to the usual suspects.
As a result of the unwritten rule, civil servants focus on the usual suspects, while at the same time obtaining wider information so as not to be unpleasantly surprised. He approaches the usual suspects when he considers it necessary.

When civil servants are dealing with key people/institutions with influence on politicians and on the field, sometimes, when gathering information, they need to go beyond merely 'consulting' (participation level: <u>how</u> do you involve actors). They are interdepartmental colleagues and/or recognized and trustworthy usual suspects who are respected by the Ministers and/or higher echelons in the line. These usual suspects are given a full part in policy development at the level of advising. Otherwise, it can lead to situations in which something cannot land in the field, which can cause trouble for the Minister and the hierarchy.

In terms of networks, these are more equal, but closed collaborations, with the characteristics of 'respecting and maintaining relationships' and 'negotiating'. This is called *'hard on content and soft on the relationships'*.

The 'being soft on relationships' and at the same time 'negotiating' was expressed by the interviewees as follows:
- *'Cherish the relationships with colleagues from other Ministries (not just with those in your own Ministry).'*
- *'Don't do too much via e-mail. When sensitive issues are involved, face-to-face is better. You have to be able to look each other in the eye'.*
- *'Take what you can take away from other Ministries that does not cause trouble for the Mister.'*

If someone is able to play that game well, they have a career as a civil servant ahead of them. A connection can be established with desired forms of visibility, managing relationships and moving ahead in the policy hierarchy, as one civil servant stated: *'People who move ahead in the administrative hierarchy are people who are strategically strong. They have the right answers to the following questions: What will contribute to the policy of the Ministry? What are the political risks? How can you negotiate with other Ministries (usual suspects) and safeguard your Ministry's bottom line?'*

7.5   Do unwritten rules restrict openness?

Based on the research results, the conclusion is justified that unwritten rules emphasize vertical organization and restrict horizontal organization. Looking up is more important than looking out. In addition, it appears that the four unwritten rules reinforce each other in their emphasis on verticality and closedness. If the Minister needs to score in his system, the line scores by letting the Minister score. The civil servant needs to be visible to the line to count. The three rules focus on the inside rather than on the outside. The focus on the outside is limited primarily to usual suspects. Sometimes, unwritten rule 4 (Cherish your network. Your network is crucial) yields exceptions beyond usual suspects, to detect potential risks and/or opportunities for the Minister and for policy.

TABLE 19: ASSUMED MUTUAL EFFECTS OF UNWRITTEN RULES

	Serve the Minister	Be visible to the line	Meet your deadline	Cherish your network
Serve the Minister		+	+	+-
Be visible to the line	+		+	+-
Meet your deadline	+	+		-
Cherish your network	+	+-	+-	

The rules restrict openness above 'consulting' and beyond 'experts who are not usual suspects' (level of exclusion-inclusion). In the case of politically sensitive problems, at the most, usual suspects are involved. Sometimes, with parties who are perceived as 'More Exclusive', things go beyond consulting, especially when they are powerful actors with political influence.
The tendency, based on the hard unwritten rules, to develop policy with the same parties (the 'standard interests'), the likelihood increases that the own policy theories are not tested sufficiently. This can threaten knowledge integrity, pushing things into a direction that matches the interests of the 'More Exclusive' network.

TABLE 20: EFFECT OF HARD UNWRITTEN RULES ON LEVEL OF OPENNESS

HARD UNWRITTEN RULE	OPENNESS	
	PARTICIPATION LEVEL	LEVEL OF INCLUSION/EXCLUSION
Be aware, we serve the Minister here (via the line)	Only **consulting** and retain 'power' over end result.	Only **usual suspects**. They have political power that Ministers (and line) have to take into account.
Be visible tot he line	Only **consulting**, maintain 'power' over end result and score in a positive way in the line.	A civil servant is visible in the line in a positive way if he shows that goes on at **usual suspects** and they have been consulted.
Meet your deadline	Only **consulting** so that your are ready in time and can determine the end result	Only internal, administrative environment and main **usual suspects**. Under time pressure, that is safe and responsible.
Cherish your network	With authoritative people/institutions that affect politie/media and field, there is a need for **partnership** (formal and informal).	Bad relationships and insufficient coodination with **usual suspects** can pose political risks for Ministers. For new ideas, sometimes **experts are consulted who are not usual suspects.**

7.6 Conclusion research phase I

What are hard unwritten rules that civil servants are expected to observe in their own organization?
Four hard unwritten rules emerged that can be seen as the core of the organization:

1. Be aware, we serve the Minister here (via the line).
    Closely observe the personality/character traits and interests of the Minister (and the hierarchy). How does he like to be served. Take those into account.
2. Be visible to the line.
3. Make your deadline, especially with things that are politically important, because those in particular will be under a magnifying glass.
4. Cherish your network. Your network is crucial.

What discrepancy is there between the required openness in policy development and the internal hard unwritten rules?

The second conclusion is that hard unwritten rules restrict openness. Participation levels beyond 'consulting', combined with levels beyond 'experts who are not usual suspects' (level of exclusion-inclusion) rarely occur. In the case of politically sensitive problems, at the most, the 'More Exclusive' usual suspects are involved. Sometimes, with parties who are perceived as 'More Exclusive', things go beyond consulting, especially when they are powerful actors with political influence.

The rules make openness not self-evident. In the next chapter, we address the question what civil servants can do. What coping strategies do they have at their disposal to deal with hard unwritten rules and enable openness in policy development?

Chapter 8

Combining openness and hierarchy

Chapter 8   Combining openness and hierarchy

In this chapter, we discuss the research results that answer the central research question:

> *'What coping strategies are available to civil servants to deal with hard unwritten rules and enable open policy development?'*

A coping strategy is described as a structured set of actions to deal with a problem or realize a goal and the principles on the basis of which actions take place (operating principles). First, a set of coping strategies is discussed and the action set of the respondents are addressed, before examining the underlying operational principles.

Finally, we pay attention to the integrity of civil servants who want to realize an open approach. Integrity 1.0 does not appear to relate well to open policy development. We close by addressing the question how the tension between vertical and horizontal can be translated into a constructive connection.

8.1   Coping strategies for realizing openness in hierarchy

Hard unwritten rules reinforce the tendency civil servants have to stay inside internal playing fields, in terms of 'participation' and 'partners'. At the same time, civil servants apply OMSPD. How do they manage to do that with certain hard unwritten rules? Although the hard unwritten rules restrict openness, civil servants have ways of dealing with unwritten rules and realize open policy development. It turns out that the coping strategies identified in this study are not 'eccentric findings'. On closer inspection, they meet three criteria:

1.   They are part of the ideas of civil servants and can be recognized as such.
2.   They can be implemented quickly and usually do not require any long-term planning.
3.   They do not have a tendency to place a civil servant in a visibly exceptional position in relation to the hierarchical line.

The respondents were asked about the coping strategies, underlying operating principles and generic (desired) convictions with the following questions (see end interview protocol Appendix 9):

•   What is a possible coping strategy for enabling a higher degree of openness (how can you do that in concrete terms, making openness possible)?
•   What are the assumptions underlying this potential coping strategy? ('Operating principles') (Herold, 2012).
•   What does the use of such a coping strategy tell you about the convictions of the person applying the coping strategy?

At the same time, we asked the respondents in phase I is they knew colleagues who had managed to realize openness. This new group of respondents as approached in phase II for an in-depth interview in line with the protocol of the skill analysis method.

This research has elicited these strategies inductively, with a rich yield of 62 coping strategies, which were ranked and written out in Appendix 6. They can be seen as a pallet of possibilities: what can a civil servant apply when he wants to develop OMSPD-proof policy?

To shed light on the ranking of coping strategies, we return to the insights provided by Ledeneva (2001), who indicated that written and unwritten rules can be followed or utilized.

TABLE 21: WRITTEN RULES /UNWRITTEN RULES /WHAT TO DO WITH THEM?

Written rules	Hard unwritten rules: (collectively shared)	What to do with them
		Follow
	XXXXXXXXXXXXXXXXXXXXXXX	Utilie

For this chapter, the coping strategies that, based on Ledenava's thinking, are 'merely following' or 'just doing, without looking at the consequences of what you do in the internal organization', are less interesting. They merely confirm our earlier conclusions. Of greater interest are the strategies that deliberately utilize or circumvent hard unwritten rules to realize open policy development.

TABLE 22: (SUB)DVISION COPING STRATEGIES GENERAL

Main categories Coping strategies	Follow or use unwritten rules?
Non-influencing oriented strategy	Follow
The 'cover' strategy	Follow
The 'Just-do-it!'-strategy	Not follow/not use
Strategies aimed directly at influencing	Use
Strategies aimed indirectly at influencing	Use

The shaded coping strategies that deliberately utilize hard unwritten rules to realize openness are the focus of this chapter.

8.2   Coping strategies without influencing

Coping strategies in the non-shaded part respect and adhere to the unwritten rules. There is no focused influencing or deliberate use of hard unwritten rules in favor of openness. Based on the empirical research, three categories of these coping strategies were identified:

- Not aimed at influencing.
- Following and covering.
- Just do it.
- *The 'not aimed at influencing' strategies*

This type of strategy conforms to the top-down decision-making authority of the line. Decisions are submitted to the line and leadership determines and selects. Although the civil servant does draw attention to the field, he does not do so without covering himself and matching the preconditions that a hierarchy has with regard to a policy theme, which determine the playing field for what can be discussed with outsiders. Only then does the question arise: 'What is possible in terms of OMSPD?'

This strategy starts with approaching the manager to find out what he thinks is important about the policy theme. The civil servant asks the manager that comes to mind first to involve in policy development. The civil servant asks colleagues additional questions like 'Who is involved in this internally? What all is involved? Who are the people involved on an interdepartmental level?' The list of people provide by colleagues is then submitted to the manager, after which a selection takes place. After this thorough exploration of 'who to involve', the participation level is discussed.

A memo that supports an OMSPD approach has all the necessary initials. In the memo, the Director-General can be asked who else he wants to involve. That can be done in a meeting with him. After this formal coordination, the contacts with the field are organized via representative bodies, usual suspects who are not overlooked. In meetings that are part of the process of policy development, if necessary, the service of professional facilitators are used. Where possible, whatever is said is checked via research and in-depth explorations.

If the immediate manager asks to build a network of interested parties and knowledge experts, the Internet is useful in finding contacts/experts/interests and determine how the problem is linked to adjacent knowledge areas. Sometimes, it is necessary to appear to be 'helpful' to the outside. In other words, there may be issues that the field finds it hard to solve. The civil servants presents that to the line and asks if the Ministry can make a contribution via OMSPD. With this strategy, the hard unwritten rules and adherence to them can be seen as the underlying operating principles.

- *The 'cover yourself' strategy: Record and stick to the rules*

Sometimes, a manager proposes a closed policy development project where the civil servant senses that things can go wrong and create a political discussion. The unwritten rules show a pattern whereby, if things go wrong in the eyes of the Minister, this lands on the desk of the civil servant, via the director and cluster manager, and the dossier in question is removed from the civil servant in question.
It is smart to record agreements with the department manager/immediate supervisor and carry out instructions in accordance with what the line prescribes. That way, the civil servant is covered and cannot simply be blamed when things go wrong. Come the next project, he can point to experiences with closed networks and thus create momentum in favor of an open approach.
With this strategy, the hard unwritten rules and adherence to them are the underlying operating principles. If the civil servant records his actions precisely and meticulously, the blame shifts to the person telling him what to do.

- *The 'just do it' strategies*

A civil servant can also just get to work without a lot of internal and external analysis. This 'just do it' approach presents the hierarchy with a fait accompli. The difference with strategy I is that, with this strategy, either the civil servant is not familiar with the unwritten rules or pretends not to be familiar with them.

A possible underlying principle with this strategy can be, in line with the thinking of a Housing Experiments Steering Group in the past:

> *'It is better to ask for forgiveness than permission'*
> (Krijger, Driest & Stoelenga, 2002).

This strategy can lead to a situation where the civil servant is deemed a 'loose cannon', which can damage his or her career. Whereas, in the case of the non-influencing-oriented and covering strategies, leadership is followed, that does not happen with this strategy and, instead, leadership is faced with a fait accompli. In the next paragraph, we take a look at strategies that do aim at realizing openness.

8.3 Directly influencing coping strategies and unwritten rules

The first category of strategies designed to realize OMSPD consists of 'direct influencing'. In line with Frazer & Summers (1984), direct influencing involves civil servants analyzing the interests and priorities of the hierarchical line themselves and determining how to respond. Without using third parties and playing the game 'via the cushion'. The strategies that belong to this main category use the hard unwritten rules. They are the inductive result of empirical research. A civil servant looks at how the hierarchical line can be influence *without* using colleagues and third parties. The civil servant analyzes the situation, the hierarchical line, possible connections and actors involved, focusing on the question: 'How do I get this past the Director-General as key to politics?'
The interviews yield a wide range of influencing strategies (see coping strategies 5-46 in Appendix 6). A civil servant goes to work and focuses on influencing the hierarchical line on his own, without sparring with colleagues. Below, we present the data that provide insight into the way in which hard unwritten rules are combined with OMSPD. We call them connection rules.

Connection rule I: Determine how Minister (and line) can score with OMSPD

The unwritten rule *'Be aware, we serve the Minister here (and the line)'* means that the Minister has to be able to score politically. He has to be able to show results. If a civil servant wants to deploy OMSPD, he has to show how a Minister can score with it and/or distinguish himself in a positive sense from other politicians. For instance by identifying new policy options that makes it easier to implement policy (which requires support and practical insights) and/or increase long-term sustainability. In addition, media exposure plays a role as well. How can OMSPD improve the Minister's image in the media? Intermediate layers in the hierarchy also look at the layer immediately above them wants. In Chapter 7, as an addition to the hard unwritten rule 'Be aware, we serve the Minister here (and the line)', respondents added: *'Closely observe the personality/character traits and interests of the Minister (and the hierarchy). How does he like to be served. Take those into account.'* Applying this rules starts with the Ministers at the top of the hierarchy. What do they say in the media and how can that be used in OSMPD? And what do relevant internal 'superiors' say, and how can a civil servant use that when he wants to apply OMSPD? In addition to the media and information and 'incidents', the civil servant can also look at the coalition agreement, legislation, departmental documents (including reports) and recognized (preferably scientific) literature, looking for clues on how to get the hierarchy to agree to an OMSPD proposal. Clues that answer the question: 'How do I translate the OMSPD proposal into language and texts that the Minister and hierarchy themselves could have expressed or have indeed expressed and to which they are sensitive?'

A next step is to determine whether the hierarchy itself can improve its image through OMSPD, for instance by positioning OMSPD as something new within the Ministry, even though it has already been applied elsewhere. The latter reduces the feeling of risk and puts OMSPD in a positive light by comparing it to 'how others do it', in particular when those 'others' have been successful, that can reduce the risk perception and create a sense of 'we are running behind'. That helps reconcile hard rules and OMSPD.

Internal acceptance depends on making it clear that an open approach cannot lead to a situation where promises have to be made that cannot be kept *and* where other public authorities do not comment on the approach. The latter also do not want to get into trouble. The policy issue and OMSPD have to be formulated in such a way that no promises are made to third parties during the process. That also covers any risks. Emphasizing the added value of new stakeholders or utilizing incidents that have to do with the policy themes in question and bring other parties into the picture also help reconcile the rules and OMSPD.

Public remarks by authoritative stakeholders with which an open approach can be supported also help. In addition, it helps to frame OMSPD as 'informal', which is where the unwritten rule *'Cherish your network. Your network is crucial'* comes into effect. Should a civil servant meet with authoritative stakeholders 'informally', and they suggested additional parties (unusual suspects), these suggested can be 'exaggerated' to own management.

Another coping strategy is to label OMSPD as research. Research is important in the development of policy and provides a sense of 'thoroughness'. With an open approach, the research is exploratory in nature. In addition, researchers have more freedom than employees working 'in the line'. In addition, calling it research makes it possible to outsource the OMSPD, which means that, should the results be unwelcome, 'not the civil servant, but someone else is to blame'.

Furthermore, civil servants can decide to gain experience with OMSPD by tackling 'niche' issues. They are politically speaking less sensitive or not at all. This allows him to show how OMSPD works. After a few successes, trust in open approaches grows and a foundation is laid for 'doing things differently'.

Finally, the civil servant can write a memo and divide the memo in two parts. The first memo is used to gain approval for an OMSPD-proof approach and, if that is given, the second memo can be used to ask for funds and capacity.

Connection rule II: Check how you can avoid or reduce risks for the Minister

The Minister and the hierarchical line are not only served by allowing them to score, but also by shielding them from potential risks. Sometimes, that is possible by staying at the participation level of consulting and not going further on the participation ladder. In the case of consulting, a deliberate distinction is made between policy exploration and policy decisions. In the policy exploration, there is a further option to focus above all on content. The number of stakeholders to be involved can be expanded, but the Ministry remains leading and a Minister can still have the final say.

There are stakeholders that are considered politically risky, but that have interesting policy insights. It is possible to consider ways to involve them in a politically responsible way in policy development, keeping in mind that not involving them can also be a political risk.

A political risk of an entirely different kind are the usual suspects who also need to bring something home for their own constituency. That will also have to be taken into account in the organization. For instance by the abovementioned distinction between 'substantive exploration' and 'decisions'. They can play a somewhat different and freer role in the exploratory phase than in the decision-making phase.

It is also important to organize the policy exploration in such a way that it does not turn in a 'Polish country fair' and one-sided influencing by one or a few parties is prevented. Furthermore, risk perception can be reduced by giving OMSPD, in the way it is organized, an 'informal character' and to call it that as well. The perceived risk of involving more parties in the policy development is also reduced if the civil servant tells the hierarchical line that he knows the unusual suspects. That gives the hierarchy confidence in a good result when these new actors participate in policy development.

Other ways to further reduce risks and risk perception in policy development is to incrementally increase the number of participants, as well as organizing lots of smaller meetings, starting with a closed (Internet) group on the basis of invitation and, last but not least, subdividing a policy development project and seeing which parts of the development process is suitable for an open approach. In the latter case, it is possible, for example that the solution phase in a policy project can be open, because the causes of a policy problem are sufficiently clear and no elaborate exploration is necessary.

Finally, for the organizational manageability, it is important to know how much money and capacity an OMSPD-proof approach costs. A cost-benefit analysis is useful in that regard.

Connection rule III Will you meet your deadline when you want OMSPD?

The hard unwritten rule 'Meet your deadline' often clashes with the assumption that OMSPD costs more time. It is, therefore, good to disprove that assumption by giving examples where a well-chosen form of OMSPD actually speeds things up. On the one hand, that can be for the policy development itself, but also by pointing to the implementation of policy measures *after* the policy development. If bad policy is being developed, that may cause problems over time, which means the Minister will have to address Parliament to discuss the negative side-effects.

The interviews provide various coping strategies for dealing with the factor time in a smart way. An example is to claim more time at the start of a policy trajectory by indicating all the parties that you need to involve. Or by emphasizing 'carefulness' in the policy development and claiming more time for that. If that is not possible, there is always the possibility of designing an OMSPD that can be carried out quickly. Think, for instance, at a combination of open online Internet consulting and group decision meetings that can be organized relatively simply and quickly.

Another form suggested by the respondents is to start as early as possible, so that you have optimum room. You can also point out that talking about OMSPD means losing time and that it would be better to get started right away.

If direct influencing should fail, there are always indirect ways.

TABLE 23: RELATIONSHIP 'DIRECTLY INFLUENCING' COPING STRATEGIES AND HARD UNWRITTEN RULES (VIA CONNECTION RULES)

Category	Connection rule/ way to use for OMSPD
Directly influencing coping strategies	*Determine how Ministers (and line) can score with OMSPD:* · Find political connections between OMSPD and what is politically relevant to Ministers · Show how a Minister can use OMSPD for positive media coverage · Use what media say for OMSPD · Indicate that new policy options have to be found · Use the practicability of policy · Use what relevant internal 'superiors' say for OMSPD · Use the coalition agreement, legislation, departemental documents (including reports) and acknowledged (preferably scientific) literature for OMSPD · Find a way in which your own leadership can use OMSPD to inncrease their profile
	Determine how risks to Ministers (and the line) can be reduced or avoided: · Make a distinction between policy exploration and policy decisions. Focus on the substance in the exploration (separate the technical and political aspects) · Determine how you can involve stakeholders who are less 'politically savvy' · Indicate that unusual suspects with a constituency can play a freer role during the exploration compared to the decision-making phase · Show it will not be a 'Polish country market' and that one or a few parties will not dominate the proceedings. · Give OMSPD an 'informal character' · Tell the hierarchical line that you know the <u>un</u>usual suspects · Build meetings incrementally in terms of the number of participants, or organize lots of small meetings · Start with a closed (Internet) group based on invitation · Split up a policy trajectory and see which part lends itself to an open approach · Provide a responsible cost-benefit analysis
	Determine how to meet/use your deadline if you want OMSPD: · Give examples of OMSPD speeding things up · Design a quick form of OMSPD · Claim time by indication who all you <u>have</u> to involve · Emphasize the 'diligence' and claim time for that · Start as early as possible, that way you have the most (political) room · Say that taling about OMSPD is what takes up time · Choose the right moment for OMSBO
	See who in your network you can use (especiall with usual suspects): · Ask authoritative stakeholders 'informally' for additional parties (unusual suspects), and exaggerate them when talking to your own management

8.4   Indirectly influencing coping strategies and hard unwritten rules

The second category consists of options to adopt an indirect approach, involving other people. There is a distinction between mobilizing internal colleagues or external stakeholders to put pressure on the hierarchy and politicians to realize OMSPD. The internal approach involves employees from the civil servant's own Ministry, while the external approach involves network contacts outside of the Ministry. If the line says 'no' to OMSPD, the external approach offers a way to get OMSPD accepted in the Ministry. This can be estimated before even talking to the hierarchy.

Connection rule: Examine who in your network can be used to get OMSPD accepted

'Cherish your network' is the unwritten rule that is the core for this main category. The network is deliberately used to put pressure on the hierarchical line and political top to adopt an OMSPD approach to policy development. That is possible by carefully planning the order in which you talk to people and use the conversation with person A when you talk to person B.
These indirect coping strategies involve organizing political support in a roundabout way, that can persuade a Secretary, Minister or Director-General to back an OMSPD approach. If that works, intermediate layers in the line will also follow, because they, in turn, serve the people above them. In that sense, there is also a connection to the unwritten rule *'Be aware, we serve the Minister here (and the line)'.*
For political support, interdepartmental and/or external 'sponsorship' can be created; a 'crowbar' in the form of a network with authoritative (and visible) people. For each policy theme, that network and who has authority can change.
To build such a network, it is examined who at the other Ministries are intensely committed to the policy themes or who experiences the blockades. Realizing informal contact with those people is important.
In the case of strategies that use an external approach, a distinction can be drawn between authoritative third parties who will act on your behalf, and parties who themselves lobby to make themselves visible. The civil servant can show them how they can make themselves visible in an effective way in terms of a specific policy theme.
Internally, it is important to build enough 'critical collegial mass' that is able to influence the line. Find out where there is internal skepticism and how to deal with it. How can you meet opponents halfway in the organization of OMSPD?

Adopting an indirect approach has characteristics of 'Strategic Selling' (Miller & Heiman, 2011), the underlying idea being that a decision to 'buy' something always involves multiple persons influencing the decision. Those persons are mapped, along with the influence they exert. In addition, an assessment is made of various decision-makers who are in favor of or against a given product (in this case: the OMSPD approach). Sponsors are 'created' for the product that needs to be sold. They influence the network and the person(s) making the final decision whether or not to buy the products.

TABLE 24: RELATIONSHIP 'VIA-THE-CUSHION' COPING STRATEGIES AND HARD UNWRITTEN RULES (VIA CONNECTION RULE)

(Sub)category	Connection rule / way of using for OMSPD
Via the external cushion	Use 'serve the Minister (and the line)' by first having Ministers influenced and then, via him, the line: · Determine who within other Ministries is closely committed tot he policy theme or experiences blockades and how to use them for OMSPD · Determine which authoritative persons have a positive attitude towards OMSPD and can serve as a 'crowbar' · Make an explicit distinction between authoritative third parties who go to bat for you, versus perties who lobby to make themselves visible · Provide them insight, if they do not know, on how to make themselves visible effectively in relation to a specific policy theme
Via the internal cushion	Determine how the line and colleagues can score with OMSPD: · Determine which internal authoritative (and visible) persons are important to the line · Determine who internally is positive about OMSPD and can serve as a 'crowbar' with regard to OMSPD · Determine where there is internal skepticism and how to deal with that · Build a çritical mass' bottom-up and move up 'through the line'. Have colleagues from other departments, their manager and their director influenced, so they can then talk to your own line about an OMSPD wish
Network development formula for internal and external cushion	Determine how you can meet/use your deadline if you want OMSPD: · Start working your network as early as possible. That takes time.
	Determine who you will use in your network (especially usual suspects): · Build a network by thinking about an <u>order in which to approach people</u>. Where you can use the conversation with person A with person B

It is not possible to turn OMSPD into a success only using coping strategies in the form of giving instructions. It takes more. An underlying foundation is desirable. A basis attitude that helps turn coping strategies into a success. That basic attitude is formed by an operating principle.

8.5   Operating principles/basic attitude

Coping strategies require underlying operating principles. They form a basis attitude to turn coping strategies into a success. A basic attitude can be described as:

> 'A fundamental attitude with regard to something or someone, the way people approach their work and their lives'
> Riepma & Van Aken, 2009: 29).

In the case of a coping strategy, the attitude and focal points are the 'operating principles' on the basis of which people act. Here, we discuss operating principles that were mentioned by the interviewees and that provide insight into a generic basic attitude of civil servants. The subject was included in every interview. In the descriptions presented below, the operating principles that the interviewees mentioned have been clustered into three blocks:

- Be entrepreneurial
- Be convinced of the added value of OMSPD
- Be convinced of the importance of respectful long-term relationships

Be entrepreneurial!

Entrepreneurship is about 'discovering and utilizing opportunities' (Bruijns, 2006: 5). OMSPD requires a civil servant to move outside of secure frameworks and think and act outside the box. For that, they need to be able to be independent and to have courage, despite the risk of rejection and disapproval.
Being entrepreneurial also means that the civil servant places his organization in a broader perspective. There is a tendency to see the world in a strictly political frame, with all the actors who have an influence on policy. But the world is more than that small political arena. It is not just about what the hierarchy, which primarily pays attention to the chain of command, wants to hear, there is also a wider world, which also has something to say. Civil servants understand that any thoughts and actions that are completely adjusted to the line run the risk of becoming rigid.
It helps to 'read between the lines'. To be able to do that well, a civil servant

is 'anti-hierarchical'. That means that, in his contacts with the outside world, he does not think in terms of hierarchies, but sees each actor as an equal, interesting party who can make a valuable contribution. On the other hand, he has a keen eye for hierarchies and knows how to use them in policy development. That changes the way hierarchy is perceived, which is not necessary in a 'vertical' way, but as way of (organizational) ordering: who decides what? From management assistants to policy specialists, they all have their own contribution to make from their particular position. If you take them all seriously, within distinction, looking at their respective contributions, hierarchy becomes less important. It becomes about 'how can we help each other?'. Being entrepreneurial means that civil servants set their own boundaries and make their own considerations; stubborn and loyal at the same time. They understand that they help realize the objectives of the coalition agreement, but not blindly and without taking insights into the policy measures to be developed into account in his approach. On the one hand, this means sticking to the OMSPD approach and, on the other hand, it means being open to new insights, with the aim of arriving at an OMSPD approach that is geared towards relevant actors.

It is important for the civil servant to understand whether he has the stamina needed to push through an OMSPD approach. If that is not the case, it is likely that he will be unable to deal with resistance. In short, relevant questions that require an honest answer are: Do I have the stamina and can I do this on my own? Is it something I feel like doing? Can I commit to the goal I am trying to realize (OMSPD)?

As one of the respondents remarked explicitly: *'You can improve your confidence by realizing that a civil servant may just be a cog in a large machine, he is an important cog that has influence on the entire machine. A "cog" that transcends the classic approach to machines and can find his own way. Convinced of the value of his OMSPD product.'*

Be convinced of the added value of OMSPD

A civil servant has to be genuinely convinced of the added value of OMSPD. He needs to understand the value of involving others than the usual suspects in policy development. Even when Ministers and larger 'policy objectives' stand in his way, the importance of 'field reality' is an integral aspect. To the civil servant, implementation, which primarily involves carrying out political objectives, equally important as shaping policy. For a civil servant, that implies an inherent curiosity about the question as to how policy works in practice.

The added value of OMSPD is that it involves all stakeholders *and* the common good. Presenting maximum differences of opinions, images and ideas and arrive at constructive insights. The assumptions is that maximum open-

ness leads to less loss of energy and fewer games. It is the civil servant's responsibility to safeguard the common good in an OMSPD process.
The added value and common interest of OMSPD can come under pressure when a party involved in the OMSPD process abuses the network. For instance, someone from a commercial company telling people that he works together with the Ministry, serving only his own commercial interests and promoting his company in the network. If that happens, the civil servant has to contact the person involved and give them feedback. Although OMSPD approaches work on the basis of trust, it is important to remain business-like.

Finally, a civil servant can be convinced that OMSPD makes the administrative role (and the role of the Ministry) more legitimate when the complexity of a theme is made visible to the outside world, creating more respect for the civil servant who has to deal with the complex theme in question. The remarks presented above make a third operating principle explicit. It is impossible to be entrepreneurial without the ability to build and maintain long-term network relationships.

Be convinced of the importance of respectful long-term relationships

Being convinced of one's own network qualities is relevant (of course, they have to exist). A civil servant has to build long-term relationships with the playing field. After all, parties have a network relationship with each other and with the Ministry. The better the civil servant is able to improve the quality of the relationships with external parties, the smaller the chance of political risk. It means that the parties trust the civil servant in question. It is easy to promote this by honoring one's agreements and not abuse, in an administrative sense, what one has heard from third parties.
Promoting network relationships also means that the civil servant in questions behave respectfully to all parties. To treat everyone equally, in terms of respect, whether policy or field, without looking at their positions and, last but by no means least, being respectful towards 'outsiders'. The core question is always: 'How are you as a human being?' Networking also about people. What else is there to say about coping strategies and underlying operating principles from an entrepreneurial point of view? What relevant information can we find in research and literature?

8.6   Reflection on operating principles

Most of the coping strategies that were mentioned have to do with the added value of OMSPD (Appendix 8). This 'added value' is mentioned multiple times by the respondents. The need to find ways to connect to Ministers and hierarchical line can be called 'vertical policy marketing', analogous to suppliers who market products in the chain 'supplier – seller – buyer' (Wuyts, Stemersch, Van den Bulte & Franses, 2004).

Marketing involves examining the needs and wishes of the customers and providing products that the customer wants to have (Verhage & Cunningham, 2004: 19). If we replace the terms customer and marketing chain by hierarchy and Ministers, this means finding out what the needs of the line are and the product (OMSPD) is tailored accordingly. A civil servant can be compared to a product manufacturer who thinks 'in between retail'.

Even though it is the hierarchy that has the ultimate say when it comes to applying OMSPD, there are other players who can either torpedo or support an OMSPD approach, which explains why 'building a critical mass' was mentioned a number of times by the respondents. There are always adjacent policy dossiers that have to be taken into account. If colleagues from other policy boards or Ministries think OMSPD is a good idea and bring that into the line, that creates the impression of coordination, which reduces the sense of risk in the line and makes it easier for director or Director-General to give their approval. At the same time, many of the coping strategies that were mentioned use 'framing'. De Bruijn (2011) talks about 'rhetorical frames', which he describes as:

> 'A substantive political message, that is used in the political debate and leads to a specific interpretation of reality. Certain aspects of reality are enlarged, others are pushed below the perception of our radar'
> (De Bruijn, 2011: 16).

Entman (1993) also states that 'framing influences thinking', which he describes as:

> 'To select some aspects of a perceived reality and make them more salient in a communicating text, in such a way as to promote a particular problem definition, causal interpretation, moral evaluation, and/or treatment recommendation'
> (Entman, 1993: 51).

Marketing, framing and creating market share (critical mass) for a certain approach, combined with the three operating principles, are based on policy entrepreneurship, which Brouwer & Huitema describe as:

> 'Entrepreneurs who, like their colleagues in the private sector, see opportunities in certain ideas and have the capacity to "sell" and "market" them'
> (Brouwer & Huitema, 2010: 10).

Bekker and Veerman (2009) additionally speak of:

> 'Civil servants who take action to create a "window" for a certain problem.
> He does so by entering into intensive contacts with relevant persons and
> organizations, organizing meetings to create a dialog, writing opinion
> pieces for a newspaper, etc.'
> (Bekker & Veerman, 2009: 47)

When the issue in question is politically sensitive, the policy entrepreneur
often uses informal contacts to create a common perception about a problem and the desired policy solution. At the same time, he adopts a wider
approach and brings people together who, previously, had little or no contact with each other (Bekker & Veerman, 2009: 28). That aspect of policy
entrepreneurship, bring people parties or individuals, is not only part of the
'practical signaling and design process', but a necessary basis for developing
OMSPD.

The policy entrepreneur can be seen as what Van Hoesel, during a meeting,
called an 'un-civil servant-like civil servant', who find the boundaries of the
unwritten rule culture. They think and act more based on what is possible
than in terms of risks. They understand the prevailing government culture,
but at the same time are able to move in networks outside government,
increase their own network and from there create opportunities and possibilities. They act on the basis of what entrepreneur Kim Spinder, during a personal meeting in mid-2011 called: 'Give a problem a network and an effective
network process!' It leads to 'win-win-win' situations for the actors involved,
although that does not change the fact that there is also a darker side to coping strategies.

8.7 Integrity: the darker side of the coping strategies

Coping strategies also have an element of what could be described as 'constructive (policy) manipulation. Market manipulation is described as:

> 'A form of improper action, whereby the price of an effect is determined
> by the manipulative transaction or information'
> (Aarnink, 2013, 3).

In that case, the coping strategies are a form of 'proper', or accepted, actions,
whereby the effect is determined by a manipulative use of contacts and information, while the market includes all the players that play a role in a certain
policy theme and do or do not compete with interests. That indicates that the

truth needs to be violated a little to do justice to the truth in the policy development process via OMSPD.

The current form of ministerial government organizations and the associated unwritten rules do not appear to stimulate the honesty and sincerity in the execution of policy-related activities. This notion echoes the thinking about integrity 3.0. Karssing & Spoor (2010) indicate that the first generation of integrity was about fraud and corruption, while the second generation involved concepts like service, functionality, independence, openness (open information), reliability and carefulness. Integrity stands for incorruptibility. Karssing & Spoor (2010) wonder whether or not an incorruptible civil servant is a good civil servant. If integrity-related policy is limited to gifts, side jobs and declarations, that does not give direction to the primary process, nor to policy development. That is where integrity 3.0 comes in. Integrity 3.0 stands for:

> 'Acting in a careful, explainable and steady way'
> (Karssing & Spoor, 2010: 76).

The authors say the following about it:

> 'Civil servants with integrity act on the basis of the responsibility that comes with their job and position, in accordance with the values, standards, rules and guidelines of the organization and society, with an eye on the well-being, the interests and the rights of citizens and other parties involved – including in new, fluid and complex situations where there are no clear guidelines (yet) … It is not the question "which action is allowed within my position?" that is at the forefront there, but "which action is fitting to my position?" … How can I do my job right?'
> (Karssing & Spoor, 2010: 76).

According to the authors, independence, morality and professionality (including 'professional pride') go hand in hand.

Finally, policy entrepreneurship, ideas and seeing opportunities, and connecting actors in networks, matches the need to stimulate government innovation, with the aim of letting government and society function better. That need for innovation touches policy development processes and the level of openness. That issue is explored in paragraph 8.8. Because that was not a core question in this study, it involves going back to an earlier internal study the researcher conducted at a Ministry and literature.

8.8   Policy innovation and policy entrepreneurship

The Netherlands has joined the Open Government Partnership (OGP), a global initiative that was initiation by the Obama administration, with the aim of letting governments function better through openness. That means more transparency about government activities, being open to initiatives from society, being accountable and using innovative technologies (Ministry for Internal Affairs and Kingdom Relationships, 2013).
There is a similarity between substantive policy innovation and innovation of the way policies are developed, and innovative thinking. There is a relationship between substantive policy innovation and new policy options and new policy theories. A policy theory is defined as:

> 'The entirety of assumptions that are the basis of a policy'
> (Hufen, 2009: 2).

They are testable (new) concepts in a certain field. Van Roosbroek (2008) refers to Thompson (1965), who described innovation as:

> 'The generation, acceptance, and implementation of new ideas, processes, products or services'
> (Van Roosbroek, 2008: 25).

The fact that The Netherlands has joined the OGP is no guarantee for successful innovation. The unwritten rules we identified display hierarchical-bureaucratic characteristics. Thompson stated that, although a bureaucracy places a strong emphasis on efficient production, it has a very limited ability to innovate. Managers in a bureaucracy want to perfect functions and processes, and control the behavior of employees in the organization. Certainty is key. In a bureaucracy, employees are cautious when it comes to innovation. If the result is undesirable, that can damage the employee.
In addition, hierarchy can block innovation. Innovation has to move up the management ladder to be accepted. But that process becomes more difficult when there are multiple hierarchical layers, which is why Thompson saw a negative relationship between innovation and the level of bureaucracy (Roosbroek, 2008; Thompson, 1965):

> 'The bureaucratic orientation is conservative. Novel solutions, using resources in a new way, are likely to appear threatening'
> (Thompson, 1965: 7).

That statement by Thompson still applies today. In a study into unwritten rules by the researcher and a colleague in 2006, a distinction was drawn between the relationships 'Management Team Board of Directors – Top Management Team Ministry' and 'employee – MT/board (member)'. It showed an 'archetypal' pattern in both relationships and can be summarized by the following assumptions:

• Docility (to the top) is rewarded, independence is punished.
• Docility is seen as 'customer orientation'.
• Docility leads to 'incident politics' within a board.

Incident politics in a board emerge when the ministerial top management is 'capricious' in what it wants and thus engages in 'incident politics'. That affects the line. Staff management that is docile and submits to the capriciousness get a negative image among other managements in the primary process. That has a negative impact on the development of craftsmanship and professionalism. The 'capriciousness' is passed on to the employees and can easily lead to an atmosphere that is not geared towards cooperation and improvement, but to people covering themselves and a game for survival. Managers do not provide their employees with a 'heat shield' for the noise from above (Weggeman, 2013: 159).

DIAGRAM 6: SYSTEMIC EFFECTS OF DOCILITY (REINFORCING FEEDBACK MECHANISM)

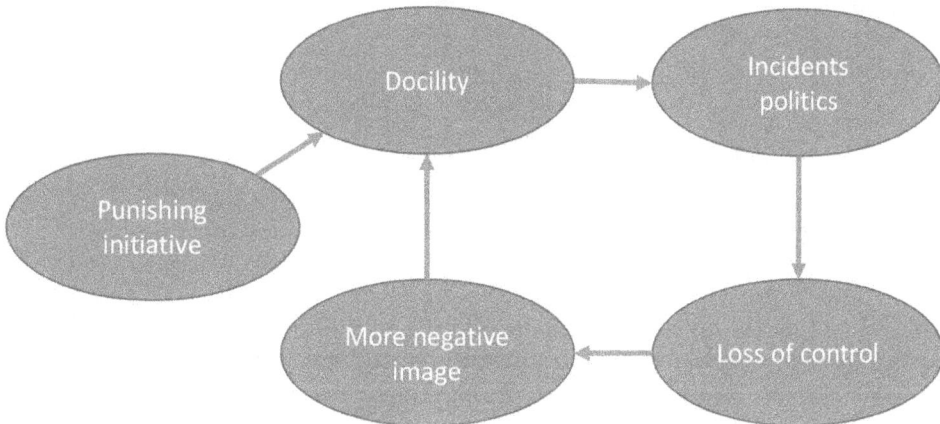

In addition, a second 'archetypal' pattern was observed:
• An employee 'claims' an expert role and fails to deliver.
• An employee is sometimes unable to live up to his expert role as a result of incident politics.

- Due to incident politics, employees are addressed less on their expert role and more on the question: 'What impression do I make, as a manager, to the administrative top?'
- That makes employees passive when it comes to developing expertise.

Analogous to Thompson (1969), in a government environment, genuine innovation and the development of expertise are difficult to realize. Experiments with OMSPD approaches can be seen as a form of administrative innovation and developing new forms of expertise. It uses a different policy 'production' paradigm (horizontal instead of vertical). The paradigm behind the unwritten rules we identified has a tendency to shape policy with usual suspects and, at the most, experts who are not usual suspects. In essence, OMSPD is the opposite. Never less than consulting and preferably one step further on the participation ladder, and always involve experts who are not usual suspects, unless ....

DIAGRAM 7: INCIDENTS, CONTROL AND EXPERTISE IN A FEEDBACK LOOP

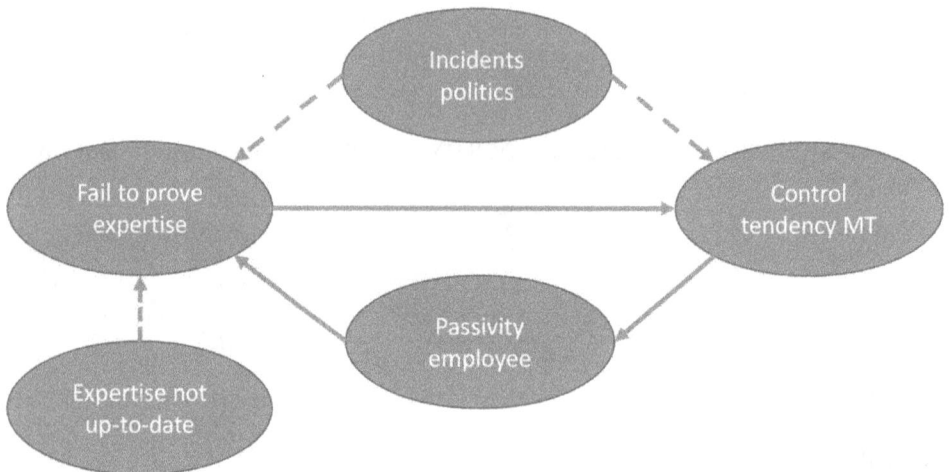

OMSPD principles undermine the need for and power of the 'intermediate trade' (hierarchy), making it more obsolete. Democracy is embedded in policy development itself. That means a shift in the role of policy managers and policy management. Mintzberg (2014) shows which way that is headed in terms of management styles. From top-down towards supportive management.

TABLE 25: MANAGEMENT BY MANAGERS SHIFTING TO NON-MANAGERS (MINTZ-BERG, 2014: 110)

Only managers → → →			No managers		
Maximum management	Participating manage-ment	Shared manage-ment	Distributed manage-ment	Supporting manage-ment	Minimum management

It is a shift from the combination 'check, followers and exchange rate man-agement' towards 'professionals manage themselves'. A development that Mintzberg (2014) considers desirable when he states:

> 'The glorification of leadership makes us look down on others. We create groups of followers who need to be motivated to perform, instead of us-ing the natural tendency people have to work together in communities. In this context, effective management can be seen as being involved to involve, being connected to connect'
> (Mintzberg, 2014: 186).

There are parallels between Mintzberg's management ideas and Pröpper's (2013: 17; table 28) overview of management styles. What Mintzberg con-siders to be desirable in managers, Pröpper sees a desirable management style for increasing openness, for 'wicked problems' that require OMSPD as a policy development style, with managers and civil servants increasingly be-coming 'webbers'. According to Roobeek, 2014: 2):

> 'Naturally networking people who can supervise horizontally and possess knowledge of multiple markets'
> (Roobeek, 2014: 2).

TABLE 26: MANAGEMENT STYLES AND INCREASING SUBSTANTIVE OPENNESS
(PRÖPPER, 2013: 17)

Increasing substantive openness → → →							
Closed au-thoritarian style	Open au-thoritarian style	Consulta-tive style	Participa-tory style	Delegat-ing style	Coopera-tive style	Facilitat-ing style
No role participant	Participant is specta-tor/recip-ient infor-mation	Participant is advisor decision	Participant is advisor from start	Partici-pant is co-de-cider	Participant is collab-oration partner	Partic-ipant takes initiative/is policy owner

The development towards facilitating matches De Geus (1996), who, in his study about long-living organizations, concludes that innovation cannot be centrally managed. It turns out that innovation thrives when it occurs in the margins *and* is self-managed (Vermaak, 2007; De Geus, 1996). Then it is possible to arrive at 'disobedient innovation', a term used by Vermaak (2007) in his study into tough issues.

When management is unwilling and/or unable to change, civil servants have to be a little 'disobedient', without losing sight of (system) morality. Which brings us to a final question: 'How can knowledge integrity, openness *and* verticality go hand in hand in political-administrative policy contexts?'

8.9   The connection vertical – horizontal

Whereas, in the previous paragraph, the focus was on the alleged dangers of and resistance to coping strategies, in this paragraph, the emphasis is on the opportunities, with a focus on neutral values underlying coping strategies. Values provide criteria for behavior or, as Dilts (1998b: 1) formulates it:

> *'Criteria refers to the values or standards a person uses to make decisions and judgments'*
> (Dilts, 1998b: 1).

From the 62 coping strategies, five criteria were deduced for the design of open policy development trajectories. Appendix 6 contains an overview of coping strategies and underlying core values, which allow us to answer the question from the Council for Public Administration (2011) in its report 'Connecting horizontal to vertical: the responses to trust in democracy':

'How can a vertically organized political administration reconnect to a horizontal society?'
(ROB, 2011: 9).

Criterion 1: political manageability/process manageability
Can OMSPD stay manageable politically? Design variations suggested by the coping strategies are:

1. Play with process characteristics like 'informal/exploring' and 'formal/deciding'.
2. When a process phase is open, informal and exploratory, more can be discussed then when something is decisive. It is about managing the expectations of the actors involved.
3. Vary between 'large-scale – small-scale' and more closed or more open. An open process can be started on small scale or closed (via 'Group Decision Room sessions') to identify a shared central issue in a policy trajectory and then, in a next phase, increase the scale and level of openness, and involve more actors in the process.
4. Organize the process in such a way that knowledge and insights from all parties are included and the process is not taken over by a dominant lobby-party.

Criterion 2: Image Minister (scoring)

The assumption is that the external political system, the internal hierarchical bureaucracy and the associated hard unwritten rules will not disappear. They can be taken into account when designing an open approach: 'How can the open process be "embedded" in scoring opportunities and statements by the Minister?' That is the message of various coping strategies and it means that the process has to be consistent with what the Ministers say in the media. Have they made any statements that count as hard conditions for the policy trajectory? Think of questions like: "Can an open policy trajectory be designed in such a way that Ministers (and the line) can score with something genuinely new and something that is sustainable in the long term?' How can Ministers and the line score with intermediate products? These are questions that can be considered together with a communications department of a Ministry.

Criterion 3: policy quality

How can the OMSPD design contribute to the quality of policy? The larger picture is important. What is the connection to other themes? How can they be included in the open policy trajectory, to prevent possible negative side-effects and stimulate desirable effects? In addition, things like new policy options (if desired), obtaining support, practicability of policy, potential savings and long-term effects also play a role with regard to the quality of policy.

Criterion 4: Process legitimacy (parties and substantive)

Coordination with important actors is crucially important, otherwise they will resist. Are the internal colleagues and important stakeholders are behind an open approach? Take that into consideration in the process design, or indicate how you have already realized that. Another aspect of process legitimacy is substantive legitimacy. How can the open approach that has been designed be connected to or embedded in the coalition agreement, framework legislation, departmental documents/departmental goals and scientific literature?
Show that there is experience with open policy approaches, and in particular the OMSPD design forms that have been selected. That will reinforce internal and external legitimacy.

Criterion 5: organizational manageability

Last but not least, there is the question as to what it costs, financially, timewise and in terms of the capacity required. A process design with a low level of financial investment, that fits within the time-frame and does not take up too much capacity has a higher chance of success.

Depending on the policy theme in question, the criteria discussed above will vary in terms of their weight and different forms of OMSPD can be explored. That changes the *'necessary manipulation to realize an open approach'* becomes the *'creativity to design an open approach based on the five criteria'.* The vertical organization (the hierarchy) connects itself to horizontal policy development and encourages civil servants to work with an OMSPD approach, giving rise to management questions like:

- Where is there room for openness?
- How can you organize OMSPD, taking into account the five criteria?
- From an integrity 3.0 perspective, how can we safeguard knowledge integrity and system morality?

8.10   Conclusions research results phase II

The central research question is:

'What coping strategies are available to civil servants to deal with hard unwritten rules and enable open policy development?'

We identified 62 coping strategies, divided into strategies that are aimed at 'directly influencing', 'indirectly influencing via the departmental cushion' and 'indirectly influencing via the external cushion'. From the 62 coping strategies, a meta-strategy can be distilled, which connects to the hard unwritten rules we identified.

1. Use that to which the line is sensitive, what they 'obey' or what they think they can use to score.
2. Find to what extent an open trajectory has process legitimacy and can be kept manageable.
3. Make sure that your colleagues/other internal parties know and share your ideas about openness.
4. Frame/translate in the words of the Minister/line.
5. Empower who you need to empower (empower third parties to support OMSPD).

OM, SPD cannot be made into a success with these steps alone. An underlying foundation is required, in the form of operating principles. From the interviews, three operating principles were distilled:

*   Be entrepreneurial.
*   Be convinced of the added value of OMSPD.
*   Be convinced of the importance of respectful long-term relationships.

Finally, it was argued that coping strategies can be somewhat dubious in terms of integrity (manipulation), but that, within the idea of integrity 3.0, they can also be looked at in a positive way.

Chapter 9

Conclusions

Chapter 9   Conclusions

The core reasoning underlying this research was summarized in the introductory chapter in three hypotheses to be tested:

1. *Openness is necessary in policy development for the solution of 'wicked problems'; these are problems in which increasing numbers of actors play a role in a context of diminishing knowledge certainty.*
2. *Hard unwritten rules restrict openness in policy development.*
3. *There are coping strategies (How to's) that civil servants, if they want, can use to enable openness anyway.*

These three hypotheses were translated into three research (sub-)questions:

1. *Why does the approach to 'wicked problems' require open policy development?*
2. *What are the hard unwritten rules that civil servants are expected to follow in their own organization?*
3. *What discrepancy is there between the required openness in policy development and the internal hard unwritten rules?*

With the central research question:

> *What coping strategies are available to civil servants to deal with hard unwritten rules and enable openness in policy development?*

9.1   General impression research results

This thesis offers a contribution to scientific theory formation, research methods and administrative practice.

Despite many government studies and experiments, OMSPD has as yet not been generally accepted. This study shows how hard unwritten rules restrict openness. Unlike earlier studies, this study looks above all to what this means for policy-makers in departments. The study shows what coping strategies are for civil servants who want to apply OMSPD, recognizing and using the hard unwritten rules. It is possible to connect the vertical orientation of the rules to the horizontal characteristics of OMSPD. The study offers civil servant insight into the possible combinations, while offering their managers in the vertical line insight into the way they can manage openness without coming into conflict with the rules.

The 'added bonus' of this study is a new policy typology of openness based on the level of inclusion and the nature of the involvement of the actors. The typology offers insight into the range of closed and open policy trajectories.

9.2   Conclusion 1: openness necessary for 'wicked problems'

Sub-question 1: Why does the approach to 'wicked problems' require open policy development?

Although this study focuses in particular on the internal rules that restrict openness and the question on how to deal with this, attention was also paid to the question whether or not openness is needed. The underlying reasoning here is that society develops in such a way that the number of 'wicked problems' is growing. According to many authors, this changes the context for government organizations. Dijstelbloem (2008), referring to Habermas (1985), talks about 'new obscurities' and complexities, Frissen (2002) about pluralism, variety and fragmentation.

According to Noordegraaf (2004: 50), the current playing field for public organizations has three conditions: *'diffuse knowledge, headstrong citizens and powerful companies.'* More and more actors can, if they so desire, influence policy development. The amount of information with which civil servants have to deal is growing.

Sargut & McGrath (2012: 45) see a development *'from complicated systems to complex systems'.* Complicated systems have moving parts, which interact, but according to a fixed pattern. It is still possible to make (accurate) predictions about the behavior of the system. Complex systems contain functions that may operate according to certain patterns, but with changing interactions. This has four consequences:

- What happens when parts of the context interact cannot be predicted. Identical starting conditions can cause different results.
- Apparently simple actions can have unexpected consequences.
- Manager can no longer understand the system, and can refuse to admit their ignorance.
- Rare events can become more significant and can occur more often than expected compared to average events.

In complex systems, problems become 'wicked problems'. They are impossible to describe with accuracy. *'The boundaries of the problem are diffuse, so it can hardly be separated from other problems'* (Hisschemöller & Hoppe, 1995: 43). It is not exactly clear which knowledge is relevant, which is one of the reasons it is unclear in which directions to look for solutions, which in turn affects the kind and type of actor involvement. These problems involve many stakeholders, with different values, standards and ideas about goals and means.

'Wicked' problems have a multiple rationality *and* can no longer be grasped by one person or organization. Houppermans (2011) establishes a connection to openness: when a problem lies about the 'wicked' line, with a multiple rationality, openness should play an important and necessary role in policy development. That way, relevant tacit knowledge, practical experiences and other relevant knowledge is included in policy development in a respectful way. Houppermans (2011: 283) calls that 'respectful participation'. It is on the basis of that insight that this thesis was written.

9.3   Conclusion 2: the restrictive effect of hard unwritten rules

Sub-question 2: What are the hard unwritten rules that civil servants are expected to follow in their own organization?

Although there is external pressure to arrive at a more open approach, the way policy is developed does not change overnight and perhaps not at all. This thesis assumes that there is a *'deep structure'* in government organizations that resists openness. The structure limits the approach:

'First to prevent the system from generating alternatives outside its own boundaries, then to pull any deviations that do occur back into line' (Zuboff & Maxim, 2002: 19; Gersick, 1991: 19).

Mintzberg (2010) also observes that restriction, when he states that, over decades, much has stayed the same in organizations:

'The more things change, the more they stay the same'
(Mintzberg, 2010: 208).

Mintzberg argues that the Internet and social media, although they may have a superficial effect, the effect they have does not run deep.

'Internet does not change the practice of management fundamentally, but it establishes the characteristics with exists for decades'
(Mintzberg, 2010: 208).

This thesis has revealed the implicit deeper structure using the modified approach by Scott-Morgan (1995). We have managed to elicit a large number of formulations of unwritten rules, that yield observations similar to those by Mintzberg (2010). Four hard unwritten rules were distilled from the many formulations, as a core of 'unwritten deep value system rules' of Ministries:

- Be aware, we serve the Minister here (and the line)!
  Closely observe the personality/character traits and interests of the Minister (and the hierarchy). How does he like to be served. Take those into account.
- Be visible to the line.
- Meet your deadline, especially with things that are politically important.
- Your network (in particular with the usual suspects) is crucial!

There are indications that the four hard unwritten rules that apply to large (government) organizations have not changed over the course of decades. When we look at popular literature like Parkinson's Law (Parkinson, 1955), Sex and the Single Girl (Landin, 2014; Gurley Brown, 1962), The Pyramid Climbers (Packard, 1963), The Peter Principle (Peter, 1969), Peter's Panacea (Peter, 1973), The Peter Principle After Fifteen Years (Peter, 1985), and The Peter Pyramid (Peter, 1986), we see similarities with the four hard unwritten rules. In 'The Peter Principle After Fifteen Years', Peter says about that:

'What do Murphy's Law, Parkinson's Law and the Peter Principle all have in common? They were the result of careful observations of true events and yielded a generalization that gave a new meaning to all those events'
(Peter, 1985: 35-36).

The following table contains advices and commands by Brown (1962) and Packard (1963). They show a remarkable similarity with the hard unwritten rules identified in this study, to which both managers and employees are subjected.

> 'Bureaucrats can rise inside the hierarchy through negative qualities. Their competence is measured against the extent to which they do not violate rules and do not rock the boat. In an organization where this condition exists, the boss is only a figurehead. There is little difference between the behavior of the leader and that of the follower'
> (Peter, 1973, 67).

A decade later, Peter (1986) states:

> 'Because the first principle of the bureaucracy is to maintain the bureau, a great deal of value is attached to the care people take to avoid any actions that might embarrass the organization. Authority, promotions and carefulness and the associated feeling .... These things are put in danger by independence, decisiveness or almost any hasty action. If someone tries to break through the regular course of events to get something done, he is accused of "overstepping his authority", "bypassing his superiors", "ignoring the proper guidelines" or, in extreme cases, "being disloyal to the department, management or the organization". Needless to say, under these conditions, the true bureaucrats emerge – the hierarchically ranked men or women. They are a perfect match for the structure. They conform to the authority and are obedient to their superiors in the pecking order, while being authoritative and meddlesome with regard to those with less authority – ultimately the public'
> (Peter, 1986: 85-86).

The fact that nothing has changed is also a recent observation by Homan (2013):

> 'First of all, I ask myself if all the management tales about successful organizations, organizations 3.0, post-hierarchical organizations, network organizations, etc., really deliver what they promise. As far as I am concerned, the answer is: no. Despite the fancy packaging, research shows that our organizations are moving backwards rather than moving ahead. Backwards in the sense of: more Taylor-like, more control, more management, more managerialism and instrumentalism. The management message and reality would appear to contradict each other in that respect'
> (Homan (2013: 1).

Or, as he puts it at a later point: 'Despite lots of fancy-sounding variations, it would appear that the bureaucratic organizational archetype is in fact unchanged' (Homan, 2013: 7). As such, whether or not there will be more room for open policy processes in the future remains to be seen. Following Drucker (1994: 101), we can assume that a bureaucratic 'Theory of the Government' will not last forever and sooner or later will (gradually) show signs of wear:

'But eventually every theory (of business) becomes obsolete'
(Drucker, 1994: 101).

TABLE 27: RECOMMENDATIONS AND COMMANDMENTS OF GURLEY BROWN AND PACKARD (1962/1963)

Gurley Brown (Landin, 2014; Gurley Brown, 1962)	Packard (1963)
You have to <u>admire</u> your boss.	*Be a dedicated worker.* Conclusion research Amercan Business Asociation: 'A man who wants to reach the top, better get himself some blinders to close himself off from everything that does not have to do with his organization.'
You must <u>NEVER criticseze</u> your boss!	*Be loyal.* This is translated as: 'It is your duty, no matter your personal feelings, to support and help execute management decisions.' *You improve your chances if you* shield your boss from the consequences of his own mistakes, maintain the authority delegated by him, are satisfied with your role as subordinate, see your boss as he likes to be seen and don't do anything unexpected.
Be <u>enthusiastic about all his decisions</u>.	*Be malleable.* Malleable means adjusment. A study in Nation's Business (april 1959) magazine called this 'the creative conformist'. The study tells the story of a promising, but unconventional young employee who is warned to adjust if he wants to keep his job.
Give him hem <u>compliments</u> and tell him office gossip as a sign of your love.	*Be deferential in a low-key manner.* A study concludes that 'there are virtually no organizations that object to the caste system'. The behavior in the hierarchy 'make a certain deference towards authority necessary'.

Current developments appear to deprive bureaucracies of exactly those advantages that they had. According to Naím (2015):

> *'Large organizations were more effective because they applied centraliza-*
> *tion and stored resources; but resources like raw materials, information,*
> *human talent and customers are easy to find and serve these days.*
> *Large organizations have an aura of authority, modernity and refinement;*
> *these days, newspapers are full of stories about newcomers challenging*
> *superpowers'*
> (Naím, 2015: 114).

So there was a reason we used the term 'hard' unwritten rules in this thesis. They have existed for a long time, are deeply embedded and have changed little, and are unlikely to disappear any day soon. And at the same time, there are wicked problems to solve.

9.4   Conclusion 4: Unwritten rules, discrepancy and necessary openness

Sub-question 3: What discrepancy is there between the required openness in policy development and the internal hard unwritten rules?

The four hard unwritten rules echo Houppermans (2011), who concludes:

> *'It has become clear that politics, like the will of the Minister, serves as a*
> *kind of disclaimer for the policy analyst: the room for, or rather the bound-*
> *aries of, an optimal policy preparation are to a large extent determined by*
> *the influence of politics'*
> (Houppermans, 2011: 306).

The conclusion is that there is a discrepancy between unwritten rules and openness, with regard to (the combination of) levels of participation beyond 'consulting' and levels beyond involving 'experts who are not usual suspects'.

The rules indicate that, in the perception of the civil servants, the vertical system is more important that open horizontal policy development.

In the case of politically sensitive problems, it is at the most the usual suspects who are involved. Sometimes, when parties are involved who are perceived as being 'More Exclusive' (interdepartmental and usual suspects), things can go a little further than consulting.

TABLE 28: EFFECT OF HARD UNWRITTEN RULES ON LEVEL OF OPENNESS

HARD UNWRITTEN RULE	OPENNESS	
	PARTICIPATION LEVEL	LEVEL OF INCLUSION/EXCLUSION
Be aware, we serve the Minister here (via the line)	Only **consulting** and retain 'power' over end result.	Only **usual suspects**. They have political power that Ministers (and line) have to take into account.
Be visible tot he line	Only **consulting**, maintain 'power' over end result and score in a positive way in the line.	A civil servant is visible in the line in a positive way if he shows that goes on at **usual suspects** and they have been consulted.
Meet your deadline	Only **consulting** so that your are ready in time and can determine the end result	Only internal, administrative environment and main **usual suspects**. Under time pressure, that is safe and responsible.
Cherish your network	With authoritative people/institutions that affect politice/media and field, there is a need for **partnership** (formal and informal).	Bad relationships and insufficient coodination with **usual suspects** can pose political risks for Ministers. For new ideas, sometimes **experts are consulted who are not usual suspects.**

9.5   Conclusion 4: coping strategies

Central research question: What coping strategies are available to civil servants to deal with hard unwritten rules and enable openness in policy development.

Although the hard unwritten rules have a tendency to be less open, civil servants who really want OMSPD can use the rules to enable openness. We identified 62 coping strategies that help civil servants. They can use them as levers to enable OMSPD, especially when they show that an OMSPD approach is successful in terms of policy options and support. It is important to connect to Ministers and the hierarchical line by using 'hooks'.

From the 62 coping strategies, we deduced five directional criteria that connect horizontal and vertical: (1) political manageability/process manageability, (2) image, (3) policy quality, (4) process legitimacy and (5) organizational manageability. These five stimulate civil servants to think and act on the basis of what is possible. They create opportunities to play with the design of open policy issues. It is important to develop an OMSPD approach for each issue or policy dossier that creates a 'win-win-win' situation for the civil servant himself, the hierarchy within a Ministry, politics and society. Managers can encourage establishing a constructive connection to the directional criteria. At the same time, that places demands on the same managers. Mintzberg calls that 'minimal management', Pröpper calls it a facilitating style.

Civil servants need to become familiar with the various methods and techniques to involve actors. Varying from the use of so-called Group Decision Rooms and social media applications to the Klinkers method, Future Search, futures explorations, World Café and Appreciative Inquiry. Methods that can be applied in part or in their entirety, or they can be combined. That is where, in addition to knowledge about how to conduct scientific research, the future lies for the profession of civil servant when it comes to dealing with 'wicked problems'. From that perspective, politics and government could establish a better connection to the network society or, as the Council for Public Administration (ROB) formulates it:

> '... be brought onto the track of the horizontalized network society'
> (ROB, 2010: 21).

According to ROB (2010: 23), so far, Dutch politics has yet to give a concrete answer to the equalizing effects of social democracy, when it writes:

> 'As such, the representative democracy suffers from the same ill as all vertical organizations: the formal authority no longer covers the position in a public democracy .... How can the legitimacy of our democratic system be increased?' (ROB, 2010: 39). 'How can the vertically organized public administration be reconnected to the horizontal society?' (ROB, 2010: 40). 'What is the difference between a vertical administration that is not connected and a vertical administration that is connected with the horizontal public space?'
> (ROB, 2010: 41).

A recommendation for stimulating the connection is to translate openness into the policy function structure.

As a bonus, this study yielded a typology of policy processes:

1. The 'classic' closed policy consultancy/advice process.
2. Closed policy consultancy/advice process by invitation.
3. The 'classic' closed policy – co-creation – process.
4. Practical signaling and design process (half open – half closed).
5. Open consultancy/advice process.
6. Open co-creating knowledge (sharing) process, for instance of best practices.
7. Open co-creating vision process.

The seven types of policy processes can be translated into functional descriptions to realize a focused match with 'wicked problems'. That way, Ministries can pay serious attention to translating OMSPD into the functional structure. In an analogy with Meuleman's hierarchy, market and network, that can be done as follows:

- *The classic civil servant*
  Matches the more closed forms of policy development; works predominantly with usual suspects and science.
- *Policy entrepreneur in two forms*
  Matches the more open forms of policy development.
  - The policy marketer who constantly moves around in the field and picks up and tests signals, respectively.
  - The policy entrepreneur who handles policy processes in such a way that the end result is a product for a problem in a target group.
- *The OMSPD civil servant*
    An expert in the application of open consultation and co-creation methods in policy processes.

9.6 Core contribution managerial scientific theory formation

If the conclusion are summarized in a managerial theory about the tension between vertical and horizontal, the following picture appears:

I *Axiom 1: 'Wicked problems' require open policy processes as an expression of more horizontal relationships*
  This means that other actors, besides the usual suspects, need to play a more serious role in policy development.

II *Axiom 2: There are hard written rules*
  Hard written rules are fundamental formal rules that determine the de-

sign of an organization. Think, for instance, at mandates and procedures as a 'phenomenon'. They have generic (bureaucratic) characteristics. Mandates, for instance, structure the organization in a top-down, hierarchical layering with associated accountabilities. For the national government, they are the written standards of the democratic state, to with the political primacy, ministerial responsibility, the rule of trust and administrative loyalty.

III   *Axiom 3: There are unwritten rules in organizations*
These are the result of written rules and the way in which leadership behaves. The result is expressed in the way written rules are interpreted (based on their motivators) and given shape by employees in everyday practice.

IV   *Axiom 4: As there are hard written rules, there are also hard unwritten rules*
These are collectively shared and acknowledged unwritten rules in an organizational segment that are hard to change. They can be seen as interpretations, based on the employees' motivators, of fundamental written rules and, contrary to Scott-Morgan's definition of unwritten rules, are not determined by the style of leadership.

V   *Axiom 5: There are coping strategies for civil servants for dealing with hard unwritten rules*
Coping strategies are principles on the basis of which people act (operating principles) *and* an associated structured set of actions for dealing with a problem or realizing an objective.

By defining openness via participation level and level of inclusion, this thesis offers science a new way of determining when a policy development trajectory is open or closed.

In the case of Open Multi Stakeholder Policy Development (OMSPD), policy is developed in collaboration and interaction with citizens, social organizations, companies and/or other governments. On the participation ladder, that happens from the consultation level (Table 7) onwards. With regard to exclusivity/inclusivity, it happens from level 4 (Table 8) onwards. In terms of time, OMSPD focuses on involving stakeholders at an early stage (Pröpper & Steenbeek, 1998; Boedeltje & De Graaf, 2004) and preventing one-sided lobbies.

DIAGRAM 8: OPEN MULTI STAKEHOLDER POLICY DEVELOPMENT

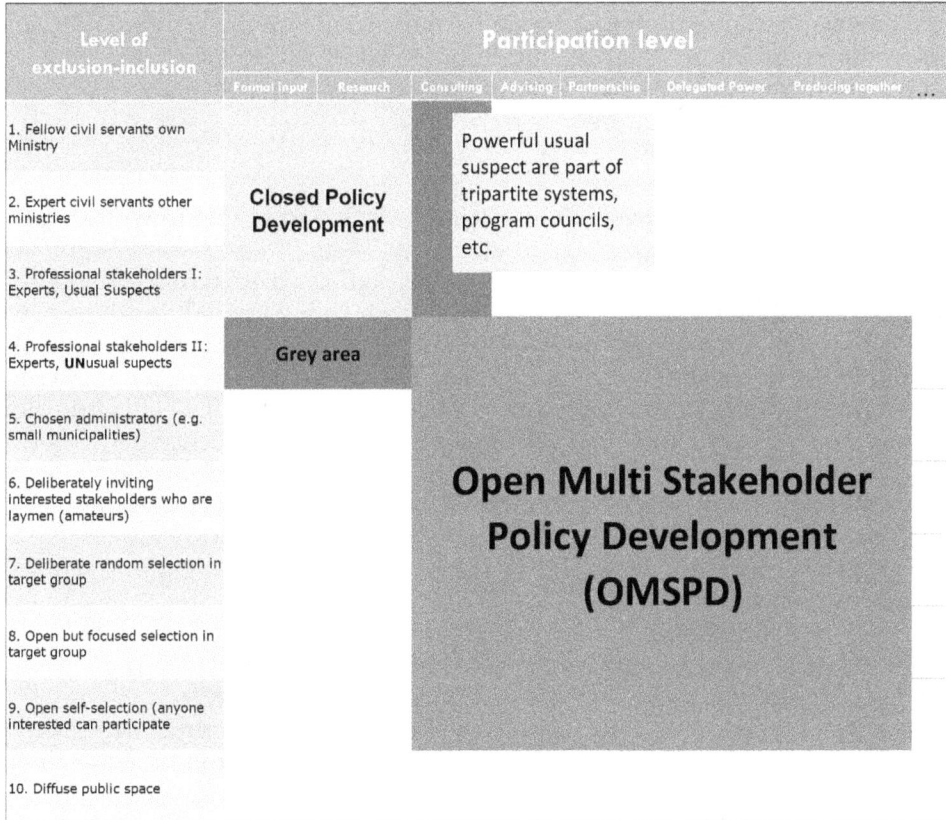

Level of exclusion-inclusion	Participation level							
	Formal input	Research	Consulting	Advising	Partnership	Delegated Power	Producing together	...
1. Fellow civil servants own Ministry				Powerful usual suspect are part of tripartite systems, program councils, etc.				
2. Expert civil servants other ministries	**Closed Policy Development**							
3. Professional stakeholders I: Experts, Usual Suspects								
4. Professional stakeholders II: Experts, **UN**usual supects	**Grey area**							
5. Chosen administrators (e.g. small municipalities)								
6. Deliberately inviting interested stakeholders who are laymen (amateurs)			**Open Multi Stakeholder Policy Development (OMSPD)**					
7. Deliberate random selection in target group								
8. Open but focused selection in target group								
9. Open self-selection (anyone interested can participate								
10. Diffuse public space								

By identifying hard unwritten rules, this thesis adds a new element to scientific literature about organizational cultures and the tension between vertical and horizontal. These rules stand in the way of an open approach and are hard, and difficult or impossible to change. It would appear they have changed little in recent decades.

The coping strategies to enable openness in policy development, given the hard unwritten rules, are a third contribution to managerial theory formation. In paragraph 9.9, the contribution of this thesis to theory formation is summarized. In the discussion paragraph (9.10), the question is answered what to with constitutional law in relation to open processes.

The division of coping strategies adds a new name to research and literature about coping for the target group civil servants.

In methodological terms, the thesis contains three innovative elements: (1) adjusting the method of Scott-Morgan to examine causal relationships between unwritten rules and openness, (2) the addition of the concept of 'hard unwritten rules' and (3) a structured approach (skill analysis) to make tacit knowledge explicit. Analyzing hard unwritten rules and skill analyses are a suitable way to shape culture research.

9.7   Discussion 1: Integrity 3.0 - basic attitude & darker side unwritten rules

Integrity 3.0, as an enabler of OMSPD for 'wicked problems', requires people who are able to create open networks in which human relationships can realize honest, open shared analyses and find creative new combinations of solutions. As one of the respondents stated, it means assuming a neutral position between the Ministry and actors and together look for what is true, how things are structured and what can be done in terms of solutions.

The vertical orientation of civil servants adhering to the hard unwritten rule becomes a problem with integrity 3.0. The hard unwritten rules support integrity 1.0 and 2.0, but undermine their own morality, because 'looking up in the hierarchy' and 'following' are the central elements, revealing a dark side of the hard unwritten rules.

On the one hand, the hard unwritten rules, combined with an integrity 3.0 style of leadership, can stimulate the development of a different implementation of morality and encourage people to take responsibility, but on the other hand, they can as easily have the opposite effect. In that regard, Luyendijk (2015) provides a deeper insight, when he draws a distinction between immorality and amorality:

> 'Being a-moral does not mean being bad or im-moral. Amoral means that the concepts of "good" and "evil" never enter discussions in the first place. We do not care if a plan is morally sound, we just care about the potential "reputational damage"'
> (Luyendijk, 2015: 88).

People's own functioning is, wherever possible, stripped of words that can create a (personal) ethical discussion, he argues. As discussed earlier, the unwritten rules have not changed in decades. Looking at older studies, there are doubts about the moral capacities of civil servants in situations in which the hard unwritten rules are used by managers, enabling them to create a regime of fear. As Todorov (1996: 183) puts it:

> 'The hierarchical relation has become a power relation'
> (Todorov, 1996: 183).

Creating regimes of fear can be seen as a form of derailing leadership. Based on integrity 1.0, which states that assignments need to be carried out loyally, amoral behavior then becomes immoral behavior. In a general sense, Korsten (2015) states that explanations for forms of derailing leadership can be found with:

> 'The person himself (his psychological characteristics), with the followers (an uncritical "court" or a fan club) and with the environment (which is not critical enough)'
> (Korsten, 2015: 2).

The hard unwritten rules offer a deeper explanatory interaction mechanism between the three system components 'manager(s) – employee(s) – organizational environment' and the occurrence of possible moral derailments, of which cases can be found in literature. One case is described by Dohmen & Wester (2014), who edited the desire to function in a morally correct way and the tragic suicide of Arthur Gottlieb at the Dutch Care Authority, who had to be 'pushed out the door' with subtle games, based on the information that Gottlieb has left. Personal image of managers was more important that the actual information and cases of fraud that had been detected.

The study by Todorov (1996) goes a level deeper and provides a clear picture of morality because he looked at situations of extreme organizational fear in concentration camps, drawing a distinction between two kinds of values, 'vital values' and 'moral values', of which he says:

> 'Vital values dictate that saving my own life and furthering my well-being are what matters most; moral values tell me that there is something more precious than life itself'
> (Todorov, 1996: 40).

Incidentally, the differences between everyday life and camps, in his view, are less sharp that one might assume at face value:

> 'In everyday life the contrast of which I have been speaking are not clearly apparent. Egocentric acts pass themselves off as ordinary and routine behavior, and furthermore, less is at stake because human lives don't depend on them. In the camps, however, where it is sometimes necessary to choose between holding on to one's bread and holding on to one's dignity, between starving physically and starving morally, everything is out in the open'
> (Todorov, 1996: 42).

The hard unwritten rules are primarily connected to 'vital values', which Todorov (1996: 43) nuances by stating:

> 'Most of the time individuals opt for vital values without necessarily losing a sense of morality'
> (Todorov, 1996: 43).

Hendry (2014) refers to the same moral phenomenon, via sociologist Zygmunt Bauman (2013), who was quoted earlier:

> '... who pointed out that the bureaucratic organization made the Holocaust possible; an example of the dehumanizing effects of the bureaucratic technology'
> (Hendry, 2014; Zygmunt, 1989).

Until the 1970's, historians wrote that a war criminal like Eichmann was an average bureaucrat (Arendt, 2009). Arendt researched and described Eichmann's legal trial in Israel. Expecting to see a ruthless 'monster', what she encountered was a clumsy, bespectacled little man who, when he no longer had to follow orders, suddenly changed into a peaceful citizen. And that made her think. Arendt writes:

> 'The trouble with Eichmann was precisely that so many where like him, and that the many where neither perverted nor sadistic, that they were, and still are, terribly and terribly normal'
> (Todorov, 1996: 124; Arendt 1979: 276).

She warns us that there is a little bit of Eichmann in each of us. In the 'case 40/61', some social scientists wonder:

> '... what the best explanation was, not just of Eichmann, but also of the police officer and civil servant who helped in the deportation of the Jews .... They found that explanation in Milgram's theory, which would show that anyone striving for conformity with the "group" could become an Eichmann'
> (Arendt, 2009; Mulish, 2010: 105).

Remarks by Eichman were written down by Arendt (2009) and Todorov (1996) from countless war criminals that pointed to the diligent following and working on the basis of the unwritten rules, the core being:

> 'We were only following orders'
> (Todorov, 1996: 165).

Eichmann described himself as:

> 'A pawn on a chessboard....Throughout my entire life I've been used to obeying.... My guilt lies in my obedience, in my respect for discipline, for my military obligation in wartime, for my oath of loyalty' (Todorov, 1996: 172; Arendt, 1979: 291).

Apparently, education or intellect are immaterial:

> 'Indeed, people with university educations could be every bit as cruel as the illiterate, so long as the life of the mind was cut off from the rest of life..... as if a sense of morals were something one learns at universities' (Todorov, 1996: 145).

Todorov (1996: 129) states that ordinary employees are capable of such immoral behavior because their thinking becomes instrumental thinking that is aimed only on carrying out tasks, while Arendt (1969) indicates that they carry out those tasks without realizing what it is they are doing. In that sense, Peter (1973) remarked:

> 'The technical expert can become so docile that he becomes an Adolf Eichmann, a competent puppet who, in all quiet, can send us to the next world. He can become obsessed with his work, his existence starting and ending with what he does. Fortunately, the extreme cases are still in a minority, but none of us is able to really escape the procession effect .... Although quite a lot of people have turned into procession puppets with a trace of concern, anyone who knows anything about hierarchical relapse and the loss of one's own personality, is anything but happy. He yearns for change, while the silent majority starts displaying procession behavior and has no objection to mediocre ethics, mediocre education, halfhearted justice, bad products and a weak government' (Peter, 1973: 63-64).

It is not by definition the case that:

> '... a bureaucracy rules out moral behavior; it imposes a certain strict form of moral behavior where moral obligations (moral ethics) mean that no exceptions are allowed to the rule' (Hendry, 2013: 139).

The media also play a role. It is excellent that the new media promote transparency and make it easier to reveal immoral behavior. But at the same time, media should also look at themselves. Journalists without a sense of morality, whether or not they blindly follow their chief editor, can easily make sensational headlines of any story and deliberately destroy people.

As far as politicians and Ministries are concerned, it reinforces the effect of the unwritten rules in a negative sense and promotes closedness, which in turn can promote political-administrative nepotism, or cause employees in Ministries to display the same behavior as immoral journalists in extreme situations.

Members of Parliament must also ask themselves if all the questions they ask are beneficial to OMSPD. And the intention with which those questions are asked. Do MP's ask questions to reinforce their own position and be reelected, or is their goal to improve the long-term functioning of society? Usually, many of these questions evoke a negative response from a Ministry, to prevent any damage to the Minister's image. They accentuate the hard unwritten rules and the associated closedness.

As a final remark of this conclusion, for the design of integrity 3.0, some statements by the American management and organization expert Peter Ferdinand Drucker can be seen as relevant, to be found in the Daily Drucker (day: April 9).

- A person should never be appointed to a management position if he focuses primarily on people's weaknesses instead of their strengths. Someone who always knows exactly what people can't do, and never sees what they *can* do, undermines the 'spirit' of an organization.
- A person should not be appointed to a job when that person is more interested in the question 'who is right' than in the question 'what is right'. Asking the question 'who is right' encourages subordinates to play it safe and engage in politics in their organization. It encourages subordinates to cover things up if they may have made a mistake, rather than learning from it openly and together.
- Never put intelligence above integrity when you hire someone. Colleagues usually know quickly which other colleagues or managers have integrity and which do not.
(Drucker, 2004: 9/4).

9.8   Discussion 2: ministerial responsibility

Ministerial responsibility is one of the underlying written rules that are at the basis of the hard unwritten rules. It is a rule that is unlikely to change in the near future. But assume it could be changed, with the aim of stimulating openness in policy development, what would a new rule or new interpretation be? In political theory formation, people think about the formulation of coherent concepts and abstractions in relation to issues in society. In a pragmatic sense, this concerns political decision-making, adequacy of political procedures or the framework of constitutional principles (Dijstelbloem, 2007: 58; Wolin, 2004: 504).

An ideal democratic organizational form, in accordance with Ashby's Law and the insights by Graves, is also able to handle 'wicked problems', with suitable rules, 'policy products' and 'problem-solving networks'. If that does not happen, gradual political decay and social 'entropy' threaten to occur.

In the current state structure, government, as the executive branch, is accountable to the legislative branch. It is for that reason that ministerial responsibility was created. Lubberding (1982) states that this law offers the most important safeguard for maintaining the quality of democracy. But does that still apply in social contexts that are becoming increasingly complex? With regard to the approach of 'wicked problems', what exactly would the Minister be accountable for? The accountability could extend beyond results/solution constellations to include the (open) quality of the policy process. That should be included explicitly in the Ministerial Responsibility Act. A modified ministerial responsibility stimulates direct democracy and makes it legitimate for civil servants to apply open policy development. It would also help if MP's were to ask questions about openness, as happened once in the Willems motion. In 1993, Groen Links MP Wilbert Willems, together with other MP's, filed a motion in Parliament aimed at improving policy development by realizing the involvement of citizens:

> '... request the government to experiment with presenting social problems and policy plans to citizens in various ways' (Accepted on December 22, 1993 under number 21427 100. Deetman Committee: political administrative and constitutional innovation).

Questions that fit in with the recognition of the need for open processes are:

- Minister, <u>who</u> are involved in the development of this policy (inclusion)?
- <u>How</u> is that done (participation quality)?
  A third question involves sub-solutions in solution constellations that need to be tested.

- Minister, what is the <u>knowledge quality</u> of sub-solutions? Have the under-lying <u>policy theories</u> been tested?

Democracy then develops into a deliberative democracy in which both the involvement and participation of citizens and quality requirements and meaningful participation are important (Verhoeven, 2004). In 't Veld (2010) calls that a knowledge democracy. In his view, the robustness of policy results with regard to stakeholders and the future are central factors, while the role of validity is smaller. In the eyes of the researcher of this thesis, validity *is* an important criterion, including for open policy processes. Research quality is essential, in combination with environmental robustness and future robust-ness in increasingly complex contexts. In open policy development, a distinc-tion can be drawn of whether the relevant policy network is reflected in all its facets in the policy development *and* one-sided lobby dominance is prevent-ed. In-depth validity can be seen as additional expert knowledge that needs to be collected for the sake of specific technical sub-aspects.

If the ministerial responsibility is modified in the way outlined above, that will have consequences for political and departmental cultures, the assumption being that it will become more open and encourage an open exchange of knowledge. Boekhof, Iske and Weggeman have signaled a problem with the current Rijnland structure.

> *'The Rijnland model on which the relationships in our country are based assumes and encourages collaboration between parties, unlike the An-glo-Saxon model, where short-term gains transcend everything. Our Rijnland model is, by nature, better equipped to arrive at the exchange of knowledge, but at the same time suffers from a lack of action due to the endless consultations. Too often, we begin another study, we set up another committee of need to hear some additional people, rather than implement the findings'*
> (Boekhof, Iske & Weggeman, 2009).

In addition to modifying the ministerial responsibility, the obligation is need-ed to include openness in the memorandum of explanation of new system laws (as described in this thesis).

An example: Suppose a Memorandum of Explanation states that usual sus-pects (institutionalized consulting partners like trade unions, employers' as-sociations, etc.) need to be consulted on a given theme. Civil servants within Ministries are aware of how these partners think, and vice versa. People can take that into account and, together with the civil servants, the usual partners make up a relative closed network.

One can wonder what would happen is that same Memorandum of Expla-nation stated that the usual suspects **and** other relevant social target groups have to be consulted. In other words, a legal equalization between usual suspects and other parties that can or want to make a contribution. One would assume that this would increase the attention to openness inside Ministries.

Box: the Environment Act

The Environment Act moves in the direction of equalization of usual <u>and</u> unusual suspects. The Act, which comes into effect in 2018, integrates hundreds of laws, general administrative measures and ministerial regulations with regard to the physical living environment, including things like building, the environment, water management, spatial planning, monuments and nature. The policy letter 'Simply better' of the Ministry for Infrastructure and the Environment, which addresses this Act, places an emphasis on

> *'the importance of investing in the quality of the preparation phase. That preparation phase will contain at least: an open issue-oriented problem analysis and inventory of directions for solutions, a funneled approach in the consideration of alternatives and room for serious public participation'*
> *(Ministry for Infrastructure & the Environment, 2011).*

In the proposed version of ministerial responsibility, and transformation of system laws, knowledge development and (actively) finding/creating solution constellations with many parties involved is central. That has consequences for political and vertical lines in governments and for the administrative craftsmanship, which includes knowledge of research methods and techniques, methods to include openness in policy development *and* (interactive) futures exploration methods. That is no easy matter and requires education and experience. At the same time, in recent years, master classes were organized at three Ministries that share knowledge and experience about research expertise, futures exploration and open policy development, creating a foundation of skills that can be expanded in the future.

Chapter 9

9.9   Looking ahead: the future of OMSPD in the Netherlands

At the end of this thesis, the question remains: 'What is the future of OM-SPD in the Netherlands?'

The development, quality and structure of regular institutions have been an important factor in the development of democracy and economic standards in Western countries. These institutions are (among those) responsible for a balance between elites and citizens and the extent to which these elites were able to claim resources (De Soto, 2000; Acemoglu & Robinson, 2012). A balance that, over the centuries, has shifted towards openness (increased influence of more actors on the government of a country), and enabled a broad development of prosperity. For that to happen, the actors involved also had to have possessions of their own. De Soto (2000: 11) zooms in on the formal legislation and registration of private property:

'The Western nations have so successfully integrated their poor into their economies that they have lost even the memory of how it was done, how the creation of capital began back when, as the American historian Gordon Wood has written, 'something momentous was happening in the society and culture that released the aspirations and energies of common people as never before in American history.' The 'something momentous' was that Americans and Europeans were on the verge of establishing widespread formal property law and inventing the conversion process in that law that allowed them to create capital'
(De Soto, 2000: 11).

Acemoglu & Robinson (2012: 74-75) agree with De Soto, but add a successful variable that explains the shift in the balance between elite and citizens: inclusion and associated inclusive institutions, which they describe as:

'Those that allow and encourage participation by the great mass of people that make the best use of their talents and skills and that enable individuals to make the choices they wish ...... Inclusive economic institutions require secure property rights and economic opportunities not just for the elite but for a broad cross-section of government'
(Acemoglu & Robinson, 2012: 74-75).

Acemoglu & Robinson (2012) then define politics as:

'The process by which a society chooses the rules that will govern it'
(Acemoglu & Robinson, 2012: 79).

The form of the political institutions, and the way they govern, is a result of that process. The institutions determine who has power over what in society, and how that power can be utilized. The question raised if new inclusive institutions are desirable.

An assumption is 'inclusion' in the approach of 'wicked problems' has to be interpreted more broadly, because there are more stakeholders and less knowledge certainty. There are other possible reasons why inclusion is important. For instance because 'inclusion' can be a political tool to counter the increasing inequality Piketty (2014) signals. Acemoglu & Robinson (2012) show that, should increasing inequality lead to a restriction of the distribution of political power, there will be serious economic repercussions. They write:

> 'Inclusive political institutions that distribute power widely often put an end to economic institutions that exploit the majority of the people, create barriers to economic activities and oppose the functioning of the market so that only a few can benefit …. Inclusive economic institutions in turn are a result of inclusive political institutions'
> (Acemoglu & Robinson, 2012: 86-87).

The two authors show that, in countries with 'extractive institutions' (a limited number of parties controlling and benefiting from the economy), innovation is obstructed and the old is preserved to safeguard vested positions.

In that sense, the idea that our existing institutions, with their limited levels of inclusion, are ready for a revision, in part due to the emergence of social media and other technologies, makes sense. According to Dijstelbloem (2007), who refers to Beck (1992), going back is not the way forward. If political legitimacy is facing a crisis:

> 'The idea that national parliaments could catch up by bringing the different forms of politics back under central democratic control, according to Beck, is doomed to fail, because, in modern society, there is no longer a central controlling body that can bring together all the information flows and impose its steering power on society'
> (Dijstelbloem, 2007: 18).

This study shows that there appears to be a 'system inertia', that expresses itself in hard unwritten rules. According to Dijstelbloem, there is no way back, but in moving forward, it is important to take the hard unwritten rules into account. In that framework, it seems sensible to recommend professionalizing OMSPD at an institutional level, by setting up an Institute for Safeguarding Participatory Democracy, a government organization that periodically checks the quality and professionalization of OMSPD in other government organizations, for instance through Appreciative Inquiry-like visitations.

The aim of the Institute for Safeguarding Participatory Democracy is to professionalize participatory democracy beyond updating representative democracy. The aim is not to punish government organizations for what they do not to in terms of OMSPD, but to look at what they are doing well and how that can be expanded through 'positive visitations' on a legal basis, analogous to the 'appreciative inquiry', about which Van de Wetering (2008: 3) writes:

> 'Appreciative inquiries establish a relationship with the story about a situation that contains the experience and intrinsic motivation of people. The experience contains the feeling that mobilizes people. "Wow, that's what I do it for!", "That's what I really find important!', "That moves me!". That stimulates the intrinsic motivation to want to improve things. Looking for the causes of problems during internal audits can cause employees to assume a defensive attitude. Uncertainty and fear that the person will be held to account also discourages people from learning. A positive question is appreciative and gives the person confidence about the subject and themselves. It stimulates reflection, which is the first step on the way to a climate of improvement. The starting point of appreciative inquiries in an audit is the idea that the glass is "half full", not "half empty". The question as it were transfers that glass half full notion to the thoughts of the other person'
> (Van de Wetering, 2008: 3).

This way, the hard unwritten rules we identified are used to serve democratic innovation. Based on the insights provided by Acemoglu & Robinson (2012) and others, an 'acknowledged' inclusion of unusual suspects in policy processes is realized. In addition to an Institute for Safeguarding Participatory Democracy, it is desirable to create support structures that can help in the design of OMSPD approaches in the form of so-called Future Centers. For almost a decade, a so-called Future Center was operating in the Ministry for Social Affairs and Employment (SAE) which, at an underlying level, contributed to the design and realization of less closed approaches. Dvir, Schartzberg, Avni, Webb & Lettice (2006) write the following about Future Centers:

> 'The first future center was conceptualized by Leif Edvinsson and established by Skandia, a Swedish insurance company, in 1997 (Edvinsson, 2003). Since then, additional public and commercial future centers have been created. Although little has been written on them in the literature, future centers are known in practice as facilitated working environments which help organizations prepare for the future in a proactive, collaborative and systematic way. They are used to create and apply knowledge, develop practical innovations, bring citizens in closer contact with govern-

ment and connect end-users with industry. They are used by government organizations for developing and testing citizen-centered, future-proof policy options with broad acceptance by stakeholders'
(Dvir, Schwartzberg, Avni, Webb & Lettice, 2006: 111).

A Future Center helps with practical solutions and is a knowledge center for open approaches. According to Castelein (2011):

'An FC is an organization that has the ability to approach important developments outside of the box'
Castelein (2011: 25).

That makes it possible to shape and implement challenging process designs. Together with clients and other relevant and interesting internal and external stakeholders. A Future Center provides:

'Business as usual that adds value to the primary process'
Castelein (2011: 25).

The insights provided in this thesis offer tools for designing an Institute for Safeguarding Participatory Democracy and setting up Future Centers for the professionalization of a participatory democracy and the design of an inclusive society. Finally, it would be worthwhile considering an update to twenty-year-old Willems motion.

This motion can still be seen as a stimulus and opportunity for civil servants of the national government to legitimately explore and develop new ways of policy development. Looking at the unwritten rules we have found, executing the Willems motion turns out to be easier said than done.
If Parliament has unanimously carried the motion, Parliament can be reminded to help put the motion in practice, to contribute to the further distribution and application of OMSPD and, in doing so, create a new level of professional inclusion in society. The 'political primacy' should become more the 'primacy of participation'. In balance with a central authority that can continue to execute its enforcement duties in a responsible way.

Literatuur

Aarnink, E. (2013) Misbruik van voorwetenschap. Verkregen op 4 april 2014 via http://hdl.handle.net/1820/5072

Academie voor wetgeving (2011) Rapport van het symposium: De risico-regelreflex in het openbaar bestuur. Verkregen op 28 februari 2014 via http://tinyurl.com/q5546s2

Acemoglu, D. & Robinson, J.A. (2012) *Why Nations Fail: The Origins Of Power, Prosperity, And Poverty*. New York: Crown Business.

Adams, D. and Hess, M. (2001) 'Community in public policy: fad or foundation?', Australian Journal of Public Administration, Vol. 60 No. 2, pp. 13-23.

Aken, J. V., & Andriessen, D. (2011) *Handboek ontwerpgericht wetenschappelijk onderzoek: wetenschap met effect*. Den Haag: BoomLemma.

Van Aken, J. (2013) *Design Science Research in Management Combining Rigour with Relevance to Support Informed Management Action*. Eindhoven: University of Technology.

Allio, R. J. (2003) Russell L. Ackoff, iconoclastic management authority, advocates a 'systemic' approach to innovation. *Strategy & Leadership, 31*(3), 19-26.

Anderson, M. S. (2007) Collective openness and other recommendations for the promotion of research integrity. *Science and Engineering Ethics, 13*(4), 387-394.

Anderson, C. (2013) *Makers: de nieuwe industriële revolutie*. Amsterdam: Uitgeverij Nieuw Amsterdam.

Andriessen, D. (2011) Wat is jouw onderzoeksparadigma? Verkregen op 21 september 2013 via http://www.onderzoekscoach.nl/category/publicaties/

Arnstein, S.R. (1969) A ladder of citizen participation. *Journal of the American Planning Association, 35*(4), 216-224.

Ashby, W.R. (1956) *Introduction to Cybernetics* London: Chapman & Hall.

Ambrosini, V., & Bowman, C. (2001) Tacit knowledge: Some suggestions for operationalization. *Journal of Management Studies, 38*(6), 811-829.

Ankersmit, F. (2008) De plaag van de transactiestaat. In: Ankersmit, F. & Klinkers, L. red. (2008). In: *De tien plagen van de staat: de bedrijfsmatige overheid gewogen.* Amsterdam: Van Gennep.

Argyris, C. & Schön, D. (1974) *Theory in practice: increasing professional effectiveness.* San Francisco: Jossey-Bass.

Argyris, C. & Schon, D. (1978) Organizational Learning: A theory of action approach. *Reading, MA: Addision Wesley.*

Arendt, H. (1979) Eichmann in Jerusalem. A Report on the Banality of Evil. Harmondsworth: Penguin.

Arendt, H. (2009) *Eichmann in Jeruzalem. De banaliteit van het kwaad.* Amsterdam: Olympus.

Australian Public Service Commissio (2007) *Tackling Wicked Problems: A Public Policy Perspective* Australia: Commonwealth of Australia.

Babiak, P., & Hare, R. D. (2009) *Snakes in suits: When psychopaths go to work.* HarperCollins.

Bandler, R., & Grinder, J. (1975) *The Structure of Magic: A book about language and therapy.* Palo Alto. *CA:* Science and Behaviour Books.

Bang, H., P. (2002a) *Cultural Governance: A New Mechanism for Connecting System and Lifeworld,* ECPR Joint Sessions of Workshops, Workshop 6, Turin, 22-27 March 2002.

Bang, H., P. (2002b) *Cultural Governance and Everyday making: A New Systems Strategy Meeting a New Tactics of Self-Governance,* XV World Congress of Sociology, RCo3, 7-13 July 2002, Brisbane, Australia.

Barker, J. (1992) *Paradigms: The business of discovering the future* NY: HarperBusiness.

Barker, J. (1996) *Paradigma's: mentale modellen voor de toekomst.* Schiedam: Scriptum.

Barker, J. A. (2002) *The new business of paradigms.* Star Thrower Distribution. Verkregen op 26 september 2013 via: http://www.thenewbusinessofparadigms.com/media/preview/Transcript21stCentPreview_NBOP.pdf

Bateson, G. (1979) *Mind and nature: A necessary unity* (p. 38). New York: Dutton.

Batens, D. (2012) Bedoelingen en principes: een onverwachte relatie. *Door denken en doen: essays bij het werk van Ronald Commers*, 93-106.

Bauman, Z (2002) *Society under siege*. Oxford: Polity Press.

Bauman, Z. (2013) *Modernity and ambivalence*. John Wiley & Sons.

Beck, D. & Linscottt, G. (1991) *The Crucible: Forging South Africa's Future*. Denton: New Paradigm Press.

Beck, D.E. & Cowan, C.C., (1996) *Spiral Dynamics: Mastering Values, Leadership and Change*. Oxford: Blackwell Publishers.

Beck, U. (1992) *Risk Society*. London: Sage.

Bekkers, V. (2007) *Beleid in beweging: achtergronden, benaderingen, fasen en aspecten van beleid in de publieke sector*. Den Haag: Uitgeverij LEMMA.

Bekker, M. & Veerman, L. (2009) *Gezondheidseffectschatting: wetenschappelijke onderbouwing en beleidscoördinatie van intersectoraal gezondheidsbeleid*. Assen: Van Gorcum B.V.

Benedictus, R.J. (2013) Hannah Arendt: Eichmann en de 'banaliteit van het kwaad'. Verkregen op 6 maart 2015 via http://www.isgeschiedenis.nl/citaat-uit-het-nieuws/hannah-arendt-eichmann-en-de-banaliteit-van-het-kwaad/

Berger, P. L., & Luckmann, T. (1991) *The social construction of reality: A treatise in the sociology of knowledge* (No. 10). Penguin UK.

Berkum, M. (2009) Ik netwerk, dus ik ben: een explorerend onderzoek naar netwerkmanagement. Enschede: Universiteit Twente.

Boedeltje, M. & Graaf, L. de (2004) Draagvlak nader bekeken: Een verkenning van het begrip draagvlak binnen interactief beleid op lokaal niveau vanuit een normatief en instrumenteel perspectief. Paper voor het politicologenetmaal, 26 en 27 mei 2004, Antwerpen.

Boekhof T., Iske P. & Weggeman M. (2009) Kenniseconomie vraagt actieve houding. Verkregen op 17 april 2016 via

http://www.volkskrant.nl/archief_gratis/article978923.ece/Kenniseconomie_
vraagt_actieve_houding?service=Print[28-7-2010

Boogers, M. J. G. J. A., Schaap, L., van den Munckhof, E. D., & BA, N. K. M.
(2009) Decentralisatie als opgave. *Bestuurswetenschappen, 63*(1), 29-49.

Brouwer, S., & Huitema, D. (2010) Beleidsondernemers in het waterbeheer. *H
2 O, 43*(1), 10.

Bruijn, J.A. de & Heuvelhof, E.F. ten (1995) *Netwerkmanagement.* Utrecht:
Lemma.

Bruijn, J.A. de & Heuvelhof, E.F. ten (1998) Procesmanagement, *Bestuurswetenschappen,* 52 (2). pp. 120-134

Bruijn, J. A. de, Heuvelhof, E. ten, & Veld, R. J. in 't (2002) *Procesmanagement.
Over procesmanagement en besluitvorming.* Schoonhoven: Academic Ser-
vice.
Bruin, H. de & Heuvelhof, E. ten (2007) *Management in netwerken.* Den Haag,
Uitgeverij Lemma.
Bruins, A. (2006) Ondernemerschap en strategie in het MKB. *Zoetermeer:
EIM.*

Bruijn, H. de (2011) *Framing. Over de macht van taal in de politiek.* Amsterdam: Atlas.

Bovens, M. e.a. (1996) *Openbaar bestuur: beleid, organisatie en politiek.* Alphen aan den Rijn: Samsom.

Burns, T. R., Flam, H., & De Man, R. (1987) *The shaping of social organization.*
London: Sage Publications.

Castelein, A.I.M. (2011) Samenspel tussen leren en werken – concept Learning & Future Center. *NSCU, december 2011, 24-25.*

Castells, M. (1996) *The rise of the networksociety. The information age: Economy, Society and Culture, Volume I.* London: Blackwell.

Castells, M. (2000) Materials for an exploratory theory of the network society
British Journal of Sociology Vol. No. 51 Issue No. pp. 5-24 ISSN 0007 1315.

Christensen, C. M. (2003) *The innovator's dilemma: the revolutionary book that will change the way you do business* (p. 320). New York, NY: HarperBusiness Essentials.

Conger, J. A., & Kanungo, R. N. (1988) The empowerment process: Integrating theory and practice. *Academy of management review, 13*(3), 471-482.

Cooperrider, D. L., & Srivastva, S. (1987) Appreciative inquiry in organizational life. *Research in organizational change and development, 1*(1), 129-169.

Cooperrider, D. L., Whitney, D. K., & Stavros, J. M. (Eds.). (2003) *Appreciative inquiry handbook* (Vol. 1). Berrett-Koehler Store.

Cooperrider, D. L., Whitney, D. K., & Stavros, J. M. (Eds.). (2003) *Appreciative inquiry handbook* (Vol. 1). Berrett-Koehler Store.

Cowan, C. & Todorovic, N. (2000*)* Spiral dynamics: the layers of human values in strategy. *Strategy & Leadership, 28 (1),* 4-12.

Cowan, Christopher C. and Todorovic, Natasha (eds.) (2005) *The Never Ending Quest: Dr. Clare W. Graves Explores Human Nature*. Santa Barbara, CA: ECLET Publishing.

Crozier, M. (1964) *The bureaucratic phenomenon*. Chicago, IL: University of Chicago Press.

Daemen, H. H. F. M., & Thomassen, J. J. A. (1989) Afstand tussen burgers en overheid. In A. Hoogerwerf (Ed.), *Overheidsbeleid*. Alphen aan den Rijn: Samsom.

Dahrendorf, R., & Dahrendorf, R. (Eds.). (1982) *Europe's economy in crisis*. Weidenfeld and Nicolson.

Damme, J. van, & Brans, M. (2008) Over het design en management van inspraakprocessen. België: Katholieke Universiteit Leuven.

Denzin, N. K., & Lincoln, Y. S. (Eds.). (2005) *The SAGE handbook of qualitative research*. Sage.

Denzin, N. K., & Lincoln, Y. S. (Eds.). (2011) *The SAGE handbook of qualitative research*. Sage.

Dick, B. (2001) Action research: action and research. In Sankaran, S., Dick, B., Passfield, R. and Swepson, P. (Eds). *Effective Change Management Using Action Learning and Action Research.* Lismore: Southern Cross University Press.

Diefenbach, T. & Sillince, J.A.A. (2011) Formal and Informal Hierarchy in Different Types of Organization *Organization Studies 2011 32(11): 1515-1537 DOI: 10.1177/0170840611421254*

Diefenbach, T., & By, R. T. (Eds.). (2012) *Reinventing Hierarchy and Bureaucracy: From the Bureau to Network Organisations* (Vol. 35). Emerald Group Publishing.

Dijstelbloem, H. O. (2007) *De democratie anders: politieke vernieuwing volgens Dewey en Latour.* Amsterdam: Universiteit van Amsterdam.

Dijstelbloem, H. (2008) *Politiek vernieuwen: op zoek naar publiek in een technologische samenleving.* Amsterdam: Uitgeverij Van Gennep.

Dickens, L., & Watkins, K. (1999) Action research: rethinking Lewin. *Management Learning, 30*(2), 127-140.

Dilts, R., & Zolno, S. (1991) Skills for the New Paradigm: Lessons from Italy. Proaction Associates.

Dilts, R. (1994) *Strategies of Genius: Volume I.* California: meta Publications.

Dilts, R. (1998a) *Modeling With NLP.* California: Meta Publications. P. 28.

Dilts, R. (1998b) Article of the month. Calfornia: Nlpu.com. Verkregen op 17 januari via http://www.nlpu.com/Articles/artic15.htm

Dohmen, J. & Wester, J. (red.) (2014) *Operatie 'werk Arthur de deur uit' - Dagboek van een ongewenste werknemer.* Amsterdam: Bertram + de Leeuw uitgevers.

Drucker, P. F. (1993) *De post-kapitalistische maatschappij: onze maatschappij van organisaties, het staatsbestel en kennis.* Scriptum, Schiedam.

Drucker, P. F. (1994) The theory of the business. *Harvard business review, 72*(5), 95-104.

Drucker, P. F. (2004) *The Daily Drucker: 366 Days Of Insight And Motivation For Getting The Right Things Done* Peter F. Drucker, Publish.

Dvir, R., Schwartzberg, Y., Avni, H., Webb, C., & Lettice, F. (2006) The future center as an urban innovation engine. *Journal of knowledge management*, *10*(5), 110-123.

Dynamiek, P. (2008) Vormgeven aan de strategische functie bij de overheid. *M&O*, nr. 1,5-19.

Ebeling, W., & Schweitzer, F. (2002) Zwischen Ordnung und Chaos. Komplexität und Asthetik aus physikalischer Sicht. *Gegenworte, Zeitschrift für den Disput über Wissen. Berlin-Brandenburgische Akademie der Wissenschaften, Heft ,Wissenschaft und Kunst'*, 46-49.

Edelenbos, J., & Monnikhof, R. (1998) *Spanning in interactie: een analyse van interactief beleid in lokale democratie*. Amsterdam: Instituut voor Publiek en Politiek.

Edelenbos, J. (diss.) (2000), *Proces in vorm: Procesbegeleiding van interactieve beleidsvorming over lokale ruimtelijke projecten*. Utrecht: Lemma.

Edelenbos, J., Teisman, G.R., & Reudink, M. (2003) *De 'LAT-relatie' tussen interactief beleid en besluitvorming: Naar een handreiking voor het organiseren van verbindingen tussen informele interactieve processen en formele overheidsbesluitvorming*. Rotterdam: Centrum voor Publieksmanagement.

Edelenbos, J. (2005) Institutional Implications of Interactive Governance: Insights from Dutch Practice. *Governance: An International Journal of Policy, Administration, and Institutions, 18 (1)*, 111-134.

Edelenbos, J. & Klijn, Erik-Hans (2005a) Managing stakeholder involvement in decision making: A comparative analysis of six interactive processes in the Netherlands, *Journal of Public Administration Research and Theory*, 16, pp. 417-446.

Edelenbos, J en E.H. Klijn, (2005b) De impact van organisatorische arrangementen op de uitkomsten van interactieve beleidsvorming, in: Bestuurswetenschappen, 2005, nr. 4, pp. 281-305.

Edelenbos J., Klok, P.J., Domingo, A. & Van Tatenhove, J. van (2006) Burgers als beleidsadviseurs: een vergelijkend onderzoek naar acht projecten van interactieve beleidsvorming bij drie departementen. Amsterdam: Instituut voor publiek en politiek.

Edwards, E. (2002) Public Sector Governance – Future Issues for Australia. *Australian Journal of Public Administration, 61(2),* 57-59.

Einstein, A. (2005) Albert Einstein Quotes. *Brainy Quote: http://www. brainy-quote.*

Entman, R. M. (1993) Framing: Toward clarification of a fractured paradigm. *Journal of communication, 43*(4), 51-58.

Erlandson, D. A. (Ed.). (1993) *Doing naturalistic inquiry: A guide to methods.* Sage.

Frazier, G. L., & Summers, J. O. (1984) Interfirm influence strategies and their application within distribution channels. *The Journal of Marketing,* 43-55.

Frenkel, D. (1994) De tweede jeugd van entropie. In *Radar* (pp. 145-162) Aramith uitgevers.

Fiol, C. M., & Lyles, M. A. (1985. Organizational learning. *Academy of Management review, 10*(4), 803-813.

Fluit E. van der, Van Nistelrooij, A., De Wilde, R. & Van der Zouwen, T. (2013) Van transities naar fundamentele verandering in het sociale domein. Verkregen op 3 februari 2014 via http://www.alignment.nu/over-ons/artikelen/

Frissen, P.H.A. (1999*) De lege staat.* Amsterdam: Uitgeverij Nieuwezijds.

Frissen, P.H.A. (2002) *De staat.* Amsterdam: De Balie.

Frissen, P.H.A. (2009) *Gevaar verplicht: over de noodzaak van aristocratische politiek.* Amsterdam: Van Gennep.

Fukuyama, F. (2011) *De oorsprong van onze politiek. Van de prehistorie tot de Verlichting.* Amsterdam/Antwerpen: Amsterdam: Uitgeverij Contact.

Fuller, R. W. (2001) A new look at hierarchy. *Leader to leader. Hesselbein & Company,* 6-12.

Fuller, R. W. (2003) *Somebodies and nobodies: Overcoming the abuse of rank.* B. J. Sandesara (Ed.). Gabriola Island, BC: New Society Publishers.

Fuller, R. W. (2006) *All rise: Somebodies, nobodies, and the politics of dignity.* Berrett-Koehler Publishers.

Fung, A. (2006) Varieties of Participation in Complex Governance. *Public Administration Review, 66,* 66-75.

Geertz, C. (1973) *The interpretation of cultures: Selected essays* (Vol. 5019). Basic books.

Geertz, C. (1994) Thick description: Toward an interpretive theory of culture. *Readings in the philosophy of social science,* 213-231.

Gersick, C. J. 1991. Revolutionary change theories: A multilevel exploration of the punctuated equilib-rium paradigm. Academy of Management Review, 16: 10-36.

Geus, A. de (1997) *Levende ondernemingen.* Schiedam: Scriptum.

Gilbreth, F.B. & Gilbreth L.M. (1917) Applied Motion Study: a collection of papers on the efficient method to industrial preparedness.

Gilsdorf, J. W. (1998) Organizational rules on communicating: How employees are-and are not-learning the ropes. *Journal of Business Communication, 35*(2), 173-201.

Glaser, B. G., & Strauss, A. L. (2009) *The discovery of grounded theory: Strategies for qualitative research.* New Jersey: Transaction Books.

Goulding, C. (2002) *Grounded theory: A practical guide for management, business and market researchers.* CA: Sage.

Graaf, G. de, & Huberts, L. (2011). Integriteit in het Nederlands openbaar bestuur.
Verkregen op 5 februari via https://www.researchgate.net/profile/Gjalt_Graaf/publication/236677415_Integriteit_in_het_Nederlands_openbaar_bestuur/links/545a01910cf26d5090ad40f3.pdf

Graaf, H. van de & Hoppe, R. (1992) *Beleid en politiek: een inleiding tot de beleidswetenschap en de beleidskunde.* Muiderberg: Coutinho BV.
Graaf, L. de (2007) *Gedragen beleid: Een bestuurskundig onderzoek naar interactief beleid en draagvlak in de stad Utrecht.* Delft: Eburon.
Graves, C.W. (1965) Man: An Enlarged Conception of His Nature, *paper presented before the Second Annual Conference on the Cybercultural Revolution at the Hotel Americana in New York City, New York on May 27, 1965.* Verkregen op 11 april 2014 via http://www.clarewgraves.com/articles_content/1965/1965_enlarged_conception.html

Graves, C. W. (1970) Levels of Existence: an Open System Theory of Values. *Journal of Humanistic Psychology, 10*(2), 131-155.

Graves, C. W. (1974) *Human Nature Prepares for a Momentous Leap*. The Futurist, april, pp. 72-87.

Graves, C.W. (1981) *Summary statement, the emergent cyclical, human nature model of the adult human biopsychsoicial systems*. Verkregen op 29 april 2013 via http://www.clarewgraves.com/articles_content/1981_handout/1981_summary.pdf

Grit, R. (2005) *Projectmanagement*. 6e druk, Noordhoff Uitgevers BV.

Guba, E. G. (86) & Lincoln, YS (1989) *Fourth generation evaluation*.

Guba, E. G., & Lincoln, Y. S. (1994) Competing paradigms in qualitative research. *Handbook of qualitative research, 2*, 163-194.

Gurley Brown, H. (1962) *Sex and the single girl*. New York: Geis.

Haanel, C.F. (1924) *The New Psychology* U.S.: C.F. Haanel.

Habermas, J. (1985) *Die Neue Unübersichtlichkeit*, Frankfurt am Main: Suhrkamp.

Habermas, J. (1997) *Vom sinnlichen Eindruck zum symbolischen Ausdruck* (Vol. 1233). Frankfurt am Main: Suhrkamp.

Hales, C. (2002) Bureacracy-lite and Continuities in Managerial Work. *Britisch Journal of management, Vol. 13(1): 51-66.*

Hakvoort, L.M. & Heer, M. de (red.) (1994) *Departementen in beweging*. Den Haag: VUGA.

Harris, M. (1976) History and significance of the emic/etic distinction. Annual review of anthropology, 5, 329-350.

Heldeweg, M. A. (2006) *Bestuursrecht en beleid*. Groningen: Wolters-Noordhoff.

Heffen, O. van (1993) Beleidontwerpen en omgevingsfactoren: vier alternatieve strategieën. In O. van Heffen & M.J.W. Twist (red.), *Beleid en wetenschap. Hedendaagse bestuurskundige beschouwingen* (pp. 67-81).

Hendriks, F. (2012) *Democratie onder druk: over de uitdagingen van de stem-mingendemocratie* Amsterdam: Uitgeverij Van Gennep.

Hendriks, F. & Tops, P.W. (2001) Interactieve beleidsvorming en betekenisver-lening. *Beleid en Maatschappij, 28*(2), p. 106-119.

Hendry, J. (2013) *Management* Amsterdam: University Press.

Herold, M. (2005) The 'Knowledge Based Networking Nation'. Verkregen op 5 juli 2013 via http://www.managementissues.com/globalisering/globalisering/the_'know-ledge_based_networking_nation'._20050424289.html

Herold, M. (2007) *De spiraal van waarden en denken.* Amstelveen: Uitgeverij Symbolon.

Herold, M. (2008a) *Ondernemen natuurlijk!* Leiden: Managementissues.com

Herold, M. (2008b) De waarden/competentieverwarring. Verkregen op 17 januari via http://www.managementissues.com/index.php/kennismanage-ment/79-kennismanagement/490-de-waardencompetentieverwarring

Herold, M. (2009) Netwerken: evolutie of noodzakelijke revolutie. Verkregen op 13 september 2014 via http://www.managementissues.com/index.php/spiral-dynamics/73-spiral-dynamics/545-netwerken-evolutie-of-noodzakelij-ke-revolutie

Herold, M. (2011) Modelleren als basis voor het ontwerpen van protocollen. In: Aken, J. V., & Andriessen, D. (red.) *Handboek ontwerpgericht wetenschap-pelijk onderzoek: wetenschap met effect.* Den Haag: Lemma.

Herold, M. (2012) Scientific (Knowledge)Management Next Generation. Ver-kregen op 31 januari 2016 via http://www.managementissues.com/index.php/organisatiemanagement/76-management/763-scientific-knowledgema-nagement-next-generation

Herold, M. (2013) 'Beleidsambtenaren, ongeschreven regels en openheid in de beleidsontwikkeling', *Beleidsonderzoek Online*, 2013-05, DOI: 10.5553/Beleidsonderzoek.000022

Heylighen, F. (2002) Complexiteit en evolutie. *Cursusnota's 2003-2004.*

Hisschemöller, M. (1993) *De democratie van problemen: de relatie tussen de inhoud van beleidsproblemen en methoden van politieke besluitvorming.* VU uitgeverij.

Hisschemöller, M., & Hoppe, R. (1995) Coping with intractable controversies: the case for problem structuring in policy design and analysis. *Knowledge and Policy*, 8(4), 40-60.

Hoesel, P. van (2008) *Partij voor eenvoud: een zoektocht naar kwaliteit van overheidsbeleid* Den Haag: SDU uitgevers.

Hofstede, G. & Hofstede G.J. (2005) *Allemaal andersdenkenden: omgaan met cultuurverschillen.* Amsterdam: Uitgeverij Contact.

Homan, Th. (2013) *Het Et-Cetera principe.* Den Haag: Academic Service.

Hoogerwerf, A. (1987) Beleid berust op vooronderstellingen: de beleidstheorie. In: Lehning, P. e.a. (red.) *Handboek Beleidswetenschap.* Meppel/Amsterdam: Boom, pp.23-40.
Houppermans, M. K. (2011) *Twee Kanten van de Medaille: een onderzoek naar de kwaliteit van de beleidsvoorbereiding.* Faculty of Social Sciences (FSS).

Hufen, J.A.M. (2009) Het Nationaal Innovatiesysteem. Zoekende naar een beleidsperspectief voor onze kenniseconomie. Verkregen op 4 mei 2014 via www.qaplus.info

Hupe, P. (2007) *Overheidsbeleid als politiek: over de grondslagen van beleid.* Assen: Van Gorcum.
Iersel, W. van, Bouwhuis, B. & Herold, M. (2007) Spiral Dynamics & Compliance. Verkregen op 23 juni 2013 via http://www.managementissues. com/spiral_dynamics/spiral_dynamics/spiral_dynamics_%26_compliance._20070117418.html

Ikerd, J. (1997, January). Understanding and managing the multi-dimensions of sustainable agriculture. In *Southern Region Sustainable Agriculture Professional Development Program Workshop.*

Jackson, P.Z. & MacKergow, M. (2003) *Oplossingsgericht denken.* Zaltbommel: Uitgeverij Thema.

Jolly, R. D. (2003) *De lerende bureaucratie? Een onderzoek naar de betekenis van ICT voor leren in het openbaar bestuur* (Doctoral dissertation, Erasmus University Rotterdam).

Jong, J. de et al. (2008) *Kafka in de polder:* Handboek voor opsporen en oplossen van overbodige bureaucratie. Den Haag: SDU.

Kalk, E. (1998) De geest is uit de fles. Slotbeschouwing. In: Edelenbos, J. & R. Monninkhof (red.), *Spanning in interactie* (pp. 210-214). Amsterdam: Institiuut voor Publiek en Politiek.

Kaplan, A. (1964) The Conduct of Inquiry: methodology for behavioral science (San Francisco, Chandler).

Karssing, E.D. & S. Spoor (2010) Integriteit 3.0. Naar een derde generatie integriteitsbeleid. In: E.D. Karssing & M. Zweegers (red.), *Jaarboek Integriteit 2010.* Den Haag: BIOS, p. 7281.

Kats, E., Glastra, F. Gussen-Benthem, I. & Lakerveld, J. van (2013) Praktijkgericht onderzoek en professioneel handelen: een voorbeeld van een onderzoeksstrategie. In: Jong, H. de, P. Tops & M. van der Land (2013*). Prikken in praktijken. Over de ontwikkeling van praktijkonderzoek.* Den Haag: Boom Lemma uitgevers.

Kettl, D.F. (2000) *The Transformation of Governance: Globalisation, Devolution and the Role of Government'.* Discussion paper, National Academy of Public Administration, June, Albuquerque.

Kickert, W. J. (2003) Beneath consensual corporatism: Traditions of governance in the Netherlands. *Public Administration*, 81(1), 119-140.

Kim, D.H. (1993) The link between individual and organizational learning. *Sloan Management Review Fall,* 37-50.

Kim, B. (2001) Social constructivism. In M. Orey (Ed.), *Emerging perspectives on learning, teaching, and technology.* Available Website: http://www.coe.uga.edu/epltt/SocialConstructivism.htm

Klijn, E.H. (2005) Netwerken als perspectief op beleid en de uitvoering van beleid
Beleidswetenschap, nr. 4, 32-54.

Klok, H. J. (2009). Van idee tot CJG (Master's thesis).
Verkregen op 4 februari 2017 via http://dspace.library.uu.nl/bitstream/hand-le/1874/35783/scriptie%20Joost%20Klok.pdf?sequence=2

Koohang, A, Harman, K. & Britz, J. (eds.) (2008) *Knowledge Management: Theoretical Foundations.* Santa Rosa, California: Informing Science Press.

Klinkers, L. (2002) *Beleid begint bij de samenleving.* Den Haag: Boom Juridi-sche Uitgeverij.

Koppenjan, J., Bruijn, J. de, Kickers, W. (1993) *Netwerkmanagement in het openbaar bestuur: over de mogelijkheden van overheidssturing in beleids-netwerken.* Den Haag: VUGA.

Koppenjan, J., Kars, M. & Voort, H. van der (2007) Verticale politiek in horizon-tale beleidsnetwerken: kaderstelling als koppelingsarrangement. Gepubli-ceerd in: *B&M. Tijdschrift voor beleid, politiek en maatschappij, jaargang 34, nr. 4, 2007, pp. 210-225*
http://repub.eur.nl/res/pub/22607/Verticale%20politiek%20in%20horizonta-le%20netwerken%2028-10-07.pdf

Kor, R., Wijnen, G., & Weggeman, M. (2007) *Meesterlijk organiseren: handrei-kingen voor ondernemende managers.* Kluwer.

Korsten, A.F.A (1999) Rivaliteit en strijd tussen ambtelijke bureaus Bureaupolitiek, verkokering, stammenstrijd, samenwerking. Verkregen op 22 augustus via
http://www.arnokorsten.nl/PDF/Organiseren%20en%20mgmt/Rivaliteit%20en%20strijd%20tussen%20ambtelijke%20bureaus.pdf

Korsten, A. (2001) Wat een manager doet met een beleidsprobleem? Ver-kregen op 5 mei via http://www.arnokorsten.nl/PDF/Beleid/Wat%20een%20manager%20doet%20met%20beleidsproblemen.pdf

Korsten, A. (2003) Inleiding in de bestuurskunde. Verkregen op 5 mei via http://www.arnokorsten.nl/PDF/Bestuurskunde/Inleiding%20in%20de%20bestuurskunde.pdf

Korsten, A. (2007) Samenwerken in ketens en ketenmanagement. Retrieved on june 5, 2011, from http://arnokorsten.nl/PDF/Organiseren%20en%20 mgmt/Samenwerken%20in%20ketens%20en%20ketenmanagement.pdf

Korsten, F.A. (2015) Bestuurders tegenspreken noodzakelijk. Verklaring voor de val van bestuurders en de betekenis van gebrek aan tegengeluiden daarbij? Verkregen op 6 maart 2015 via http://www.arnokorsten.nl/PDF/Bestuur/ Bestuurders%20tegenspreken.pdf

Korzybski, A. (1948): *Science and sanity: an introduction to non-Aristotelian systems and general semantics* (3rd edn). Lakeville, CT: The Internal Non-Aristotelian Library.

Korzybski, A. (1994) *Science and sanity: An introduction to non-Aristotelian systems and general semantics*. Institute of GS.

Kovecses, Z. (2010) *Metaphor: A practical introduction*. Oxford University Press.

Kreijveld. (2013) *Samen Slimmer. Hoe de 'wisdom of crowds' onze samenleving zal veranderen*. Den Haag: Stichting Toekomstbeeld der Techniek.

Krijger, E., Driest, P., & Stoelenga, B. (2002) De integrale medewerker. Stuurgroep Experimenten Volkshuisvesting (SEV).

Kuiper, D. T. (1992) Christelijk onderwijs in een ontzuilende samenleving. *Christen democratische verkenningen*, 137.

Kupchan, C. A. (2012) Democratic Malaise: Globalization and the Threat to the West, The. *Foreign Aff.*, *91*, 62-67.

Kuypers, P. (2001) Rooksignalen: opstellen over politiek en bestuur. Amsterdam: de Balie.

Lakoff, G., & Johnson, M. (1980a) The metaphorical structure of the human conceptual system. *Cognitive Science*, *4*(2), 195-208.

Lakoff, G., & Johnson, M. (1980b) Conceptual metaphor in everyday language. *The journal of Philosophy*, *77*(8), 453-486.

Landin, M. (2014) Secretaresse is de baas. *Historia, 9(8)*. Verkregen op 3 januari 2015 via http://www.managementissues.com/index.php/cultuuranalyse/80-cultuuranalyse/865-flirt-je-een-weg-omhoog-in-historisch-perspectief

Ledeneva, A. (2001) Unwritten rules: How Russia really works. Verkregen op 10 september 2015 via http://cer-staging.thomas-paterson.co.uk/sites/default/files/publications/attachments/pdf/2011/e246_unwritten_rules-2203.pdf

Leede, J. de (1997) *Innoveren van onderop: over de bijdrage van taakgroepen aan product en procesvernieuwing* Enschedé: Twente Publications.

Levy, S (2011) Steve Jobs, 1955-2011. Verkregen op 22 september 2013 via http://www.wired.com/business/2011/10/steve-jobs-1955-2011/all/1

Lincoln, Y. S., & Guba, E. G. Naturalistic inquiry. 1985. *VALLES, M. Técnicas.*

Linden, A. & Perutz, K. (1997) *Mindworks.* New York: Berkly Books.

Lipietz, A. (1996) The New Core-Periphery Relations: the Contrasting Examples of Europe and America. In: *The State and the Economic Prosess.* Naastepad, C.W.M & Storm, S. (red.) UK: Edward Elgar Publishing Unlimited.

Lipsky, M. (1980) *Street level bureaucracy and the dilemmas of the individual in public service.* New York: Russel Sage Foundation.

Lubberdink, H. G. (1982) *De betekenis van de ministeriële verantwoordelijkheid voor de organisatie van het openbaar bestuur* (Doctoral dissertation, University of Groningen).

Luhman, N. (1984) *Soziale Systeme. Grundrisse einer algemeinen Theorie.* Frankfurt Am Main: Suhrkamp.

Luyendijk, J. (2010) *Je hebt het niet van mij, maar...* Amsterdam: Uitgeverij Podium B.V.

Luyendijk, J. (2015) *Dit kan niet waar zijn.* Amsterdam: Uitgeverij Atlas Contact.

Mak, G. (2013*) In Europa (deel I).* Amsterdam: Uitgeverij Olympus.

Mak, G. (2012) *Mijn land: een minigeschiedenis voor beginners.* Maartensdijk: B for Books.

Magnée, M. J., Cox, I. M., & Teunisse, J. P. (2015) eHealth onderzoek ter ondersteuning van mensen met autisme: Op weg naar richtlijnen voor praktijkgericht onderzoek. *Stem-, Spraak- en Taalpathologie, 20.*

March, J. G. (2010) *Rediscovering institutions*. SimonandSchuster. com.

March, J. G., Schulz, M., & Zhou, X. (2000) *The dynamics of rules: Change in written organizational codes*. CA: Stanford University Press.

Oost, H., & Markenhof, A. (2002) Een onderzoek voorbereiden. *Baarn: HB Uitgevers*.

Martens, R. (2007) Science, knowledge, and sport psychology. *Essential Readings in Sport and Exercise Psychology*, 457-69.

Martín, M. A., & Rey, J. M. (2000) On the role of Shannon's entropy as a measure of heterogeneity. *Geoderma, 98*(1), 1-3.

McDermott, I., & O'Connor, J. (1996) *Practical NLP for managers*. Gower Publishing, Ltd.

Meindertsma, B. A. (2013) Van heilig huisje tot bodemloze put, de rol van de media in het Nederlandse publieke en politieke debat over ontwikkelingssamenwerking tussen 1995 en 2010.

Mertens, F. (1996) *Vriendelijk converseren en krachtig optreden. Over vakmanschap in de beleidsadvisering*. Rotterdam: Erasmus Universiteit.

Metze, M. (2010) *Veranderend getij: Rijkswaterstaat In Crisis: 'Log, Te Duur, Te Ondoorzichtig', De Nieuwe Man, Een Nieuwe Koers, De 'Generaal', De Heren Zeventien, De Coup, De Leegloop, Het Verzet. Het Verhaal Van Binnenuit*. Amsterdam: Balans.

Metze, T., & Turnhout, E. (2014) Politiek, participatie en experts in de besluitvorming over super wicked problems. *Bestuurskunde, 23*(2), 1-48.

Meuleman, L. (2006) Internal meta-governance as a new challenge for management development in public administration. *Director, 31*(6), 21827020.

Meuleman, L. (2008) *Public management and the metagovernance of hierarchies, networks and markets: the feasibility of designing and managing governance style combinations*. Springer Science & Business Media.

Meuleman, L. (2009) Metagovernance: Publiek management voorbij de nieuwste managementmodes. Verkregen op 19 februari 2012 via http://www.managementissues.com/organisatietools/organisatietools/metagovernance%3a_publiek_management_voorbij_de_nieuwste_management-modes._20090926607.html

Meijer, A. J., Curtin, D., & Hillebrandt, M. (2012) Open government: connecting vision and voice. *International Review of Administrative Sciences*, *78*(1), 10-29.

Miles, M. B. & Huberman, A. M. (1994) *Qualitative data analysis: An expanded sourcebook*. CA: Sage.

Miller, G.A., Galanter, E. & Pribram, K.H. (1986) *Plans and the Structure of Behavior*. New York: Adams-Bannister-Cox.

Miller, R.B. & Heiman, S.E. The New Strategic Selling: The Unique Sales System proven Succesful by the World's best Companies. London: Kogan Page.

Ministerie van Binnenlandse Zaken en Koninkrijksrelaties (2013) Visie Open Overheid. Den Haag: Ministerie van BZK.

Ministerie van Infrasttructuur en Milieu (2011) Beleidsbrief Eenvoudig Beter. Verkregen op 28 juni 2016 via www.rijksoverheid.nl/onderwerpen/omgevingswet/documenten/kamerstukken/2011/06/28/beleidsbrief-eenvoudig-beter

Ministerie van Sociale Zaken en Werkgelegenheid (2010*) Handout Masterclass Van Buiten naar Binnen*. Den Haag: Ministerie van SZW.

Mintzberg, H. (2003) *Mintzberg over management*. Amsterdam: Atlas Contact.

Mintzberg, H. (2006) *Organisatiestructuren*. Pearson Education.

Mintzberg, H. (2010) *Managing*. Amsterdam/Antwerp: Business Contact.

Mintzberg, H. (2014) *Simply managing*. Amsterdam/Antwerp: Business Contact.

Mitchell, G. J. (1999) Evidence-based practice: Critique and alternative view. *Nursing Science Quarterly*, *12*(1), 30-35.

Mortelmans, D. (2007). *Handboek kwalitatieve onderzoeksmethoden*. Leuven: Acco.

Mulisch, H. (2010) *De zaak 40/61*. Amsterdam: Uitgeverij De Bezige Bij B.V.

Naím, M. (2015) *Het einde van macht* Amsterdam: Carrera.

Nederland T., Huygen, A. & Bouttelier, H. (2009) *Governance in de WMO: theorie en praktijk van vernieuwde governance modellen* Utrecht: Verwey-Jonker Instituut.

Neuberger, V. J. (2011) A Nudge in the Right Direction won't Run the Big Society. *The Observer, 17*.

Nieuwenkamp, R. (2001) *De prijs van het politieke primaat: Wederzijds vertrouwen en loyaliteit in de verhouding tussen bewindspersonen en ambtelijke top*. Eburon.

Noordegraaf, M. (2000) *Attention! Work and behavior of public managers amidst ambiguity*. Eburon.

Noordegraaf, M. (2004*) Management in het publieke domein: issues, instituties en instrumenten*. Bussum: Uitgeverij Coutinho.

North, D., C. @?@ (1990) *Institutions, Institutional Change and Economic Performance*. Cambridge, Cambridge University Press.

Nuys, O. (2010) Parallellen tussen twee werelden. In: Heijden, J. van et al. *Combineer wat je hebt* Delft: Eburon p. 32-33.

O'Connor, J. & Seymour, J. (1993*) Introducing NLP: psychological skills for understanding and influencing people*. California: The Aquarius Press.

Oosterhout, D. van (2010) *Procesregie: creatief sturen op gedragen besluitvorming*. Culemborg: Van Duuren Management.
Ott, J. Steven (2012) Understanding Organisational Culture. In: Shafritz, J.M. & Hyde, A.C. (2012) *Public Administration: Classic Readings* Wadsworth: Cengage Learning.

Paauwe, J. (2004) *HRM and performance. Achieving long term viability*. Oxford: Oxford University Press.

Paauwe (2004) HRM and performance. Achieving long term viability Oxford University Press in: Steijn, B. & Groeneveld, S. (2009) *Strategisch HRM in de publieke sector* Den Haag: Uitgeverij Van Gorcum, p. 13.

Packard, V. (1963) De piramidebeklimmers. Amsterdam: Uitgeverij H.J. Paris.

Parkinson, C.N. (1955) *Parkinson's law, and other studies in administration.* Houghton Mifflin.

Peter, L. J., & Hull, R. (1969) *The peter principle* Uitgeverij: W. Morrow.

Peter, L.J. (1973) *Peter's Panacee: hoe te zorgen dat het goed gaat.* Deventer, Uitgeverij Kluwer.

Peter, L.J. (1985) *Waarom altijd alles verkeerd gaat. Het Peter principe van vijftien jaar* Utrecht/Antwerpen: Veen.

Peter, L.J. (1986) *De Peter Piramide* Utrecht/Antwerpen: Veen.

Peters, G. & Pierre, J. (2001) Developments in intergovernmental relations towards multi-level governance. *Policy and politics 29 no 2:131-5 The Policy Press.*

Peters, M., & Robinson, V. (1984) The origins and status of action research. *The Journal of Applied Behavioral Science, 20*(2), 113-124.

Pleij, H. (2014) *Botte Hollanders.* Maartensdijk: Uitgeverij B for NBooks.

Piketty, T. (2014) *Capital in the 21st Century.* Harvard University Press.

Poorter, M. (2005) *Democratische legitimiteit van governance networks: Een studie naar de democratische legitimiteit van governance networks in het Groene Hart en de Driehoek RZG-Zuidplas.* Diss. Msc. Universiteit van Amsterdam, p. 8.

Pröpper, I.M.A.M. & Steenbeek, D.A. (1998) Interactieve beleidsvoering: typering, ervaring en dilemma's. In: *Bestuurskunde,* jrg.7, nr. 7. pp. 292-301.

Pröpper, I.M.A.M. & Steenbeek, D.A. (1999) *De aanpak van interactief beleid: elke situatie is anders.* Bussum: Coutinho.

Pröpper, I.M.A.M. & Steenbeek, D.A. (2013) *De aanpak van interactief beleid: elke situatie is anders.* Bussum: Coutinho.

Quinn, J.B., Managing Innovation: controlled chaos – big companies stay innovative by behaving like small entrepreneurial ventures, Harvard Business Review, May June pp 73-92.

Raad voor Openbaar Bestuur (2010) *Vertrouwen op democratie.* Den Haag: ROB.

Raad voor het openbaar bestuur (2011) *Horizontaal met verticaal verbinden. De reactie op de reacties op* Vertrouwen op democratie. Den Haag: ROB.

Rainey, H. G. (2009) Understanding and managing public organizations. Wiley. com.

Reason, P., & Rowan, J. (Eds.) (1981) *Human inquiry: A sourcebook of new paradigm research.* Chichester, UK: J. Wiley.

Reeves, M. & Deimler, M. (2012) Adaptability: The New Competitive Advantage. *Boston Harvard Business Review pp. 52-58.*

Redder, T. & Woolcock, G. (2004) In municipals True Participation of the Council Organizing feedback to the municipal council commitment from political officeholders. *Australian Journal of Public Administration, 63(3),* 75-87.

Ridder, J. de & Struikema, N. (2008) De kern van de zaak? Eindrapport in het kader van de pilot kernbepalingen *Vakgroep Bestuursrecht en Bestuurskunde van de Rijksuniversiteit.*

Riege, A., & Lindsay, N. (2006) Knowledge management in the public sector: stakeholder partnerships in the public policy development. *Journal of knowledge management, 10(3), 24-39.*

Riepma, R. & Aken, T. van (2009) Schitterende converSatieruimteS. *IPMA ProjectieMagazine, mei pp. 26-31.*

Rijksdienst Voor Ondernemend Nederland (2012) Veiligheid Kleine Bedrijven.
Verkregen op 18 mei 2014 via http://www.rvo.nl/subsidies-regelingen/veiligheid-kleine-bedrijven?gclid=CPbl2aPXtb4CFWqWtAodEGkAEw

Rijksoverheid (2015) Integriteit Overheid. Verkregen op 27 maart 2015 via http://www.rijksoverheid.nl/onderwerpen/kwaliteit-en-integriteit-overheidsinstanties/integriteit-overheid

Rijkswaterstaat (1995) Secundaire literatuuranalyse deel I: Het rapport-Glasbergen Grote wateren en het WRR-rapport Grote projecten. Haarlem, Rijkswaterstaat. Verkregen op 10 januari 2015 via
http://www.google.nl/url?sa=t&rct=j&q=&esrc=s&frm=1&source=web&cd=1&ved=0CCEQFjAA&url=http%3A%2F%2Fpublicaties.minienm.nl%2Fdownload-bijlage%2F60488%2F362865.pdf&ei=iiSxVNKsKci4OPHDg-ZgB&usg=AFQjCNHD1cunbJr0xN43UnhleulDyyLrfQ

Rijnja, G. W. (2012) *Genieten van weerstand*. Universiteit Twente.

Rittel, Horst W. J. (2013) Melvin M. Webber (1973) Dilemmas in a General Theory of Planning. *Policy Sciences* **4**: 155-169. Retrieved 25 April 2013.

Rhodes, R. (1997) *Understanding Governance: Policy Networks, Governance, Reflexivity and Accountability.* Buckingham: Open University Press.

Robbins, D. (2014) Danger of Hierarchy in a Fast-Moving World. Verkregen op 5 mei 2014 via
http://www.huffingtonpost.com/debbie-robins/danger-of-hierarchy-in-a-_b_5187316.html?utm_campaign=Socialflow&utm_source=Socialflow&utm_medium=Tweet

Roemischer, J. (2002) The never-ending upward quest: An interview with Dr. Don Beck. *EnlightenNext Magazine*.

Rolfe, G. (2006) Validity, trustworthiness and rigour: quality and the idea of qualitative research. *Journal of advanced nursing, 53*(3), 304-310.

Roobeek, A. (1992) Een toekomst voor de verzorgingsstaat? In: Klooosterman, R. & Knaack, R. (red.) Het Nederlandse model: Kansen en bedreigingen voor de verzorgingsstaat. Amsterdam: Amsterdam University Press.

Roobeek, A. (1994) Strategisch Action Research in de praktijk. In: Veendrick, L. & Zeelen, J. *De toekomst van de sociale interventie.* Groningen: Wolters-Noordhoff.

Roobeek, A. (1996) Comment: The many Faces of Post-Fordism. In: *The State and the Economic Process.* Naastepad, C.W.M & Storm, S. (red.) UK: Edward Elgar Publishing Unlimited.

Roobeek, A (2008) InterCompanyLab: Strategieontwikkeling in een Netwerkproces. Verkregen op 13 juli 2013 via http://www.meetingmoreminds.com/artikelen/

Roobeek, A. & Grotenhuis, F. (2011) De barrage naar het Andere Werken in de publieke sector. In: *Management in beweging*. Karssing, E, Bossert, H. & Meuleman, L. (red.). Assen: Uitgeverij Van Gorcum.

Roobeek, A. & Swart, J. de (2013) *Sustainable Business Modeling: een besluitvormingsinstrument voor duurzame bedrijfsvoering*. Den Haag, Academic Service.

Roobeek (2014) Nederland moet collectieve intelligentie naar een hoger plan tillen. Headlines pp. 2-3.

Roosbroek, S. van (2008) *Kwaliteitsmanagement als innovatie in de lokale besturen in Vlaanderen*. Leuven: Steunpunt Bestuurlijke Organisatie Vlaanderen.

Rosenthal, U., Geveke, H. & Hart, P. 't (1994) Beslissen in een competitief overheidsbestel: bureaupolitiek en bureaupolitisme nader beschouwd. Acta Politica, juli pp. 309-335.

Rotmans, J. (2003) *Transitiemanagement; sleutel voor een duurzame samenleving*. Assen: Koninklijke Van Gorcum. P. 22.

Rozemond, K. (2012) kritische lezing van Hannah Arendts, Eichmann in Jerusalem. De complexiteit van het kwaad. *Netherlands Journal of Legal Philosophy, 41*, 1.

Ruijters, M. (2006) *Liefde voor leren: over diversiteit van leren en ontwikkelen in en van organisaties*. Deventer: Kluwer.

Sandelowski, M. (1993) Rigor or rigor mortis: The problem of rigor in qualitative research revisited. *Advances in nursing science, 16*(2), 1-8.

Sargut, G. & McGrath (2012) Learning to live with complexity. In: Boston Harvard Business Review, pp. 44-50.

Schrijver, J. (3013) *Wachten op het omslagpunt (Expeditie bestuursbeleid): verkenning van het governancedenken in bestuursbeleid bij het ministerie van Binnenlandse Zaken*. Amsterdam: Universiteit van Amsterdam.

Schein, E. (2010) *Organization culture and leadership*. CA: Jossey-Bass. Verkregen op 10 september 2010 via http://www.ehs-club.com/Files/lin-li_mary/file/20150211/20150211124427_6412.pdf

Schön, D. & Rein M. (1994) *Frame reflection: towards the resolution of intractable policy controversies*. Basic Books, New York.

Scott, J.C. (1999) *Seeing like a state* New Haven: Yale University Press.

Scott-Morgan, P. (1993) Removing Barriers to Change:
The Unwritten Rules of the Game. Verkregen op 23 juni 2013 via
http://www.adlittle.com/prism-articles.html?&no_cache=1&view=104

Scott-Morgan, P. (1995) *De ongeschreven regels van het spel*. Groningen: Boekwerk.

Senge, P. (1990) *The fifth discipline: The art & Practice of The Learning Organisation*. New York: Doubleday.

Shafritz, J.M. & Hyde, A.C. (2012) *Public Administration: Classic Readings*. Wadsworth: Cengage Learning

Schillemans, T. (2008) Regelruimte. Over de logica van verkokering en alternatieven voor ontkokering. Verkregen op 21 maart 2015 via http://dspace.library.uu.nl/bitstream/handle/1874/236036/2008%20Regelruimte.pdf?sequence=1

Smaling, A. (2010). Constructivisme in soorten. *Kwalon 43, jaargang, 15*.

Schmidt, E., & Cohen, J. (2013) *De digitale lente*. Business Contact.

Slingerland, E. (2014) *Proberen niet te proberen*. Amsterdam: Maven Publishing.

Schumpeter, J. A. (1934) *The theory of economic development: An inquiry into profits, capital, credit, interest, and the business cycle* (Vol. 55). Transaction publishers.

Soest, J. L. (1960) Orde en wanorde. *Statistica Neerlandica, 14*(3-4), 249-258.

Sørensen, E. & J. Torfing (2004) *Making governance networks democratic* Denmark: Centre for Democratic Network Governance.

Soto, H. de (2000) *The mystery of capital: Why Capitalism Triumphs in the West and Fails Everywhere Else*. London: Black Swan Books.

Spreitzer, G. M. (1995) Psychological empowerment in the workplace: Dimensions, measurement, and validation. *Academy of management Journal, 38*(5), 1442-1465.

Steijn, B. & Groeneveld, S. (2009) *Strategisch HRM in de publieke sector.* Assen: Van Gorcum.

Stephenson, K. (2005) Trafficking in trust. Verkregen op 11 augustus 2013 via http://www.drkaren.us/pdfs/chapter15.pdf

Stoker, G. (1998) *Governance as a theory: five propositions* International Social Science Journal, No 155, pp 119-131.

Stoker, G. (2006) *Why Politics Matter. Making Democracy Work.* Hampshire/New York: Palgrave MacMillan.

Stone, C. N. (1989) *Regime politics: governing Atlanta, 1946-1988.* Lawrence, KS: University Press of Kansas.

Taibbi, M. (2015) A Whistleblower's Horror Story. Verkregen op 6 maart 2015 via http://www.rollingstone.com/politics/news/a-whistleblowers-horror-story-20150218

Taleb, N.N. (2012) *Antifragiel: dingen die baar hebben bij wanorde.* Amsterdam: uitgeverij Nieuwzijds.

Team, B. I. (2013) Applying behavioural insights to charitable giving. *London: Cabinet Office.*

Teisman, G. (2005) *Publiek management op de grens van chaos en orde: over leidinggeven en organiseren in complexiteit.* Den Haag: Sdu Uitgevers bv.

Thomas, W.I. & Thomas, D.S. (1929). The child in America. New York: Knopf.

Thompson, V. A. (1965) Bureaucracy and Innovation. *Administrative Science Quarterly, 10,* 1-20.

Todorov, T. (1996) Facing the extreme. *Moral Life in the Concentration Camps.* New York: Metropolitan.

Tops, P. (2004). Regimetheorie en Rotterdam. De relevantie van regimetheorie voor de analyse van ontwikkelingen in een grote Nederlandse stad. Een eerste verkenning.
Verkregen op 4 februari 2017 via
http://www.politologischinstituut.be/pe2004/documents/12tops.pdf

Tops, P. (2007), *Regimeverandering in Rotterdam*. Rotterdam: Atlas.

Trappenburg, M. (2011) Waarom het allemaal niet lukt. In: J.H. van Tol, I. Helsloot & F.J.H. Mertens (red.), *Veiligheid boven alles? Essays over oorzaken en gevolgen van de risico-regelreflex* (pp. 37-51). Den Haag: Boom Lemma uitgevers.

Van der Arend, S.J. (2007) *Pleitbezorgers, procesmanagers en participanten.* Delft: Eburon.

Van der Heijden, J., Van Doorn, K., Van Griethuijsen, M., Groeneveld, M., Haasnoot, G., Schrijver, J., & Van der Wiel, T. (2005) *Recombinatie van overheid en samenleving. Denken over innovatieve beleidsvorming.* Eburon: Delft.

Van Hout, E., Oude Vrielink, M., & Putters, K. (2006) *Governance van lokale zorg- en dienstverlening.* Paper voor het TSPB Congres Betovering in een onttoverde wereld. Efteling, Kaatsheuvel, 2 november 2006. Tilburgse School voor Politiek en Bestuur, Universiteit van Tilburg.

Veen, W. (2009) *Homo Zappiens.* Amsterdam: Pearson Education Benelux.

Veenswijk, M. (1996) *Departementale cultuur.* Delft: Eburon.

Veerman, G.J. (2011) Juridische observaties. In: *Rapport van het symposium: De risico-regelreflex in het openbaar bestuur.* Den Haag: Academie voor wetgeving. Verkregen op 28 februari 2014 via http://tinyurl.com/q5546s2

Veld, R. in 't (2010) *Kennisdemocratie – Opkomend stormtij.* Den Haag: Academic Service.

Verhage, B., & Cunningham, W. H. (2004) *Grondslagen van de marketing.* Stenfert Kroese.

Verhoeven, I. (2004) 'Veranderend politiek burgerschap en democratie', blz. 55-78, in E.R. Engelen & M. Sie Dhian Ho, *De staat van de democratie. Democratie voorbij de staat*, Amsterdam: Amsterdam University Press.

Vermaak, H. (2009) *Plezier beleven aan taaie vraagstukken: werkingsmechanismen van vernieuwing en weerbarstigheid.* Deventer: Kluwer.

Vliegenthart, R. (2012) *U kletst uit uw nek - Over de relatie tussen politiek, media en de kiezer.* Amsterdam: Uitgeverij Bert Bakker.

Weber, M. (1924) Legitimate authority and bureaucracy. *Organization Theory: Selected Readings*, 3-15.

Weber, M. (1922) Bureaucracy. In: Sharitz, J.M. & Hyde, A.C. (2012) *Public Administration: Classic Readings* Wadsworth: Cengage Learning.

Weber, M. (1946) *Essays in Sociology* New York: Oxford University Press.

Weggeman, M. (1997) *Kennismanagement, Inrichting en besturing van kennisintensieve organisaties.* Schiedam: Scriptum.

Weggeman, M. (2013*) Leidinggeven aan professionals? Niet doen!* Schiedam: Scriptum.

Weick, K. E., & Roberts, K. H. (1993) Collective mind in organizations: Heedful interrelating on flight decks. *Administrative science quarterly*, 357-381.

Wetering, A. van de (2008) Waarderend auditten met behulp van Appreciative Inquiry. Verkregen op 30 januari 2015 via: http://www.managementissues.com/index.php/ontwikkelingstools/77-ontwikkelingstools/510-waarderend-auditen-met-behulp-van-appreciative-inquiry

Willems, W. (2012) De motie-Willems. Verkregen op 28 april 2012 via: http://www.politiek-digitaal.nl/nieuwedemocratie/demotiewillems/index.html.

Wit, K. (2008) *Universiteiten in Europa in de 21e eeuw: netwerken in een veranderende samenleving.* Leuven: Academia Press.

Wijnberg, R. (2013) *De nieuwsfabriek.* Uitgeverij De Bezige Bij.

Wolin, S. (2004) Politics and Vision, Princeton: Princeton University Press.

WRR (2006) *Lerende overheid: een pleidooi voor probleemgerichte politiek.* Amsterdam: Amsterdam University Press.

Wuyts, S., Stremersch, S., Van den Bulte, C., & Franses, P. H. (2004) Vertical marketing systems for complex products: A triadic perspective. *Journal of Marketing Research*, *41*(4), 479-487.

Yeager, J., & Sommer, L. (2007) Linguistic mechanisms cause rapid behavior change part two: how linguistic frames affect motivation. *The Qualitative Report*, *12*(3), 467-483.

Yin, R. K. (2009) *Case study research: Design and methods* (Vol. 5). Sage.

Yperen, T.A. van & Veerman, J.W. (2008; red.). *Zicht op effectiviteit. Handboek voor praktijkgestuurd effectonderzoek in de jeugdzorg*. Delft: Eburon.

Zamfir, C.M. (2009) The metamodel: the NLP Map of Language. *BAS, British and American Studies, Vol. XV.*

Zarif, M. J. (2014) What Iran Really Wants Iranian Foreign Policy in the Rouhani Era. *FOREIGN AFFAIRS*, *93*(3), 49-59.

Zi, Z. (2010) *Zhuang Zi-De volledige geschriften*. Atlas Contact.

Zuboff, S. and J. Maxim (2002) *The Support Economy*. New York: Viking.

Appendix 1: Overview literature bureaucracies and network organizations

1 Differences between traditional bureaucracies and network organizations
Authors emphasize the characteristics of and differences between hierarchies/bureaucracies and network organizations. Hierarchies/bureaucracies are seen as vertical organizations, network organizations as horizontal organizations. De Bruijn & Ten Heuvelhof (2007) identify the differences between the two types of organizations as follows:

TABLE 29: HIERARCHY VERSUS NETWORK (DE BRUIJN & TEN HEUVELHOF, 2007: 18, 32)

Hierarchy	Network
Uniformity	Pluriformiteit
Unilateral dependencies	Multilaterial dependencies
Open/receptive to hierarchical signals	Closed to hierarchical signals
Stability	Dynamics
Regular and linear	Irregular and no clear list of activities
Phases (project)	Rounds (process)
Actors are stable	Actors come and go
One arena: process (project) has clear start and end point	Multiple arenas: no isolated start and end point
Substance problem stable	Substance problem shifts and changes
Stimulus to see problem as structured	Stimulus to see problem as unstructured
Consistency and predictability	Flexibility and unpredictability

The studies offer insight into hierarchy and network and make it clear why networks, as an organizational form, are a better fit for contextual complexity and the associated unpredictability and for more openness.

Stephenson (2005: 250) shows that, even with an organization with a formal hierarchy, the real value of the organization depends on social networks. She describes the following network roles:

- *Knowledge hubs*
  A knowledge hub is someone who has such connections with others (networks) that he is important in keeping the flow of information going. He is a point of collecting *and* sharing. If that is removed from an organization, a great deal of its tacit knowledge disappears.

- *Pulse takers*
  Pulse takers cultivate relationships that enable them to monitor the health of the organization and of its top management. They have a good feel for the organization.
- *Gatekeepers*
  Gatekeepers are information bottlenecks, who determine the flow of contacts to a certain part of the organization.

The roles are a concrete expression of the *'informal principle of communicative dominance'* of Diefenbach & Sillince (2011). They are not only played by managers and, in light of their influence, they can sometimes compete with hierarchical management roles. De Bruijn & Ten Heuvelhof (2007) describe network management strategies to reinforce the informative and strategic position. Civil servants can use those strategies to achieve results that are desirable from their position. An example is providing a redundant network. Relationships with functional, extra-functional, strong and weak actors are maintained, which reinforces the own information and strategic position in a network.

The studies show that networks, as a form of horizontal approaches and openness, also play a role in hierarchies and vertical management. Their specific goal is to maintain and reinforce the own position.

In this thesis, when it comes to openness/OMSPD, the focus is less on reinforcing the own position, and more on using the collective intelligence in a network and letting it do its work as a network (Roobeek, 2014) in service of the quality of policy.

2 Development lines from bureaucracies to network organizations

In this thesis, we discussed Roobeek (1996) and Castells (2000). Diefenbach & Sillince (2011) provide a division of organizational forms in a climbing scale from bureaucratic/orthodox organizations to network organizations. The studies provide insight into organizational forms that fit an increasing level of openness and social context complexity.
Diefenbach & Sillince (2011) mention a sequence of different organizational forms on the way to a network organization: from bureaucratic/orthodox organization via professional organization to representative democratic organization, followed by a hybrid/post-modern organization and, finally, a network organization. Even network organizations have bureaucratic characteristics. Hales talks about 'bureaucracy-lite' versions of organizations (Hales, 2002: 52). Diefenbach & Sillince (2011), with regard to the 'bureaucracy-lite' Hales

(2002) talks about, also indicate that network organizations possess – decreasing – bureaucratic features. They occur in two forms, to wit (1) hierarchical communication with a 'center-to-periphery' structure and (2) systematic patterns of addressing certain issues.

Bureaucratic/orthodox organizations are synonymous with a formal hierarchy, rule-based specialization and division of tasks under a single authority. All position are located along top-down lines of command and control. They refer to Crozier (1964):

> *'A bureaucratic organization, therefore, is composed of a series of superimposed strata that do not communicate very much with each other. Barriers between strata are such that there is very little room for the development of cliques cutting across several categories'*
> (Diefenbach & Sillince, 2011: 1521; Crozier, 1964: 190).

Professional organization

In professions, the formal hierarchical order is translated into the principle of seniority. Of seniors supervising juniors. Vertical and horizontal integration is realized via formal diplomas and official codes of conduct. Juniors have to obey the written and unwritten rules of the profession. Whereas, in bureaucratic-orthodox organizations, the maxim 'obedience or out' applies, in the professional organization, the adage is 'up or out'. Professional organizations do have informal ways of bypassing the formal hierarchy, as well as initial forms of network development.

> *'Professionals, therefore, also use informal ways in order to practice the kind of professional autonomy they believe in and to by-pass formal hierarchical structures. For example, they initiate networks and informal collaboration with (like-minded) colleagues within and outside the organization they work for those colleagues may be at the same or at different levels (according to their formal degrees or official position)'*
> (Diefenbach & Sillince, 2011: 1523).

Representative democratic organization

The representative democratic organization is designed to make decision support processes more cooperative and democratic, not to supersede or replace hierarchical structures. Line responsibilities continue to exist. Managers are selected and appointed, not chosen. Most of the decisions are made by 'superiors' and carried out by subordinates. The work becomes harder for the subordinates, because they have to take multiple 'superiors' into account that they have to coordinate with or obey. Although democratic principles trump hierarchical principles, the latter stay in effect. However, the quality of the network with relevant parties/network relationships becomes more important with regard to getting things done.

Hybrid/post-modern organization

In hybrid/post-modern organizations, employees work in temporary of more permanent project teams. The teams are organized along orthodox principles: functional and hierarchical. Project members guard and regulate each other's contributions. That leads to strong informal control, coupled with indirect formal hierarchy on the basis of functional roles, next to the formal hierarchy.

> *'Favoritism and political manoeuvring were present in the older style bureaucracies......... In the hybrid organization actors must strive for informal dominance, or at least participate to some extent in the daily struggle for survival because their formal positions do not automatically provide security anymore. Over time, the internal struggles produce informal leaders and followers (either in line or in contrast to their formal positions) and lead to informal hierarchy and to further social dynamics around it. Hence, one might say that in hybrid organizations there is a strong informal principle of continuous hierarchical positioning at work'*
> (Diefenbach & Sillince, 2011: 1527).

Network organization

> *'The internal network organization is conceived as a loose federation of informally constituted, self-managing, often temporary, work units or teams within which there is a fluid division of labour and which are coordinated through an internal market, rather than rules, and horizontal negotiation and collaboration, rather than hierarchy .... Instead of a hierarchy of vertical reporting relationships there is a 'soft network' ... of informal lateral communications, information sharing and temporary collaboration based on reciprocity and trust'*
> (Diefenbach & Sillince, 2011: 1528; Hales, 2002: 54).

In such an organization, although the formal hierarchy is avoided, usually two forms of hierarchy develop over time:

> 'One was hierarchical structures of communication, i.e. official communication channels representing a very clear centre-to-periphery structure. And the other was the content of communication, i.e. members developed systematic patterns of addressing certain issues in unequal ways and of using rhetoric in order to signal superiority or inferiority, dominance or submissiveness'
> (Diefenbach & Sillince, 2011: 1529).

Diefenbach & Sillince (2011: 1529) talk about the 'the informal principle of communicative dominance'.

Appendix 2: Ashby's Law and the insights of Graves

Complex problems require different skills. The art of 'managing' a multitude of stakeholders, who have influence, combined with less equivocality in knowledge. That requires openness in policy development: involving more stakeholders and more equality in the way in which they are involved. The need for openness is supported by Ashby's Law and the insights of Clare W. Graves.

Ashby's Law of Requisite Variety states that, if a system wants to be stable, the number of 'realization options' of its management system need to be greater than or equal to the number of 'realization options' of the system being managed. To put it succinctly: *'Variety can destroy variety'* (Ashby, 1956: 207).

Formulated differently, Ashby's Law indicates that the level of variety in a context can be managed if the managing mechanism is able to match that context variety. That is a hard condition. If the context variety increases, the managing mechanism will have to adjust in terms of its own variety.
That means that an open system – like an organization – can only respond effectively to variations in its environment if the organization's ability to respond is adequate (Leede, 1997). If regulation is to be adequate, the regulatory system has to have at least the same variety in ways to respond at its disposal as the system to be regulated (Ridder & Struikema, 2008).
This can be applied to government. If actors in society have enough variation of alternative actions to bypass the control mechanism of a government, with its array of alternative actions, that government has a problem in terms of managing a problem, and it will have to look for forms of dealing with social problems that 'match' the variety of alternative actions of social actors.

According to Ashby's Law, unstructured problems cannot be handled with organizations that are too structure (many procedures, hierarchy and control mechanisms). There is simply not enough organizational leeway available to develop the variety required to deal with unstructured problems.

Graves: ordering of ways to solve problems in relation to changing contexts

Ashby's Law, multi-angulation and the associated ways or problem-solving can be put into perspective via the work by Graves (Herold, 2009). Graves (1974, 1981), founder of a model called 'The Emergent Cyclical Levels of Existence Theory' (ECLET) (Cowan & Todorovic, 2005), states:

'The biopsychosocial development of a mature man arises from the inter-action of a double helix complex of two sets of determining forces, the environmental societal determinants (THE EXISTENTIAL PROBLEMS OF LIVING) and the neuropsychological equipment of the organism (THE NEUROPSCHOLOGICAL EQUIPMENT FOR LIVING)'
(Graves, 1981: 1).

Graves points to an interaction between context and its demands for being able to function in that context and the abilities/capacities of people. If those abilities/capacities do not match the existential problems in the context and there is no 'fit', it becomes difficult to exist. In Table 31, 'deep value systems', capacities and contexts are connected. That matches Teisman (2005), who, along with Reeves & Eimler (2012), points to the ability to establish connections in chains, networks and composite processes, even where there are no direct possibilities. Connections are organized with regard to opportunities that arise and incidental combinations that occur. Roobeek (2014: 2) supports that:

'Solving a large complex issue is not at individual achievement, like skating 5 kilometers, which can only be done when the knowledge of the collective reaches a higher level. Super-specialists often lose sight of larger issues'
(Roobeek, 2014: 2).

TABLE 30: LEVELS OF GRAVES, WAYS OF SOLVING PROBLEMS AND TYPES OF PROBLEMS

Level Graves	Coping skills / characteristics of way of solving problem	Suitable for contexts with:
1. *Hierarchical, obedient, absolutist/ thinking in dichotomies*	A problem 'deviates from a (uniformly desired) norm'. *Solving problems from vertical management and norms, rules and guidelines that are in (written) handbooks.*	Problems that are clear or somewhat complicated.
2. *Individualistic, personal profiling, thinking in options*	Thinking/acting based on options and choosing 'best' alternative based on collecting as much information as possible. *Solving problems /finding the best solution through competition*	Problems that are complicated.
3. *Empathy, relationships, equal, relativistic*	Us-oriented actions based on the idea that there is no best solution but a constellation of solutions that emerges from connections/relationships in the network through open/transparent co-ordination. *Solving problems through horizontal approaches.*	Problems that are complex and can no longer be solved with available knowledge (unstructured problems).
4. *Knowing and feeling systemically withour wanting to leave a footprint*	Me-oriented *problem-solving by knowing and feeling a system with the people involved positioned and acting in different places in a system to experience how it is connected to other parts of the system. Focus on long-term solutions.*	Problems that are (very) complex and can no longer be solved with available knowledge (unstructured problems).

Reeves & Deimler (2012), Teisman (2005) and Roobeek (2014) can also be positioned in Graves' diagram in the transition from contexts with complicated problems to contexts with unstructured problems (level 2 to level 3).

Looking at developments (with the required problem-solving skills), Graves talks about *'increase in conceptual space'* (Graves, 1981: 2). Dichotomous (either/or) thinking and acting become optional thinking and acting, followed by relativistic thinking and acting. In the latter case, knowledge connects itself from empathy and equality between people, creating combinations of solutions in and from a network. Finally, the table contains a systematic way of thinking, feeling and acting. A thought foundation that allows people to learn to know and feel connections that are unable to know and feel through the other thought foundations. Linear causal thinking has to make way for thoughts and actions from experiencing complexity in a multitude of systemic connections. That has consequences for the top-down (vertical) organization from a central point. According to Frissen (1999: 50-51):

> 'Linearity is a development towards more and more, better and better, faster and faster .... The linear process can best be seen as a process of branches that become increasingly detailed .... (structural differentiation)' (Frissen, 1999: 50-51).

> 'All these developments make the idea of linear progress from a singular starting point, unidirectional and managed from one center, problematic. Although these developments can be described as hyper-differentiation, the singularity and central management are lost. In a cultural sense, there is even a rupture with modernist rationality' (Frissen, 1999: 52).

Where Graves argues that changing contexts require new values and associated problem-solving skills, the opposite can also be argued: new problems can be handled with the same values and coping skills. Value systems and coping skills that can easily handle new types of problems. If open policy approaches are seen as new skills for dealing with new types of problems that can fit within the current political and administrative problem-solving framework (i.e. political-administrative paradigms for policy development), there is no problem.

Should such a fit be absent, there is a need for a more fundamental change, about which Graves (1974) made the following remark:

> 'My research indicates that man is learning that values and ways of living which were good for him at one period in his development are no longer good because of the changed condition of his existence. He is recognizing that the old values are no longer appropriate, but he has not yet understood the new' (Graves, 1974: 72).

That creates a need for a new thought foundation with new rules for solving problems, resulting from changes in the context, that cannot be understood from the old thought foundation and require new problem-solving skills.

Appendix 3: Unstructured problems: comparison authors

TABLE 31: UNSTRUCTURED PROBLEMS

Rittel en Webbers (1973: 161-167)	Schön, D. and M. Rein (1994)	Australian Public Service Commission (2007)	Korsten (2001: 2)
There is no definitive problem formulation.		Unstructured problems are hard to define precisely. Different stakeholders have different problem descriptions.	There is a debate about what problem is. People rarely agree about *problem definition*. Visions fight for priority.
You don't know exactly when they end.	*'Intractable policy controversy.'* Differences in values lead to differences in searching.	Unstructured problems have dependencies and are multi-causal. Often there are conflicting goals in the problem field.	Because there are conflicts about values and desirable goals.
Solutions cannot immediately be classified as either true or false and not as good or bad.		Unstructured problems can lead to chronic policy failures, for decades.	
There is no ultimate test for a solution.			
Every solution is a 'one-shot operation'. It is not possible to learn through 'trial and error'. All attempts tell us something.		Attempts to solve the problem usually have unforeseen effects.	
Unstructured problems have no exhaustive set of potential and accurately describable solutions.		Unstructured problems have no clear solution.	The knowledge to map the problem is usually limited.
Each unstructured problem can be seen as a symptom of another problem.			

Rittel en Webbers (1973: 161-167)	Schön, D. and M. Rein (1994)	Australian Public Service Commission (2007)	Korsten (2001: 2)
There are more explanations for unstructured problems. The explanation steers decisions and solutions.	Actors have to find each other in negotiations about problem descriptions and possible solutions.	'Solutions' to unstructured problems require coordinated action from more stakeholders.	
		Unstructured problems are rarely the responsibility of one organization.	
		Unstructured problems are no stable, but evolve.	
		Unstructured problems require a change in behavior and innovative approaches.	

Appendix 4: Participation ladders Edelenbos, Schiphorst & Arnstein

Arnstein (1969) was the first to describe a participation ladder with 8 levels:

1. Manipulation: in the name of stakeholder participation, people are placed in 'puppets', advisory committees or advisory boards, with the aim of 'educating' them or gain their support.
2. Therapy: as a mask for stakeholder participation in policy plans, people ate subjected to clinical group therapy. Citizens are involved via intensive activities, but the aim is to cure them of their 'pathology'.
3. Informing: stakeholders are informed of rights, responsibilities and possibilities. Usually, the emphasis is on sending the information.
4. Consulting: both conducting research through questionnaires and organizing neighborhood meetings and public hearings.
5. Elaborate advice: stakeholders are offered the opportunity to give elaborate advice, but the policy-makers retain the right to decide about the legitimacy and practicability of their recommendations.
6. Partnership: planning and decision-making responsibilities are shared with stakeholders, via structures like advisory boards, planning committees and mechanisms to overcome stalemates. Once the basic rules have been set, after some negotiation, they are no longer subject to discussion.
7. Delegated power: at this level, the stakeholders hold the most important cards to execute policy. To solve differences of opinion, policy-makers have to negotiate.
8. Control by citizens: the participants can execute a program and they completely determine policy and management, as well as being able to negotiate the conditions, should 'outsiders' want to change them.

Arnstein (1969) does not call the first two levels participation:

> 'Their real goal is not to enable people to participate in planning or conducting programs but to enable powerholders to 'educate' or 'cure' the participants'
> (Arnstein, 1969: 217).

Arnstein regards levels 1, 2 and 3 as 'government', as vertical thinking and acting. Informing is often also not participation. Citizens can be informed about rights, duties and options, but the emphasis is often on sending the information,

> 'a one-way flow of information from officials to information'
> (Arnstein, 1969: 219).

The levels proposed by Schiphorst were used in 2014-2015 in the Master Classes From the Outside In at the Ministry for SAE to order interactive methods and provide insight into participation levels. Veen (2009) describes Schiphorst's levels:

1. Complete autonomy: no interaction with outsiders.
2. Formal input: parties can respond to the proposed policy plan at the end of the policy process.
3. Research: for instance questionnaires.
4. Consultation: this word has a different meaning for Schiphorst than it has for Arnstein. The civil servant invites people to advise him or her, after which the civil servant himself uses the input being provided as he sees fit.
5. Participation: stakeholders are invited personally to think about the policy being developed together with the civil servant. However, the civil servant remains responsible for the end result, although the stakeholders have the right to object to the end product.
6. Partnership: if stakeholders are invited to think about and determine policy together with the civil servant. In advance, agreements are made as to how stakeholder can object to policy ultimately being developed.
7. Self-management: within certain criteria and limitations, external parties are given the opportunity to shape both the policy process and the policy itself.
8. Free market: no intervention from civil servants.

Edelenbos & Klijn (2005b: 294) distinguish five levels:

1. Informing: politicians and administrators let stakeholders know what they are talking about.
2. Consulting: politicians and administrators set the agenda and stakeholders provide input. Politicians are not bound to use that input.
3. Advising: politicians and administrators set the agenda and stakeholders have the opportunity to complement and modify it, they play a serious role.
   Politicians commit in principle to take the input into account, but can (with good arguments) deviate from that.
4. Co-production: politicians, administrators and stakeholder together set the agenda and determine opinions and solutions. Politicians are bound by the results, provided the relevant conditions are met.
5. Co-deciding: politicians and administrators leave the development of policy and decision-making to the stakeholders, with the administrative apparatus playing an advisory role. The results of the interactive process are binding.

Tabel 32: Vergelijking participatieladders Arnstein, Schiphorst & Edelenbos

Niveau	Edelenbos & Klijn	Schiphorst	Arnstein
1	Informing: politics and administration let interested parties know what they are talking about.	Complete autonomy: no interaction with the outside.	
2		Formal input: at the end of the policy process, parties are allowed to respond to a proposed policy plan.	Informing: stakeholders are informed about their rights, responsibilities and possiblities, usually in a one-way form of communication from policy-maker.
3		Research: think of questionnaires, etc..	Consulting: conducting research via inquiries like neighborhood meetings and public hearings.
4	Consultation: politics and administration set the agenda and the interest parties take part in the talks. Politicians are not bound by the results of the talks.	Consultation: civil servant invites stakeholders for advice, after which the civil servant decides what to use for further action.	Elaborate advice: stakeholders are allowed to give elaborate advice. Decision-makers retain the right to decide about legitimity and practicability of the recommendations.
5	Advising: politics and administration set the agenda. Interested parties can add and adjust and have a meaningful role. Politicians are bound by the results, but can deviate (with arguments).	Participation: stakeholders are invited personally to reflect on policy together with civil servant. The civil servant remains responsible for end product, although the stakeholders have the right to resist.	

TABEL 32: VERGELIJKING PARTICIPATIELADDERS ARNSTEIN, SCHIPHORST & EDE-
LENBOS (CONTINUED)

Niveau	Edelenbos & Klijn	Schiphorst	Arnstein
6		Partnership: if stakeholders are invited to reflect on and determine policy together with civil servant. In advance, agreements are made about ways stakeholders can resist the eventual policy.	Partnership: planning and decision-making responsibility are shared with stakeholders via structures like advisory boards, planning committees and mechanisms to resolve stalemates. Once the basic rules have been set, after some negotiating, they are no longer the subject of discussion
7			Delegated power: at this level, stakeholders hold the main cards to implement policy. To resolve differences of opinion, policy decision-makers have to negotiate.
8	Co-production: politicians, management and interested parties together decide on an agenda, positions and solutions. Politicians are bound by the results, if they meet the conditions.	Self-management: external parties are given, within given criteria and limitations, the opportunity both to shape the policy process and to determine the substance of the policy.	

270

TABEL 32: VERGELIJKING PARTICIPATIELADDERS ARNSTEIN, SCHIPHORST & EDE-
LENBOS (CONTINUED)

Niveau	Edelenbos & Klijn	Schiphorst	Arnstein
9	Co-deciding: politicians and administration leave policy development and decision-making to stakeholders, with the admiistration playing an advisory role. The results of the interactive process are binding.		Control by citizen: participants can execute a program and completely determine policy and management, as well as negotiate about the conditions, should 'outsiders' want to change them.
10		Free market: no intervention by civil servants.	

Appendix 5: Ordering hard unwritten rules

TABLE 33: HARD UNWRITTEN RULES THAT WERE MENTIONED

Unwritten rule		Relation to
1.	You have to serve the Minister	Minister
	Look at what the Ministers (and their political parties) consider important and how they want to be served. This also applies to the Director-General, director and department head. The hierarchy is focused on Minister and politics.	Hierarchy
		Media
	The Minister has to be successful in Parliament and cannot be 'caught' on a theme. There are political dimensions to what you do. You, as civil servant, have to anticipate potential risks and opportunities. Ministers cannot be made to look bad in Parliament. You have to help them stay in the saddle. They need to be able to score political points and show that they have accomplished something. Makes sure that the Minister gets something done without running any risks.	Openness
		Expertise
		Usual suspects
	Political sensitivity has three basic components:	
	· Negative publicity: when something appears in the media, that leads to questions in Parliament.	Interdepartemental
	· Are there risks or perceived potential risks? The media are quick to jump on those.	Non-usual suspects
	· Individual positioning politicians: are there opportunities for the Minister to improve his public profile?	
	NB That always has a negative undertone.	
	The media play a very important role. You have to keep the Minister out of trouble and difficult questions from Parliament and void unpleasant discussions.	
	Be quick in establishing connections between your dossier and other current matters, by staying well-informed about:	
	· What goes on in Parliament in relation to the Minister.	
	· What goes on in the field.	
	· What goes on in the media.	
	· Developments outside the field that can directly or indirectly affect your dossier.	
	Based on the abovementioned, assess/anticipate what the Minister will or can encounter.	
	Deal with policy solutions in a flexible way:	
	· See what is possible politically.	
	· Check where the risks are for the Minister	
	· Determine where there are possible solution, given the answers on the previous two questions.	
	· Determine how a Minister can score with a particular solution.	
	If necessary, go to Business Support for questions or advice.	
	It has to be safe, or there will be trouble. Especially in the case of major issues. Don't do anything that casts the Ministry in a bad light.	
	There must be no risk to the Minister/Secretary by listening too much to society. The field can come up with things that cause problems because they do not match what we or the Minister want. If you listen to society, that is essentially undemocratic. It can go in all directions and who is to say you will hear a majority view? In that sense, it is undemocratic.	
2.	Be respectful in addressing the Minister	Minister
		Hierarchy
	You cannot offend the Minister. If you are with the Minister and he says something that is incorrect, you have to be careful with how you say it. You cannot be direct. You cannot tell him he is incorrect. You say: 'We will investigate this, but I suspect there legal details that require attention'. You recommend having Legal Services take another look at it.	Etiquette
	The higher you get, the more formal your clothing. You adjust what you wear.	

Unwritten rule		Relation to
3.	Be aware that Ministers have their own personality traits. In other words, every Minister has his own wishes. Know what is relevant, what the Minister wants to do something with (priorities). What are the REAL issues?	Minister
4.	The Director-General is the link to the Minister and politics. Be very clear about that. If you want something, make sure leadership backs you. Or else you will not be successful. You need the hierarchy to support you. They make the decisions (authority).	Minister Hierarchy
5.	The higher you get in the hierarchy, the lower the tolerance for mistakes. If something goes really wrong, and the Minister is angry, he will lash out down the hierarchy. Minister → Director-General → Director → Cluster Leader → Civil Servant.	Minister Hierarchy
6.	Nothing every leaves the department that hasn't been seen by the coordinator and department head. After the director, director-general and Communications, the department head has the final say. He will be held accountable if something is wrong. Each following person further on in the hierarchy is led more strongly by what politics wants.	Minister Hierarchy
7.	Follow the hierarchical line. Know your role. Do what you are asked. Carry out. You play it safe by just doing your job and not taking too much risk. Just do what you are asked, and do it well. When making a proposal, keep in mind what the director and director-general want. Do not antagonize your superiors, you need them to reach your goal. Never come into conflict with your director or department head. Make sure that he (manager) is satisfied with you. He is the first hurdle. Don't be critical toward the line/Minister. Go with the flow. Don't go against the system/the hierarchy. Ideally, the work processes (policy development, memos, etc.) yield information that the line itself can use and matches their direction (and the political line/coalition agreement/wishes of the Minister himself). The common thread in the hierarchy: I can do it well for you, so you can show other people you are doing it well. Make sure that, when a superior scores thanks to you, he is aware of your role. On the other hand: when things go wrong, you will get the blame as well.	Minister Hierarchy Visibility Staying inside frameworks
8.	People who move up in the administrative hierarchy have good strategic skills. They have answers to the following questions: <ul><li>What contributes to the Ministry's policy?</li><li>What are the political risks?</li><li>How to negotiate with other Ministries without compromising the bottom line of your own Ministry?</li></ul>When talking to other Ministries, never let them know what you want up front. Keep your powder dry. What you take away from other Ministries, without getting in your own Minister's way, take that. But don't do it on the hard issues. Find out where there is common ground but never go below the minimum requirements that are important to the Ministry.	Minister Hierarchy Expertise Openness Interdepartemental Interests
9.	Create visibility in the (memo) production among those who are considered important by the line and anyone who has even a little influence on the continued existence of management. If you do everything well, without producing memos, you will not be noticed. Or worse, people will criticize you for it. After all, the managers are also held accountable for what they deliver to their managers. If you are out a lot and get things done there, that's not always good for your image/internal PR.	Hierarchy Visbility Networking Usual suspects Unusual suspects
10.	Make sure to visit the MT regularly with something you have made and that can score political points.	Hierarchy Visibility

TABLE 33: HARD UNWRITTEN RULES THAT WERE MENTIONED (CONTINUED)

Unwritten rule	Relation to
11. Be visible all the way up to the director by: · Sending CC's at opportune moments. · Showing people what you have done. What you have contributed.	Hierarchy Viisibility
12. Try to be engaged in politically sensitive dossiers. Let people know you are aware of what is going on elsewhere. Establish connections to what goes on in society and your own or other dossiers. Inform your colleagues about that. Anticipate matters that affect you. If you want the managers/organization to appreciate you, make sure you are working on high-priority dossiers.	Minister Hierarchy Visibility Politically sensitive dossiers
13. You score when you have finished a trajectory/law and it has been published in the statute book. Or a General Meeting has been organized. The same with passing a major policy initiative or having contributed to it.	Minister Hierarchy Visibility
14. Meet your deadline. It is sacred. Speed of delivery: deliver documents on time. A memo that is late is not a memo. Momentum lost. Meeting your deadline: do that *especially* with things that are politically important. Be aware that those are under a bigger magnifying glass. If you fail to meet your deadline, the Minister can get angry, and nobody likes that.	Minister Hierarchy Time planning Politically sensitive dossiers
15. Your room for maneuver is determined by the leadership. The boundary of what you are allowed to say is determined by higher regions and politics. Don't voice things that are not in line with policy or the position of the Minister. Never make promise to the outside. Unless you have coordinated it up to the highest level. Keep an eye on the consequences in everything you do. Never make any promises externally that you cannot keep. Make sure that other people can't make claims based on the things you say. Be careful. Never give anything away, certainly not without checking it with the department head. Look what your mandate is before going out in relation to a substantive issue. Coordinate in advance. Who can you tell what in a conversation? No what you are and are not allowed to say. For instance, when something is in the orientation phase of policy development, you cannot voice a clear opinion about a direction or end result.	Minister Hierarchy Openness Usual suspects

Unwritten rule	Relation to
16. Make sure to mobilize opinions on the field that match politically. When you take to stakeholders, you have thought out a large part and the conversation is meant to test and see their response: Will this pass Parliament or will stakeholders write letters? The aim is to keep the process quiet. That's why you have an eye for the points of the stakeholders. You wonder if the decision is painful, how painful it is and if it will cause a commotion. Use deviating situations if that is important for the decision-making of a memo. Plan in advance where you want to end up when talking to professional stakeholders (usual suspects). When you are together, look for a common solution. From your end, you decide together when you don't want to give up and what it's worth to maintain good relationships. Who is at the table depends on how important the subject is and whether the director is interested and where it can be solved at civil servant level. You want colleagues form other departments to adjust their position so that it will match yours. You do that by sometimes being formal and sometimes being informal. You alternate. With regard to outside information, you have to have a policy story. Sometimes in favor, sometimes the opposite. The story that the department wants to present to the outside world (the broader ministerial picture). You explain why something is the way it is and show you have taken a broad range of interests into account.	Minister Networking Interdepartemental Usual suspects Unusual suspects Interests Informal
17. The more political an item is, the more closed it becomes (in terms of who is involved in the policy development). If something becomes *really* political, it is taken out of the hands of the civil servant. The level of openness is related to how sensitive a subject is. If something is politically sensitive, you are told who has to sit at the table. People do your thinking for you. If you go beyond that, people will think you're being a nuisance. In other words, please don't. In the case of 'niche subjects', you have plenty of room for consultation and interaction, provided you stay below the radar. Once you attract the attention of the director/director-general or the subject becomes more political, that room will decrease quickly. Up to that point, you have a lot of room. It has to be finished quickly, be safe for the Minister, within the rules and within budget. The more you move towards heavier subjects, the less you will be allowed to bring on 'loose cannons'. If it is sensitive in Parliament: be less open with whatever can cause the Minister trouble. If it is less politically sensitive, you have more room to speak with outsiders. Especially when it involves a specific expert subject.	Minister Hierarchy Politically sensitive Openness Interdepartemental Usual suspects Unusual suspects Time planning
18. Your network is crucial, so managing your network is too. That is especially important with usual suspects …. Without your network, you will get nothing done. Also, things go much more quickly, for example, when you talk to the usual suspects. Your network allows you to gauge informally how something will come across in a broader political sense. Also, carefully check your idea externally. How do they respond? If necessary, go beyond the regular intermediaries and interest groups. The latter will give you 'ammunition' against (conservative) interest groups. Consult informally with representatives of other organizations, checking how something can be solved. Ask: 'What do you think?' Also, ask your director about that. Build a network around political relevant themes, so you will be able to come up with concrete solutions that have support, if necessary. Or present interesting ideas. Respond quickly and adequately to questions from above is only possible when you have built a good and reliable network and know who knows and can do what. Also, network informally. Go to parties. Be aware that certain relationships are important.	Networking Usual suspects Openness Informal Minister Coordination Interests

Table 33: Hard unwritten rules that were mentioned (continued)

Unwritten rule		Relation to
19.	Policy often begins with signals from society that you, as civil servant, pick up and on the basis of which you can make proposals about what is right and wrong with policy. These days, that happens less and less. This has to do with, among other things, the fact that governments last less long, voter are more unpredictable and media influence. That makes it hard to assess the political effect of something. Certain when it involves media-sensitive subject. The following line can be seen. Increasing media influence, uncertainty with parties, short government tenure → Uncertainty among Ministers → Uncertainty in the hierarchy → Fear that something could go wrong/more carefulness/risk avoidance.	Minister Hierarchy Media
20.	Finding signals: Be reachable, talk a lot to outsiders, be on the road a lot and invest in your network! That means signaling and, where possible, connecting. Compare initiatives from outside to the internal picture and test for internal feasibility. Does it fit within how we work here, important themes and the coalition agreement. Look at what does and does not match the vision of the Minister/Secretary and whether it can be lined to that. Also look at external opinions and interests.	Networking Policy entre-preneurship
21.	There is a line between what you pick up on the outside and what you can then do with it (whether or not matching policy/politics). Maintain a certain distance to parties in the field. We make the policies and the rules, they can think and talk with us about them, but we make a decision. It is good to bring in outsiders, because you do not have all the information yourself, but there should be some distance. As civil servant, I think it is important to remain independent.	Minister Openness Coordination Interests
22.	There are three important criteria you have to deal with in policy development: - Quality of the content. - Support. - Political agreements that have been made. Familiarize yourself with everything that's in the political programs.	Minister Openness Expertise Interdepar-te-mental Usual sus-pects Unusual suspects
23.	Who you involve depends on the policy subject. Sometimes, you want to know how you can realize something. There are four criteria that play a role: · Level of independence of the (parties in the) environment for implementation/execution/realization of policy. Exploration often uses research-like structures. · Policy phase (are you at the beginning/still looking, or have decisions already been made). Extent to which Ministers already know what you want/have made up their minds.	Minister Openness Interdepar-te-mental Usual sus-pects Unusual suspects
24.	Some subjects are much more suitable to be worked out internally. Later on in the policy process, you can look at possibly problems that can occur when it is translated into law.	Openness Coordination
25.	It is better to score big once in the media than have 10 things that generate half a sentence somewhere.	Media

Unwritten rule		Relation to
26.	Show that you have an eye for the situation and that you want to give the internal communications department input that will allow the Minister to score. Show risks and opportunities.	Minister Media Coordination
27.	Never tell the Communications department 'I know how to do it'. They are the outer shell of the Minister. Treat them with respect.	Collegeagues Coordination
28.	The fact that external stakeholders (usual suspects) are getting weaker means that, as a Ministry, we have more room to do our own things.	Minister Hierarchy Openness Usual sus-pects
29.	Too much contact with the outside world is also not appreciated. People are less interested in what other people think than they seem to be. Because we want to find the shortest route from A to B, in accordance with the Minister's wishes (or the director's, or the director-general's) and in accordance with the coalition agreement. There is no longer any room to put things into perspective.	Minister Openness Usual sus-pects Unusual suspects
30.	Be aware that the director-general and directors also have their own networks, of which they are a part and which you will have to take into account. Don't enter the network of your managers or directors without prior coordina-tion. Find out the networks higher up in the hierarchy are organized. Who clicks with whom. Or not, as the case may be.	Hierarchy Openness Usual sus-pects Networking Interdepar-te-mental Unusual suspects
31.	If something in existing policy is not quite right, try to sell it so it is accepted anyway. You can't just say that something isn't right, because that will have a negative effect on your director, director-general and the Minister. In short, your superiors will be held responsible. If you make an error judgment with political consequences, it will come back to you and you will be held accountable.	Minister Hierarchy
32.	Don't volunteer ideas that deviate too much, that are too far outside the box. If you do that, people will take you less seriously. Substantive creativity and out-side-the-box thinking alone are not enough. That is not the competence that is asked for here. You will not get it passed, because you have to get the hierarchy on board. The critical elements will be removed and it becomes a run-of-the-mill memo. However, be creative when it comes to 'manipulating information'. That you write a text in such a way that people accept it. Write through the eyes of the (hierarchical) other. You need to something past them. When unsure about your own critical remarks, and how they will be received in larger meetings, voice them in smaller gatherings and let them appear in a memo. When you voice a position in a meeting that lies outside the frameworks, it is not recognized. If it were, something would have to be done with it, which means more work. Be inspired in your contributions. And bring that inspiration in line with the dom-inant framework. Show that you think in terms of possibilities, not in terms of what cannot be done. Show that you are proactive, that you do something to help the manager and the director. Don't carry out blindly. Make suggestions. If you have a spot, forget it.	Staying within frame-works Minister Hierarchy Criticism Visibility

TABLE 33: HARD UNWRITTEN RULES THAT WERE MENTIONED (CONTINUED)

Unwritten rule	Relation to
33. Don't elaborate and make things more difficult. Make things simple. Think of a solution before mentioning a problem, unless you really have hard problems.	Expertise
34. If you go successfully beyond what you have been asked to do, that is rewarded. Make sure to be willing to share the credits with someone else (including colleagues at the same level), while your own contribution remains visible (also label 'visibility').	Hierarchy Visibility Colleagues
35. Make sure not to misinterpret information from the line. It is better to ask and make sure.	Hierarchy
36. You are allowed to argue something else, provided you are correct. Especially if that helps the Minister to avoid making a mistake. If Ministers have an idea about something that is too bizarre, try to correct it via the line.	Criticism
37. With regard to higher leadership, you will get nothing done on your own. Especially when it's an outside-the-box idea. For that, you need multiple parties/civil servants who think it is a good idea.	Hierarchy Outside frameworks Coordination
38. Make sure you are easy to get along with: walk into his (director's) office, talk to him at an office party, ask him something personal and make a joke, keep it light and don't just talk politics.	Hierarchy Visibility
39. If you have done something that is not in accordance with the rules (outside legal framework) and that at some point can create a problem, make sure you coordinate with the line. If there are complaints about you from parties that are held in esteem by the vertical line (director-general, directors), make sure you are covered. Be careful of conflicts of interests.	Hierarchy Covering Usual suspects Interests
40. If it is unclear which department handles which subject, cover yourself and report a certain matter (for instance not being able to meet the planning or changes in priorities) to everybody.	Hierarchy Covering
41. Cover yourself if you are new to a department, because otherwise people may find it easy to let you take the blame, instead of themselves.	Covering
42. Try to be an independent advisor. If you follow your own path too much, you are no longer open to other insights. And that's not what they hired you for. Being able to let go of your own opinions is also part of the job.	Expertise
43. Just because you are an expert, does not mean your proposals will always be accepted. Keep in mind that other interests play a role in the higher echelons (director-general).	Hierarchy Expertise
44. If you perform normally, there is an automatic promotion pattern, depending on, among other things, how long you have been in a pay grade.	Expertise
45. Know when it is the right time to involve a director or MT member in what you are doing. That is when the impact and sensitivity start playing a role in administrative and political terms. For instance, when there are problems with a white paper, or critical items for a deadline, or when a dossier can get into trouble, or when you need a crowbar/bridge-builder to another party. However, only call in a director when it is really important.	Hierarchy Upscaling
46. If people (from other departments) are not encouraged by their director, they won't move. So, if necessary, use your own director to get them moving.	Hierarchy
47. If you really want to get something done, get people involved from higher up in the hierarchy who have some clout.	Hierarchy Networking Bypass
48. Align your goals to the coalition agreement/political goals (what is politically desirable) and the goals of the organization. Or ride along on a new policy direction of the government. If there is a new coalition agreement, read it carefully, put it next to your own ideas and see where they have something in common.	Minister Hierarchy Own goals

Unwritten rule	Relation to
49. If you know something won't get done along the hierarchical way, think of a bypass without harming the hierarchy.	Minister Hierarchy Own goals Bypass

50. What do you do with policy that is in accordance with the coalition agreement (and that the Minister wants), but that is not good for society?
  · Include above all counter-arguments in your memo
  · Find a bypass (for instance, via an interest group who opposed the policy and has connections to Parliament).
	Minister
	Hierarchy
	Own goals
	Bypass

51. What do you do when you want something that is not in line with the coalition agreement or what the Minister wants, but that is good for society: Find a bypass (for instance, an interest group with connections in Parliament).	Minister Hierarchy Own goals Bypass
52. You can want something as much as you like, but you have to do it when the time is right. When there is political support. Political momentum.	Minister Hierarchy Own goals
53. Always pay attention to who you can use to promote your line or to cover for you. Who that is, can vary greatly, for instance your department head, the director or legal services.	Hierarchy Own goals Covering
54. If you want something in terms of social effect, make sure to present something that we as directors/Minister consider to be a problem. Something for which we are responsible. More particularly, make sure that your director and director-general see it as a problem.	Hierarchy Own goals
55. Make sure you maintain good relationships with Business Support, the Minister's personal assistant and the internal network. Also make sure you have good relationships with the secretariat and employees of the director-general and the Ministers by invest time in them. Effect: you can easily reach them and get them to do something for you. Maintain good relations with support. Help them so they will help you.	Hierarchy Collegeagues
56. In the case of politically interesting dossiers. Don't think 9 to 5, even when you work part-time. Be available 24/7, in particular on your own policy area, and always be reachable. You see it in combination with people who are less available, for instance because they work 2 or 3 days. They get the regular jobs, not the major dossiers.	Minister Hierarchy Politically sensitive dossiers Time planning
57. If you want to make a career, you need to stand close to the higher echelons at parties and laugh at the jokes they make. Go to who you need to be seen with. Attend informal meetings that the leadership also attends. Also be visible by occasionally organizing something or giving a presentation about something connected to policy.	Hierarchy Visibility
58. If you want variety in your work, find out whether the subject has priority (whether there is political interest). If a subject has priority, you can apply a variety of skills. For instance legal expertise, negotiating with the sector, etc. If your subject has no priority, the work often has less variation. Switch to a different subject with a higher priority.	Minister Hierarchy Politically sensitive Expertise
59. Inform the department head a lot about sensitive dossiers or items. Communicate/inform about the state of affairs. Walk into his office. Especially regarding MR-recommendations. They do not want to be surprised.	Minister Hierarchy Politically sensitive dossiers

TABLE 33: HARD UNWRITTEN RULES THAT WERE MENTIONED (CONTINUED)

Unwritten rule	Relation to
60. Working from the outside in is only possible when there is really room for it: in terms of time and from the line. Due to a limited capacity, it is not always possible to consult with many stakeholders. And there's always the risk that people bow out.	Hierarchy Openness Interdepartemental Usual suspects Unusual suspects Capacity Time planning
61. In case of conflicting interests, we do not tend to be openly interactive. We prefer to keep things small-scale, simple and closed. If you don't do that, it's usually hard to meet your deadline.	Openness Interests Usual suspects
62. If you don't know what the end product will be (in the case of open processes), that matches in no way with deadlines, project goals, result-oriented thinking, etc. Not being able to meet deadlines can make for difficult projects when you want to work From the Outside In (OMSPD).	Openness Time planning
63. A general rule of thumb is: 'the earlier you begin, the more room you have'.	Openness Time planning Interdepartemental Usual suspects Unusual suspects
64. Trajectories can be delayed by participation/consultation, which can provide critical input. If Parliament learns of the project, it will want to know what the end result is, and that is not desirable then. For instance subject x. There is a lot of resistance to it, but the decision has already been made. That is no good. You look for what is good to get policy passed. You have to keep the Minister out of trouble and avoid difficult questions from Parliament and unpleasant discussions.	Minister Openness Usual suspects Unusual suspects
65. In the case of political decisions (as opposed to decisions that touch the internal organization), make sure to inform the Minister well with clear descriptions. Also, sometimes avoid certain terms.	Minister Politically sensitive dossiers Expertise
66. Writing skills are important to your career. That means writing: · The way the Minister wants it (because that's how the director and director-general will also want it). · Keep the message to the director (or director-general) very short and simple. He is a busy man. Tell him what you want and for what. Outline the relevant political playing field, he will listen then, and indicate what is expected of him.	Minister Hierarchy Expertise Usual suspects
67. Write flat, safe pieces with only the facts and within enthusiasm. 'To the point' and without frills. That way, people can't hold you accountable for anything that goes beyond the facts.	Hierarchy Covering

Unwritten rule	Relation to
68. If you bring a story to the director-general, it has to have support. And you have to know what the sensitivities involved are. The director-general checks whether you have coordinated it with colleagues from other departments. The standard question is always: 'Have you coordinated with other departments?'. Then you're legitimate. You cover yourself by telling him what you are doing and by coordination a lot. For instance in the case of a memo. If many people have looked at it, in principle that means shared responsibility. You cover yourself to minimize risks. There is a clear tendency to focus on risks more than on opportunities. The risks are emphasized so much that they overwhelm the opportunities. Cover yourself well, make sure you have coordinated the dossier. At any rate internally. Sometimes externally as well, depending on the subject. If you don't cover yourself and something goes wrong, you will be blamed. If everyone has agreed, there's no one to (get the) blame.	Hierarchy Coordination
69. Make sure to fully inform the director: on the substance, pros/cons alternatives, what other parties think. · That it is clear that you have coordinated with relevant parties. · With every memo, outline the context and list the issues regarding the theme inside and outside the Ministry. What is and isn't sensitive. · How something can be solved. · Clear and simple advice with a recommendation on what to do, or options for him to choose from.	Hierarchy Coordination
70. How to tell someone that what they are saying is incorrect varies per hierarchical level. Within a small department and with the department head, it is easier than with the director or director-general.	Minister Hierarchy Etiquette
71. Don't try to talk your director-general or director out of something they feel strongly about. Don't say 'this is stupid'. Be diplomatic. If the manager/director/director-general has an idea that you know to be wrong, say something like 'what if you looked at this from a different perspective? See what it looks like then'. Play with perspectives. Or say 'what would <his manager> think about it?' In other words, make a constructive contribution. Compare it to being courtier trying to please your king.	Hierarchy Etiquette
72. If you go somewhere with your director, stay in the background. But be constructive.	Hierarchy Etiquette
73. Don't become an island in your own department. It's not good for your career. Seek out your colleagues' managers and make sure you have a good working relationship. Network within the organization. Build a network of relationships with experts around you. Have coffee regularly with colleagues from other departments; get to know each other personally. Focus on little personal things that allows you to create a bond.	Collegeagues Networking
74. If you want to realize something with regard to a policy theme, don't do it radically but in small steps (silent revolutions). Then submit it to a department meeting. Do that with multiple people at the same time.	Own goals Coordination

Table 33: Hard unwritten rules that were mentioned (continued)

Unwritten rule	Relation to
75. If you have a direct line with the Minister, that can be fatal, because your director and manager are unable to check and influence what you are doing and that makes them nervous, because if something goes wrong, they are responsible. If you get a direct line, keep your director and manager fully informed about what you discuss with the Minister. The same thing happens when the director-general wants to head a project group himself, which makes the director nervous, because he wants to be in control. If the Minister/Secretary approaches a civil servant directly, that civil servant has a problem. That is suspicious. Report it immediately to the department head, director and director-general. They want to be present. The manager wants to be in control. In particular in case of direct contact with the layers above him, make sure to send him a CC.	Minister Hierarchy Bypass
76. Work on your professional development. Two things are important: 　·　How do you translate a problem and policy theory into solutions that do-able in practice and politically acceptable? 　·　How quickly are you able to get up to speed on a new dossier?	Expertise Minister Usual sus-pects Unusual suspects
77. Ultimately, it is about real practical results that are also good for the Minister.	Minister Expertise Usual sus-pects Unusual suspects
78. Emphasize the common good and stay away from the hobby horses of the ex-ternal stakeholders. Avoid saying anything foolish that may land the Minister in trouble.	Minister Networking Interests Usual sus-pects
79. The fact that external stakeholders (usual suspects) are getting weaker, means that we, at the Minister, are better able to do our own thing. Sometimes I feel powerless. Rules are always focused on inside the Ministry.	Minister Hierarchy Usual sus-pects Interests Own goals
80. Try to get a handle on how things work in another Ministry. Who is in charge of what?	Interdepar-te-mental
81. Be hard on substance and soft on relationships. Cherish your relationships with colleagues from other Ministries. Show respect to your interdepartmental col-leagues. We are in similar situations. Find out what other people find important and what you need from each other. Show an interest in your colleagues (depart-mental and interdepartmental) and others (external) in your network and connect people. You do this because you want good insights and arguments.	Interdeparte-mental Informal
82. Make sure that people know you and that you can be trusted. Consult a lot to get people on board. Trust is important. Trust is broken if you abuse the information being discussed for your own ends. Also make it clear how the information being provided will be used and how you treat each other with respect. Take each other seriously.	Informal
83. Don't ambush colleagues from other Ministries after the fact. Consult them in time and give them time to respond. But don't exaggerate.	Coordination Interdepar-te-mental

Unwritten rule	Relation to
84. If you have gone through the entire internal circuit, also take on board the external circuit.	Coordination Interdepar-te-mental Usual suspects Interests
85. Build a good relationship with stakeholders, by: · Providing information about what is important to them. · Making sure that the Minister or an important official is present during a certain meeting *And* · Asking information that is important. · Voicing support (good idea!) · Make sure you are involved early in upcoming actions that involve politic. Don't just use outsiders, but also do something in return, for instance by answering questions and making sure that answers are provided later if you don't them at the time.	Networking Informal Usual suspects
86. Preferably establish contact with stakeholders through existing contacts. If that is not possible, the fact that you are part of a Ministry is often sufficient.	Networking Usual suspects
87. Listen and show an interest, without taking on an attitude that says 'we at the Ministry know how it should be done'. Indicate what you will be taking back to the Ministry and what you will do with it. And preferably give them feedback later. Inform them what you have done with the items that you discussed with them.	Networking Trust
88. Know the interests of organizations in relation to your policy area and also know the individual interests of the people of those organizations. You need to keep a close watch on the position and interests of the various external stakeholders, what their interests are, what they fight for. They often have their own 'thing'. Usually you know, you have been there a while, so you have exchanged ideas in the past with stakeholders. But if it is important to your policy area, you talk to them. Keep in mind that what they say may be one-sided.	Minister Networking Usual suspects Interests
89. If you work with many parties, you are often the only one who oversees all the interest. You are often a network prompter (in bilateral exchanges).	Networking Informal Interests
90. Be aware that you have a dependency relationship with parties in the field. Look at 'what they want', 'what can you offer', indicate what you cannot offer. Be clear and do so in an informal setting. But contribute and give them something small if you can. If you do not do the latter, that can create a political risk.	Networking Interests Informal
91. Every time you are in contact with the outside world, check who needs to know in your own organization (colleagues, department head, director, director-general). Also ask yourself 'What are the interests of the various people/parties internally?' Make sure to discuss a certain problem with the right person, because you will be criticized if you don't.	Hierarchy Coordination Interests

TABLE 33: HARD UNWRITTEN RULES THAT WERE MENTIONED (CONTINUED)

Unwritten rule		Relation to
92.	Often, you can go further in sharing information with stakeholders than you may think. In particular parties that have been dealing with Ministries longer understand how it works. You can 'cover' yourself by saying: 'This has not yet been coordinated at an administrative level, we want to know if there is support for it.' If you want to say and discuss more, do so informally. Be honest informally. Usually, that also leads to better contacts. It's easy because, in part, you share the same culture. This is also true at an interdepartmental level. You understand why and what you do. Don't do too much by e-mail. Face-to-face works better with sensitive issues. You have to be able to keep working together.	Minister Hierarchy Networking Informal Interests Interdepar-te-mental Usual sus-pects
93.	If you want to get something done via an MP, do it indirectly (for instance via a presentation at a conference).	Bypass
94.	When dealing with a party that is not a 'usual suspect', who wants to take part in the discussion, it is best to talk to them. Three reasons: · It is a form of politeness. · If you hear them out, you avoid negative media coverage. · You will always hear something new. · When interacting with non-institutional parties, don't explain what you are doing, what your purpose for being there is and why. Guard your boundaries. Be clear about how the Ministry works. Most people don't know that.	Networking Unusual suspects
95.	Coordinate a lot, because many parties are involved. Make sure that everyone stays on board. Explain your story to relevant people often. Why is it important? What is it for, etc.	Coordination Networking Interests
96.	You can involve many parties in the exploration of a problem. Whether they will do something is another matter.	Networking
97.	Exploring a theme (one of the ways of being a policy entrepreneur) is done as follows: - Study the theme. What does literature say? Do you know the basics of what you're talking about? - Gather people around you who also have an opinion on the matter. Ask them for feedback. - Look at how expert knowledge fits into the policy. How you can translate expert knowledge into policy. - Talk to a lot of people about the theme. Ask questions like: · Should it work like that? · Why don't we do this? - Look at who does what, is the theme part of your domain? Are others better equipped? Who is adjacent? - Make sure to listen to outsiders. How does it really work? - When talking to external parties, don't be afraid to say 'I just don't know. We know what the end goal is, but not how to realize it'. Vulnerability can be rewarded.	Networking Policy entre-preneurship
98.	You can be politically active on themes for which you yourself are not responsible. That also applies when you are politically active at a local level.	Being politi-cally active
99.	Don't send too much to colleagues. Listen!	Networking Colleagues
100.	To a director-general, you give above all complementary information. That he needs. In that sense you are more reactive in relation to your director-general, compared to your manager and director.	Hierarchy/DG Expertise
101.	A director-general at a distance no longer knows what goes on in departments.	Hierarchy/DG

Unwritten rule		Relation to
102.	In relation to your director-general and director, make sure to focus on main issues, not details.	Hierarchy/ DG/ Director Expertise
103.	Make sure to give a director-general/director room to play his political game.	Hierarchy/ DG/ Director Expertise
104.	If you go to the director-general with a group, prepare that. Who will say what?	Hierarchy/DG Coordination
105.	Sometimes, a director will take a civil servant with him to a director-general and use him as a 'shield' when something goes wrong. 'It's your dossier, you tell him'.	Hierarchy/ DG/ Director Expertise
106.	Be honest to a director so he knows what you are like.	Hierarchy/ Director
107.	If a department head is not responsible for a certain policy trajectory, he won't deploy capacity. There is competition for capacity. Everyone has to score. Department heads can also be held accountable.	Minister Hierarchy
108.	If you really don't function well, you are presented with the 3-5-7/story. After three years you are told to look elsewhere.	Expertise
109.	Policy is considered more important than its implementation: those are the less well-educated who live in a smaller world.	Minister Hierarchy
110.	At this Ministry, it really is no use being part of the same political circuit as the advisors, both politically and director-general.	Minister Hierarchy
111.	If you want to realize a social goal, look for a department head who understand that social interest and quality are not always the same a political priority (although those department heads are getting fewer in number).	Hierarchy Own goals
112.	Keep your paws off other people's work.	Hierarchy Interests Coordination

Appendix 6: Elaboration identified coping strategies

TABLE 34: ORDERING COPING STRATEGIES: FROM GENERAL TO SPECIFIC

Coping strategies	Follow or use unwritten rules?	Kind of unwritten rule(s) that the coping strategies match	Specific coping strategy
Coping strategie not aimed at influencing	Follow	Serve the Minister (and the hierarchy)	
The 'covering' coping strategy	Follow	Serve the Minister (and the hierarchy)	1. Cover yourself
The 'Just-do-it!' coping strategies	Don't follow / don't use	You 'assume' that you serve the Minister (and the hierarchy) in this way	2. Think beyond the entire institutional field 3. Make an elaborate stakeholder analysis 4. Just do it!

TABLE 35: COPING STRATEGIES AIMED DIRECTLY AT INFLUENCING (SCORING WITH OMSPD)

Coping-strategies	Follow/use un-written rules?	Main un-written rule(s)	Subdivision coping strategies general	Specific coping strategy	
Coping straegies aimed <u>directly</u> at influencing	Use	Serve the Ministers (and the hierar-chy) Translated into: **How can the Minister (and the line) score with OMSPD?**	See how Ministers can score during administration in terms of 'interme-diate policy prod-ucts' and media moments	1.	See the short term in the long term
				2.	See how Ministers can score during administration in terms of'intermediate products and media moments
			Find 'hooks' that the Minister and the line can 'swal-low'	3.	Find 'hooks' that Ministers can 'swallow'
				4.	Find hooks for relevant people in the intern departemental circuit
			Look for ways the line can increase their profile with OMSPD	5.	Put the own department (next to the Ministry) on the map
				6.	Sell OMSPD approach as something new
			Use acknowl-edged written information	7.	Use the coalition agreement
				8.	Use (framework) legislation
				9.	USe departemental docu-ments
				10.	Use acknowledged literature that refers to <u>unusual</u> suspects
				11.	Use sales arguments author-itative
			Emphasize that a larger number of stakeholders yields more	12.	Contextualizer OMSPD
				13.	Exaggerate the importance of bringing on board certain new stakeholders!
				14.	Indicate what the risks are if new stakeholders are NOT included
				15.	Emphasize support (including for implementation practice)
			Use incidents	16.	Use incidents
			Connect OMSPD to conducting research	17.	Label OMSPD as research
				18.	Outsource OMSPD as research that has to be conducted inter-actively
			Compare to earli-er/other OMSPD approaches	19.	Show that, in terms of policy approach, the Ministry is lag-ging behind! Use earlier policy development experiences
				20.	Gain experience with OMSPD via niche subjects
			Spit the policy memo	21.	If you write a memo, split it up in two memos nota's

TABLE 36: COPING STRATEGIES AIMED DIRECTLY AT INFLUENCING (AVOIDING RISK WITH OMSPD)

Coping-strategies	Follow/use un-written rules?	Main unwrit-ten rule(s)	Subdivision coping strategies general	Specific coping strategy
		Serve the Min-isters (and the de hierarchy) translated into: **How to avoid/ reduce risks for Ministers with OMSPD?**	Focus on the content	22. Make a distinction between exploring and decid-ing
				23. Focus on content and substantive playing field
			Make a distinction in approach between usual suspects and unusu-al suspects	24. Give the suspects a special role
				25. See how loss of face by usual suspects can be avoided
				26. See how parties that are not politically savvy can be involved
			Start 'small', 'closed', 'informal'	27. Reduce political risk perception by giving OMSPD an 'informal character'
				28. Start small by collecting perspective and build incrementally
				29. Start with a closed group on the Internet
				30. Explicitly stick to (many) small groups
			Create an expanding, 'known' net-work	31. Create a good network with added value
				32. Tell your manager that 'you know them'
			Show how OMSPD can be kept manageable	33. Indicate that OMSPD can be controlled in an orga-nizational sense
				34. Frame the type of questions such that it is clear that you are managing expectations
				35. Show how you avoid being overwhelmed or keep one party from hijacking the discussion
			Show in which policy development phase it can be used	36. Split the policy trajectory in clear phases: in which phase is it possible?

TABLE 37: COPING STRATEGIES AIMED DIRECTLY AT INFLUENCING (HOW TO MEET/USE DEADLINEHOE FOR OMSPD)

Coping-strategies	Follow/use unwritten rules?	Main unwritten rule(s)	Subdivision coping strategies general	Specific coping strategy
		Meet your deadline	Create more time to carry out OMSPD	37. Double the time for openness for OMSPD by indicating who all needs to be involved
				38. Emphasize 'diligence' in relation to other Ministries and that that is why more parties have to be involved
				39. Start the policy development as early as possible
				40. Turn the time factor around: no discussion about OMS[D because it is that discussion that costs time!
			Show how OMSPD can save time	41. Show that OMSPD can save time
			Choose the right moment	42. Choose the right (political) moment(um)

TABLE 38: COPING STRATEGIES TO INFLUENCE INDIRECTLY-VIA-THE-CUSHION

Coping strategies	Follow/ use un-written rules?	Main unwritten rule(s)	Subdivision coping strate-gies general	Specific coping strategy
Coping strategies that influence _indi-rectly-via-the-de-partemental cush-ion (internal)_	Use	**Cherish your network Your network is cru-cial (internal)**	Create critical mass	43. Determine who you want to influence with what and where 44. Build a 'critical mass' bottom-up and work your way up 'through the line' 45. See where there is internal skepticism and how to deal with it
			Use specific authoritative internal persons	46. Use another department head 47. Use the Communications department of the Ministry 48. Approach, possibly via the political assistant, the Secretary or Minister
Coping strategies that influence _in-directly-via-the-ex-ternal-cushion_	Use	**Cherish your network Your network is cru-cial (external)**	Use specific au-thoritative 'third parties'	49. Organize a small face-to-face network meeting with people other people listen to 50. See who can further your idea for OMSPD inter-departementally (up the line) 51. Lobby an outside-the-box thinking in the usual suspect network for OMSPD 52. Join a political party 53. Approach friends at authoritative institutes to make your inights into OMSPD public 54. Approach the media for OMSBO 55. Let your idea for OMSPD come from Parliament 56. Use experts. Let the 'knowers' (experts) feed the 'powerful' and promote OMSPD
			'Empower' the field	57. Lobby informal parties to make themselves visi-ble 58. Reinforce the field outside the usual suspects

Coping strategy 1: Cover yourself

If a boss wants you to do things in a certain way (about which you may have your doubt), do them exactly as your boss has prescribed. Provide explicit feedback about the steps. If the same boss says "I do not want to receive an e-mail", make sure everything is recorded in a visible way. Including the fact that he does not want to receive an e-mail. Make sure you cover yourself in this way.

Coping strategy 2: Think further than the entire institutional field

If you want an open approach, prepare yourself well for the question 'why'? What are the advantages? What ideas and new contacts are you talking about? What will it save? Also realize that, if you present it to your colleagues, the burden of proof is always on the person who wants something new. For that 'think through the institutional field'. Look at a problem or policy theme in its broader context. That way, you will be able to see more dependency connections to other themes, which will make it easier to convince the line of the need to invite other parties, in addition to the usual suspects. Create a picture of the end-result:
- In terms of explored sub-areas/components.
- In terms of substantive result.
- In terms of the relation to reality.
- In terms of support.
- In terms of practicability.
- In terms of SMART characteristics.

Coping strategy 3: Make an elaborate stakeholder analysis for yourself and visit them informally

Make an elaborate stakeholder analysis for yourself, using the following questions:
- Who is mentioned in literature? Who is mentioned in documents, etc.?
- Who is working on the subject?
- Who does it touch?
- Who has an opinion about it?
- Who must I not overlook in answering this question? Who are really relevant?
- Where is knowledge and experience?
- Who makes/can make the difference?

And ask these people informally:
- What is important in relation to <policy theme>?
- What would the result be if <policy theme> were tackled?
- Who else could be interesting participants?
- Do we know what can be done about it?
- Why are we not doing it yet?

- What are the obstacles? What stands in the way of success?
- How can we make something of it?

Coping strategy 4: Just do it!
Working from the outside in is something you can just do. You simply assume you have a substantive question that can be answered with new parties.

Coping strategy 5: See the short term in the long term
The Minister will really score if he is able to create policy that will remain in place for years. Policy about which there is no longer a discussion about the principles, and at the most about implementation details. So never aim for result within one government term, but do look at how the Minister can score in the short term as part of a longer running project. Determine what that means for your (open) approach.
The same applies to the Director-General. What will let him score in the short term and can therefore be politically interesting.

Coping strategy 6: Determine how Ministers can score via intermediate products and media moments
Identify intermediate products, in case of an interactive trajectory that takes longer than a Minister will be at a Ministry. I.e. an intermediate step with which a Minister can score politically (and in the media).
Show what can be interesting moments for the Minister to step into the spotlight (media exposure):
- At the outset: goals and goodwill.
- Intermediate moment(s): presenting results/thanking participants.
- Presenting policy results after political consideration.

Coping strategy 7: Find media hooks of Ministers that may get a favorable response (from the line)
The core question to be answered is: 'How do make the Minister and the line feel "happy"?' See if there are (media) hooks. Hooks are points in policy or politics to which a type of approach can be connected. In terms of the media, it means following closely when a Minister says in the media and determining what can be used to support a certain approach.
Literally: 'Which sentences can I use that the Minister (and/or Director-General) says that match my proposal for realizing openness?'
That makes it possible to be a civil servant under any Minister and at the same time bring in your own accents or those of the outside world.

Coping strategy 8: Find hooks with relevant persons in the internal departmental circuit

Looking at the hierarchy, ask the question: 'What is a (plausible) connection between what you want to have done an what is relevant to the hierarchical line? What are relevant matches?

Have a chat with the managers about more stakeholders and how they can be involved, and find out what he is sensitive to.

In addition, talk to directors, consultants, assistants of the Ministers and secretaries to find what Directors-General are busy with. What are the relevant themes to them? (Also see the strategies 'Coalition agreement', 'Legislation', 'Departmental documents' and 'Acknowledged literature'.)

Also talk to the Communication board within the Ministry.

Then make a table in which you include all the parties, what the risks and opportunities for those parties are and think of various strategies to approach and involve various persons of those parties. Look at strategies like: what's in it for whom? And whether 'seducing' may be better than 'scaring'.

Finally, you can make a short list of the advantages. Show what the potential benefits are of an OMSPD approach and how the sensitivities of the hierarchical line are taken into account.

Coping strategy 9: Put your own director on the map (in addition to the Ministry)

Show that it does not only help the Minister, but that it also makes your on board visible. In other words, your own director also scores!

Coping strategy 10: Sell the OMSPD approach as something new

What do a Minister's eyes light up? When he manages to realize something real and is supported by the field and political parties. With something that has not been done before and the Minister is the first to do it.

Coping strategy 11: Use the coalition agreement

Use what is written in the coalition agreement. That is the framework within which the Minister has to think and act and to which he or she is beholden.

Coping strategy 12: Use (framework) legislation

Use legislation wherever possible. Framework legislation forces people to work together more. Some laws offer external parties the opportunity to function as a partner. In some research programs, such laws allow external parties a say in which studies need to be conducted and when instruments need to be developed. After all, they are the ones that have to work with the instruments.

Coping strategy 13: Use departmental documents
Read the staff reports and the ideas surrounding the themes that were discussed and check informally with someone who attended the meetings in question to see what 'was said around them'. In other words, gauge the people who were there and also look at their non-verbal response. Does it match what they say?
Familiarize yourself with the history. What was said before? By whom? Are there possible solutions yet or is it completely new in terms of solutions?
The annual plan of your own policy management can also provide you with leads or to see whether it fits in the 'window of management'.

Coping strategy 14: Use accepted literature which refers to unusual suspects
Use accepted (preferably scientific) articles that refer to unusual suspects.

Coping strategy 15: Use sales arguments of authoritative external stakeholders
Use sales arguments of authoritative external stakeholders. For instance, the Parliamentary Technical Committee.

Coping strategy 16: Contextualize OMSPD in such a way that it is clear that involving more stakeholders will have clear benefits
Contextualize your message in such a way that it becomes self-evident that an OMSPD-proof approach together with stakeholders will have greater benefits. Collect arguments as to why such an approach is especially beneficial with regard to this policy theme. Show how an open approach can fit well within the political context and mission/vision of the Ministry.

Use the argument that you can present the Minister with more options by involving a broader network, because a greater variety in stakeholders can lead to new insights and possible solutions. Options that, among other things, fit in with the coalition agreement and are less costly. In other words, create a 'basis of facts' that shows that involving more parties other than the usual suspects has benefits.

Make sure to ensure the approval of the Director-General by showing that this will have political benefits for the Minister, making the Director-General the key/gateway to the politicians. Make it interesting for the Director-General in particular to invite more people, by including names that a Director-General likes to hear. (You say: 'I was thinking of person X, but I am also curious about Y and Z'.)

Coping strategy 17: Exaggerate the importance of getting certain new stakeholders on board!

When conducting an informal exploration externally (see strategy: make a stakeholder analysis for yourself), deliberately ask people about who to involve and why. You can then say later that important party X thinks that Y should also be included. Exaggerate the social value of Y. Turn it into a huge circus. If we don't get so and so on board, it will not work! Sell this early on in the trajectory.

Coping strategy 18: Indicate what the risks are if new stakeholders are NOT involved

Map the risks of NOT involving new or other stakeholders. Turn it into a story. Focus on the quality of the policy. Indicate that only working with the usual suspects creates an intellectual monoculture. And that you want a balanced view. A monoculture can also be risky for the Minister. By including those (new) external parties and not ruling them out, and showing that that may prevent Parliamentary questions, you also create legitimacy among the usual suspects for involving other parties besides them as well. In short: show how expanding the number of parties to be consulted actually reduce any political risks. Also be aware that, these days, parties other than the usual suspects are able to put a Minister under pressure via social media. They can do so much more quickly these days with Twitter.

Coping strategy 19: Emphasize support (including with regard to the executive practice)

You can make a point of mentioning the importance of support. Find arguments for broadening that support/going one step further in the ladder in terms of who you involve. For instance, by remarking that you want to find smart 'catalyst' parties that are not yet part of your network.

It is important to indicate that the execution is just as important and equal to the policy and the usual suspects (if the practical execution is insufficiently represented among them). In particular when it involves a behavioral change in the field, formal rules regularly do not work.

Finally, involving parties other than the usual suspects can be useful to put something in motion, to actually realize solutions.

Coping strategy 20: Use incidents

If possible, use an 'incident' that has occurred to legitimize involving parties other than the usual suspects.

Coping strategy 21: Label OMSPD as research

Sell an OMSPD-proof approach as research. A research label increases the acceptance and legitimacy of such an approach. When you deliberately start by conducting research, you can include multiple parties that can and have to be consulted if it is a valid research. It then becomes easy to connect an interactive approach with conducting research. An example of the methodological approach that connects research and interactivity is the Klinkers Method (Klinkers, 2002).

Coping strategy 22: Outsource the OMSPD as research that needs to be conducted interactively

Outsource the process to experts who can adopt a broader approach more easily. Include that in your proposal. Tell a research agency to conduct 'interactive' research. If a civil servant feels insecure and expects political risks, this strategy makes it possible to 'outsource' the risks as well. After all, it wasn't the civil servant. In a positive sense, by obtaining and examining different representations of a problem, a civil servant gets a better picture of a policy theme. In other words, he gains a deeper insight into the core of a problem, as well as where possible solutions can be found.

Coping strategy 23: Show that, in terms of policy approach, the Ministry is lagging behind! Use previous comparable OMSPD experiences of policy development

Show that other Ministries already engage in OMSPD approaches and that 'we' are lagging behind or that the hierarchy can earn 'credits'. The Ministry ought to be ahead in its own policy area. If it is the case, show that the 'old-fashioned' approach that has been used so far has had no, or insufficient' result. Explore this. For instance by asking an open question on social media: *'How could X be approached from a process point of view?'* You can do this in a neutral and careful way.

Examine which approach has worked and where. Look for good examples that show the added value of more openness in policy development. Talk to someone who has experience involving more stakeholders or increasing the participation level. Use the successful bottom-up experiences of other Ministries.

Present those good examples *and* the fact that you have coordinated with colleagues to your department head. In other words, point to successes of other dossiers that have been handled in a similar way. And if you manage to get your department head on board, go to the director together. He is a key figure.

Coping strategy 24: Gain experience with OMSPD via niche subjects

The freedom a civil servant is allowed to use an open approach depends in part on his, or other people's, successes using a similar approach.

There is plenty of room for consultation and interaction with 'niche subjects', as long as a civil servant stays below the radar. As soon as the theme in question catches the attention of the director/Director-General, or becomes more political, that room is immediately reduced. It then has to be finished quickly, safely for the Minister, within the rules and within budget. It is easier to 'practice' with 'nice' subjects, usually items with a board time horizon, which are by definition less political. The more you move towards politically more serious subjects, the less political support there will be for bringing on board 'loose cannons'.

Coping strategy 25: If you write a memorandum, split it in two

If a memorandum is written, make sure that it will lead to a conversation that supports more openness. For instance by including a question that goes into that direction (as a kind of bait), or that allows certain parties to be involved in policy development. If that meets with approval, write a follow-up memorandum asking for money. Make sure to pay a visit to your manager first, however. Cover yourself.

Coping strategy 26: Draw a distinction between exploring and deciding

Build in steps where the Minister still has the final say. You can build in steps in the policy development in which a broad exploration of a problem is conducted at the start. The further you go into the exploration (and emphasize that in an interactive trajectory), the more you need to explore beyond the usual suspects. The early phase is clearly limited to an exploration (only brainstorming, initial orientation, sharing ideas, etc.). In other words, in the external communication, make a clear distinction between diverging/exploring/listening and deciding. The latter is a political act. In a further phase of the policy development, decisions about possible solutions can be made by the Ministers.

With regard to the hierarchical line, you emphasize that you are not making any substantive promises and that risks can be managed by managing expectations (goal, framing and expectations with regard to the interactive process). That framing creates security for the line. Be aware that what you do on the outside must not come as a surprise to the inside.

Coping strategy 27: Make sure to put the content, and the substantive playing field (the question), center stage

Start by focusing on the content. Determine the substantive playing field. What you are and are not talking about. There is a substantive, administrative phase and a political (decision) phase.

See if you can make sure that the politician also makes that distinction. It is always best to start by focusing as much as possible on the substance/facts. If you want to, you can start by aiming your open approach on that. That way, you keep the politics out of it in the early phase! Opinions and interests come later.

Coping strategy 28: Give the usual suspects a special role
If you set up an OMSPD, if necessary, give the usual suspects a specific/special role.

Coping strategy 29: Examine how you can prevent loss of face for usually suspects
If necessary, examine how an open process can produce solutions that relevant parties can take him without suffering loss of face. Think about what that means for the way you organize an open interactive process.

Coping strategy 30: Examine how parties that are not politically savvy can be included
Examine how parties that are not politically savvy can be included informally or otherwise. Focus on the question: where is the resistance when I want to open up the policy process?
- Content-related
- Political
- Person-related
- Process-related (different phases in the process have different kinds of resistance)

Choose a way to involve parties (seminar, other ways) and discuss that informally with colleagues who have insight into the issue in question, as well as with experts in open approaches.

Coping strategy 31: Reduce the political risk perception by giving the OMSPD-proof policy development process an 'informal character'
Preferably give the interactive trajectory an informal character. Keep it 'small' in the political risk perception. If you increase the scale, that creates perceived political risks in the line.

Coping strategy 32: Start small by collecting perspectives and build from there
Consultation can take place simply by collecting perspectives in the earlier/explorative phases of the policy development. Show the different sides there are to a problem and that more people are needed than just the usual suspects. Start by informally collecting perceptions surrounding the theme you can to apply an open approach to via multiple conversations with the same two or three people who (also) know about the theme. Let them do the talking. Give them room and, together, make a list of interesting people (stakeholders), if necessary via a Group Decision Room or via more informal discussions. After all, no decisions are being made. This approach allows you to gradually increase the scale of the interactive meetings. Start small (for instance a pilot) and, in discussions with others and the line, expand the ambi-

tion. If you write a memorandum at that stage, work towards a larger meeting together with all the stakeholders.

Coping strategy 33: Start with a closed group on the Internet
Start with a closed group. Your own colleagues and colleagues from other Ministries. Make colleagues aware that the group exists via e-mail.
You can do this in addition to the face-to-face meetings. If you 'just do it'/go about it in a clever way, you will not have to deal with 'bureaucratic cramp' from your own Ministry.

Coping strategy 34: Keep it explicitly to (many) small groups
Keep it explicitly to (many) small groups at research/consultation level (only exploring and listening). That allows you to be more focused in your questions. Many small consultations together make up a large consultation. That way, you can also call it 'qualitative' research. (Also see the strategy: labeling the process as research.)

Coping strategy 35: Build a good network with added value
If it has been proven that a civil servant has a good network that he has been able to use in the service of departmental objectives, in an open way, there is more that is possible. It can be shown in that case that the (extensive) network of the civil servant in question also has added value in the specific case where he or she wants to apply an OMSPD-proof approach.

Coping strategy 36: Tell the manager that 'You know them!'
Pretend you already know the newcomers. If you say that you know them, that is reassuring. You may want to sound out (new) stakeholders informally in advance.

Coping strategy 37: Indicate how OMSPD can be kept controllable in an organizational sense
The underlying question here is how you can keep it manageable (time, money, quality) and practicable. You have to look at how much money such an interactive trajectory costs and the capacity it requires. So find ways to show that it does not require a lot of capacity and is easy to execute. That way, you will be able to invite other parties more quickly. In your set-up, provide a clear division of responsibilities, make a cost-benefit analysis and check it with your manager.

Coping strategy 38: Frame the type of questions in such a way that you manage expectations
Look at the type of questions to which you want answers. Frame them in such a way that the line clearly understands that you are managing expectations

(externally as well as internally) and are not making any promises. If necessary, use a disclaimer. (Also see the strategy: The Ministry is leading.)

Coping strategy 39: Show how you avoid getting overwhelmed or prevent one party from hijacking the discussion

Show how you avoid getting overwhelmed by entire hordes, that all anarchy does not break loose once you start such a trajectory and that you will not allow one party to take over the discussion. That it remains manageable and yields good results. For instance, by the deliberate use of a Group Decision Room. A good facilitator is able to spread the energy and attention among all the participants.

Coping strategy 40: Divide the policy trajectory in distinct phases: in which phase is it possible!

If applying an open approach to an entire policy development trajectory is not possible, examine in which part it *is* possible.

Coping strategy 41: Double the time for openness for an OMSPD-proof approach by indicating all the parties that need to be involved

An argument against openness is that it costs a lot of time. One way to deal with that is to double the amount when asked to provide a time frame at the start of a policy trajectory, for instance by listing all the stakeholders that need to be involved and how much time that will cost.
Incidentally: Make sure what/who are the culprits if you fail to meet your planning.

Coping strategy 42: Emphasize 'diligence' in relation to other Ministries and that that is the reason more parties need to be involved

If another Ministry is involved, say that 'diligence' is important. Write that down in a letter of postponement. After all, it is not your fault that things are going more slowly.

Coping strategy 43: Start the policy development as early as possible

A general rule of thumb is that 'the sooner you start, the more room you have for an OMSPD approach'.

Coping strategy 44: Turn the time factor around: don't enter into a discussion about the OMSPD approach because that discussion costs time!

There is a tendency to limit contacts to the usual suspects. That way, the civil servant has done his job, it is not hard and you can do it within the regular time frame. On the other hand, usual suspects tend to want to (co-)determine how things should be done.

What is you decide NOT to start with the question what the usual suspects can think of an open process that involves them more? But instead use the fact that there is little time. Use that in a positive sense and just start a plan of approach of an open process, with the argument that 'talking about the plan of approach takes up a lot of time'.

In addition, the usual suspect are only some of the parties and you do not have to coordinate an approach with the usual suspects separately if they are only a few of the participants. Even if this is unusual and civil servants sometimes find it difficult (from a risk perspective).

Coping strategy 45: Show that OMSPD can save time
You can also gain time if you show that, in fact, an open approach reduces the policy trajectory.

Coping strategy 46: Choose the right (political) moment(um)
Don't strike the iron before it is hot. That also applies to policy themes. Above all, there is a political momentum. Present a document to the MT when the assessment is that it will pass. When there is trust in it.

Another version is the following. If a civil servant knows that a director or Director-General does not agree with him or her, make sure that the memorandum is discussed when the person in question is absent and the replacement will handle it.

Elaboration of the strategies 'Via the cushion' (internal and external)

Via the internal cushion

Coping strategy 47: Determine who you want to influence with what and where
Ask the question: What is an ideal line (people to approach and order in which to approach them) to get something through the hierarchy? In negative terms: to avoid problems with the hierarchy. In positive terms: how can I use the hierarchy? Can I send them out with the message I want?

Coping strategy 48: Build a 'critical mass' bottom-up and work your way up 'through the line'
It is no use if colleagues and the hierarchical line are unwilling to continue with an idea involving an OMSPD-proof approach. That is why you need to organize support. Take it slow, in small steps. Begin by talking/sparring with colleagues: 'What are your views?' Explore their contacts, who they find interesting. Start by looking for support among colleagues. Sound them out carefully one by one and see what questions/doubts you encounter.

In short, gauge your colleagues and use that in other conversations: 'I have heard that …, then we should also ask X.'

At the same time, ask colleagues what adjacent themes are and who, on the basis of those adjacent themes, in addition to the usual suspects, could also be interesting to include in the policy development. In other words, use the connection to other themes to gain legitimacy and invite others besides the usual suspects. At the same time, collect arguments. Why working from the outside in is a good approach for theme <X> in particular. Then you decide together that it is a good idea.

Then let it simmer in the hierarchical lie. Write a memo. Have an informal talk with the department head. If you notice that a coordinating civil servant and head object, put something to paper that you can discuss in a broader framework (department/work meeting). Then move on to an interdepartmental context and finally the usual suspects.

Coping strategy 49: Determine where there is internal skepticism and find out how to deal with it

This strategy is an addition to "Build a 'critical mass' bottom-up and work your way up through the line'.

New things evoke resistance. They mean more work and people do not know how the hierarchy will take it. Will the idea be an advantage or a disadvantage? Make sure you have the right arguments, prevent people from saying 'no' based on a feeling and keep it on the agenda.

Start by finding out where there is internal skepticism by asking around in the organization (who is working on it, what is their opinion?). Then talk to the skeptics bilaterally. Find out what they respond to and what may mellow them. Things they may respond to are:

• Studies that confirm what you are saying.
• Authoritative people who support your arguments.
• What the field wants.

Connect to what the skeptic finds important. What does he indicate? Don't send. Listen!

Coping strategy 50: Use another department head

Use another department head inside of our outside your own division who agrees with you about how to approach a theme.

Coping strategy 51: Use the Ministry's Communication division

Use the Ministry's Communication division. They have tools, for example to poll the message in society, but they could also have expertise with regard to OMSPD-proof approaches or be able to support them based on their professional expertise.

Coping strategy 52: Approach the Secretary or Minister, possibly via the political assistant
If the director/Director-General says 'over my dead body', you can always go around them. For instance at a network meeting where the Secretary/Minister is also present. Ask them informally: 'Do you understand why the director/Director-General is against this?' Another option is to call the Minister's political assistant and explain that you have an idea on how to approach the policy theme that you are almost certain the Minister will agree with, or with which he can score or prevent political risk.

Via the <u>external</u> cushion
If the line says 'no', the external line is a way to create movement. First, you need to organize political support externally. So you need to convince a Secretary, Minister or Director-General.
For that, you have to create interdepartmental and/or external 'sponsorship' that is will to question the politics and the Minister, and function as a 'crowbar' in the form of a network with authoritative (and visible) persons. Of course, that network and who is authoritative can vary per dossier. To build that, do the following: Determine who with other Ministries are involved in the issue/ feel blockades and develop a good informal contact with those people.

Coping strategy 53: Organize a small face-to-face network meeting with people other people listen to
Bring relevant people from the network together yourself (10 to 15). Make sure there are people among them that other people listen to. Look for authoritative people who subscribe the interactive process you want. If possible, also people who have already solved (part of) the problem.

Coping strategy 54: Find out who can promote your idea for an OMSPD approach interdepartmentally (move it up the line)
Find out who in the other Ministries can move the relevant them up via their line, without raising questions from a Director-General from their Ministry to the Director-General of your Ministry about the theme. The underlying tone in the communication is 'unrest and a feeling of risk'. Such that an open approach is considered necessary.

Coping strategy 55: Lobby an outside-the-box thinker in usual suspect network for OMSPD
Make sure that some well-known people who are also known to and recognized by the leadership share the ideas about involving more stakeholders than the usual suspects.
Lobby them. If necessary, find an outside-the-box thinker in your usual suspect network who has some influence. Discuss the use of and need for

involving more parties in policy development than just the usual suspects. Explore how that can be an advantage for his organization.

Then approach a manager, but do not present him or her with a fait accompli. Provide ideas and say: 'I think that it best to involve Y, do you also think that is a good idea?'

Coping strategy 56: Join a political party
Join a political party or another important network. Use the relationships in that network to exert influence towards a more open approach of the policy development surrounding a certain theme. If necessary, use the network to put pressure on the director or Director-General.

Coping strategy 57: Approach friends at authoritative institutes to make your ideas about an OMSPD approach public
Approach friends at authoritative institutes and create pressure from there.

Coping strategy 58: Approach the media for OMSPD
This can be twofold. If an issue attracts more attention because it is in the media, there will automatically be responses from other interested parties. On the other hand, the media can be approached to have them talk about the importance of an OMSPD-proof approach.

Although this particular coping strategy was not mentioned in the interviews, it can be a useful one, in light of, as Vliegenthart (2012) indicates, the influence of the media on politicians and Ministries.

Coping strategy 59: Let your sound come from Parliament
If the Minister does not want something the civil servant wants, let the sound come from Parliament, by contacting social actors who experience the problem on which you focus and encouraging them to contact (the Standing Committee of) MP's. You can also do that by contacting institutes in your network who meet with the Minister in a regular basis and have them bring it up during the meetings/put it on the agenda, or have it put on the agenda via MP's. Or let them write a letter or directly approach a Member of Parliament.

Coping strategy 60: Use experts.
Keep in mind that the 'knowers' are often the real players in the field, not the usual suspects (powerful). Sometimes, the 'knowers' are less visible to regular government/Ministry, which means they are less interesting to the line. Make sure that the 'knowers' feed the 'powerful' and support an OMSPD approach. Also keep in mind that powerful players are not always substantively active. The 'powerful' determine whether or not you make progress (traffic light).

Coping strategy 61: Lobby informal parties to make themselves visible
Approach the parties you want to involve informally and lobby them into making themselves more visible and indicating that they want to play a part.

Coping strategy 62: Reinforce the field outside the usual suspects
Explain to stakeholders in the field who are not usual suspects what their options are if they want to realize something. How they can do that. You, as a civil servant, can simply explain to them how to do that, how the roles are organized. After all, a civil servant is not a politician. Also see strategy 61 with regard to making themselves visible.

Appendix 7: Values mentioned in the coping strategies

No. strategy and value(2) (= directional criteria for behavior)
1. Process legitimacy method: The boss clinging to the old strategy: Tried and tested: not deviate from the rules
2. Policy quality: Being able to see the broader context:
   o   Costs savings
   o   Support policy
   o   Practicability policy
3. Process manageability: Distinction formal – informal
4. Policy quality: Policy options: New contacts -> New ideas
5. Policy quality: Long-term effect: Policy that will be in place for years
6. Image: Scoring with (intermediate) process products
7. Image: Media hooks indicated by the Minister
8. Policy quality: Connection to relevant themes
9. Image: Director 'on the map' (who 'scores')
10. Image: something new that is meaningful (Minister scores)
11. Substantive legitimacy: Coalition agreement
12. Substantive legitimacy: Framework legislation
13. Substantive legitimacy: Departmental documents
14. Substantive legitimacy: Acknowledged scientific literature
15. Substantive legitimacy: What do authoritative acknowledged stakeholders find interesting?
16. Policy quality: Higher yield than 'ordinary' policy process (political benefits Minister)
17. (Im)practicability
18. Policy quality less through intellectual monoculture
19. Policy quality: Support (including the execution)
20. Policy quality: Incidents (where new parties played a role)
21. Legitimacy approach (frame as participation level research)
22. Process manageability (+ running no risk): Outsourcing
23. Being out of sync/lagging behind
24. Process legitimacy: Experience with openness
25. Organizational manageability: Financially
26. Process manageability (distinction exploring/deciding)
27. Process manageability: Technical substantive exploration (no decision)
28. Image usual suspects: Recognition process role usual suspects
29. Image usual suspects: Preventing loss of face
30. (Political) Process manageability: Distinction formal – informal (small-scale) consultation
31. (Political) Process manageability: Distinction formal – informal
32. (Political) Process manageability: (Reducing) risk perception: Working from small and informal toward larger scale

33. (Political) Process manageability: From closed to open
34. Political process management: Many small ones make a big one
35. Substantive legitimacy: Departmental objectives
36. Political process management: Known and informal first
37. Organizational manageability: Time, money and capacity required
38. Political manageability: Expectation management & no promises
39. Political manageability: Not being taken over by dominant party
40. Process manageability: Divide the process
41. Organizational manageability: Time
42. Policy quality: diligence
43. Organizational manageability: Time
44. Organizational manageability: Time
45. Organizational manageability: Time
46. Image: Scoring via political momentum
46-51 Internal process legitimacy/support: You do not deviate/multiple ac-
    knowledge actors say it
52-62 Internal process legitimacy/support: You do not deviate/multiple ac-
    knowledge actors say it

Striking in the list presented above:

Political manageability/process manageability
- Phasing: Distinction informal – formal
- Phasing: Distinction exploring – deciding
- Expectation management
- Scale: Small-scale – large-scale and the possible development during a process (or from more closed towards more open and the development in that process)
- Avoiding the risk of being taken over by party that is too dominant

Image (scoring)
- *Scoring on content*
  - o   Minister: Consistent with what he says in the media
  - o   Minister: Something genuinely new and long-lasting
  - o   Minister: Scoring with intermediate products
  - o   DG/director/department manager: 'on the map'
- *Scoring in terms of process/approach*
  - o   Not being out of sync because of 'old-fashioned' process

Policy quality
- Connection to other themes
- New policy options
- Long-term effect

- Support
- Practicability
- Cost savings

Process legitimacy
- *Coordination:*
  - o Internal: What do the others think of such an open approach? Has it been coordinated?
  - o External: What do important stakeholders think of such an open approach?
  - *Substantively covered/connected to:*
  - o Coalition agreement
  - o Framework legislation
  - o Departmental documents/departmental objectives
  - o Scientific literature
- *Experience with open approaches*

Organizational manageability
- What does it cost?
  - Financially
  - In terms of lead time
  - In terms of the required capacity

Appendix 8: Coping strategies: number of times mentioned

T = number of times mentioned in specific interview round

TABLE 39: COPING STRATEGIES, NUMBER OF TIMES MENTIONED

Coping strategies (direct and indirect)	Phase 1		Phase 2	TOT
	T1	T2	T3	
Strategy 1: Think beyond the entire institutional field	2	2	6	10
Strategy 2: Make an elaborate stakeholder analysis for yourself	2	3	5	10
Strategy 3: just do it!	1	1	0	2
Strategy 4: Cover yourself	1	0	1	2
Strategy 5: See the short term in the long term	1	0	2	3
Strategy 6: Ministers score via intermediate products and media moments	1	1	1	3
Strategy 7: Finding media hooks that Ministers can respond to	2	0	3	5
Strategy 8: Finding hooks with relevant persons in the internal departmental circuit	7	0	1	8
Strategy 9: Put your own directors on the map	1	1	0	2
Strategy 10: Sell it as something new	3	0	1	4
Strategy 11: Coalition agreement	2	0	0	2
Strategy 12: Framework legislation	1	1	0	1
Strategy 13: Departmental documents	0	0	1	1
Strategy 14: Acknowledged literature that refers to unusual suspects	1	0	2	3
Strategy 15: Sales arguments from authoritative external stakeholders	0	0	1	1
Strategy 16: Contextualization: more stakeholders produces more (options) Consists of: * Contextualization: more stakeholders produces more * Find out how the Ministers and the line can score by inviting multiple people via an open approach * Being able to present multiple options to Ministers	16 2 11 3	9 0 8 1	11 2 5 4	36 4 22 8
Strategy 17: Exaggerate importance	1	0	0	1
Strategy 18: Risk of NOT involving new stakeholders	2	1	1	4
Strategy 19: Emphasize support (including regarding executive practice)	3	4	1	8
Strategy 20: Use incidents	1	0	0	1
Strategy 21: Label as research	4	0	1	5
Strategy 22: Outsourcing as research that needs to be conducted interactively	1	2	0	3
Strategy 23: Framing in terms of 'we are lagging behind'	4	2	3	9

TABLE 39: COPING STRATEGIES, NUMBER OF TIMES MENTIONED (CONTINUED)

Coping strategies (direct and indirect)	Phase 1		Phase 2	TOT
	T1	T2	T3	
Strategy 24: Gaining experience via niche subjects	2	0	0	2
Strategy 25: When you write a memo, split it in two memos	2	0	0	2
Strategy 26: The Ministry remains leading by drawing a distinction between exploring and deciding	5	0	1	6
Strategy 27: Emphasize the central importance of the substance, and the substantive field (the question)	3	0	1	4
Strategy 28: Give the usual suspects a special role	0	1	2	3
Strategy 29: No loss of face for usual suspects	0	0	1	1
Strategy 30: What to do with parties that are politically less savvy?	0	0	1	1
Strategy 31: Reduce the political risk perception by giving the open process a more 'informal character'	2	1	0	3
Strategy 32: Start small by collecting perspectives and build from there	4	5	1	10
Strategy 33: Start with a closed group on the Internet	0	0	2	2
Strategy 34: Many small ones make a big one	0	3	1	4
Strategy 35: Build a network with added value	3	0	1	4
Strategy 36: You know them!	4	2	0	6
Strategy 37: Organizational manageability	7	3	0	10
Strategy 38: Framing type of questions/expectation management	0	1	1	2
Strategy 39: Not getting overwhelmed or having one party hijack the discussion	2	0	0	2
Strategy 40: Splitting up policy process	0	0	1	1
Strategy 41: Double time	1	0	0	1
Strategy 42: Emphasize diligence in relation to other Ministries	1	0	0	1
Strategy 43: Start as early as possible	1	0	0	1
Strategy 44: Turn the time factor around	1	0	0	1
Strategy 45: More efficient policy process	0	1	0	1
Strategy 46: Playing with the factor of time. Choose the (political) momentum	0	0	1	1
Strategy 47: Determine who you want to influence with what and where	0	0	1	1
Strategy 48: From a 'critical mass' bottom-up working your way up the line	11	2	2	15
Strategy 49: Dealing with internal skepticism	1	0	2	3
Strategy 50: Via another department head or director	1	1	1	3
Strategy 51: Via the Communication division	1	1	0	2
Strategy 52: Via the Secretary or Minister	0	0	2	2
Strategy 53: Small network meeting with people other people listen to	0	0	1	1
Strategy 54: Interdepartmental	0	1	1	2
Strategy 55: Lobby outside-the-box thinker in usual suspect network	4	3	3	10
Strategy 56: Join a political party	2	0	0	2

TABLE 39: COPING STRATEGIES, NUMBER OF TIMES MENTIONED (CONTINUED)

Coping strategies (direct and indirect)	Phase 1		Phase 2	TOT
	T1	T2	T3	
Strategy 57: Friends at authoritative institutes	2	2	1	5
Strategy 58: Via the media	0	1	0	1
Strategy 59: Via Parliament/Standing Committee	3	0	1	4
Strategy 60: Use substantive experts. Let the 'knowers' feed the 'powerful'	0	0	1	1
Strategy 61: Lobby informal parties to make themselves visible	4	0	1	5
Strategy 62: Reinforce the field outside the usual suspects	0	0	1	1

Appendix 9: Interview protocol phase I: round 1

Conduct 2 interviews (both take about an hour and a half).
Interview 1:

Indicate setting:
- Results are confidential; remain in the hands of the research(s)
- Short explanation about unwritten rules
- Short explanation about the steps in the research protocol

Aim of this round is:
1. Arriving at a list of unwritten rules that affect the openness in a policy process.
2. Exploring to what level of openness the various unwritten rules lead.
3. Finding explanations for the level of openness as a result of certain unwritten rules.
4. Determining which rules (formal structures) are seen as underlying a certain unwritten rule.
5. Identifying potential coping mechanisms to increase the level of openness.

Motivators/motives
What motives do you see among your colleagues for working here?
What are your motives for working here?
Result = inventory motives.

Examples are: security, recognition, status, social commitment, substance work, compensation/reward, etc.

Unwritten rules mentioned from motives.
For each motive, ask the question: 'If motive X were important to you, what would you have to do/not do in this organization?'
Note: check if a conjunction is included,
Suppose the motive is <security>, someone says: 'You need to cover yourself for your boss in everything you do.'
Then ask the additional question … because …
Result = Unwritten rules from motives.

Authorities
Who do you need to get things done here? Who are really important? Inside/outside the DG, SAE?
Result = inventory important positions/people

Examples are: Ministers/Secretaries, DG, directors, department managers, immediate colleagues, colleagues other sections, colleagues other Ministries, FEZ employee, management consultants, political assistant.

Unwritten rules mentioned in relation to authorities
For each authority, ask the question: 'If authority <X> is important to you, what must you do/not do?'
As with motives, as additional questions like … because …
Result = unwritten rules in relation to authorities.

Levers
Ask the questions: 'Are you really held to account for this?'
When do products really score here? How can you really score with a product? What do you focus on?
Other things you are held accountable for when push comes to shove of with which you gain successes?
Result = Inventory levers.

Example can be the vision (and the words used in the vision), process descriptions often contain a large number of levers, personnel management/personal instruments, assessment criteria, career projections, assessment diagrams, etc.

For each lever, ask the question: 'If lever <X> is important to you, what do you need to do/not do?'
Again, ask additional questions like … because …
Result = Unwritten rules based on levers.

Specifically with regard to openness in policy development
Ask: which unwritten rules have to do primarily with themes like 'from the outside in', 'openness in policy development' and 'dealing with stakeholders'?
Those you have mentioned so far?
Other unwritten rules?
Result = unwritten rules with regard to openness in policy development

End of interview 1.
Interviewer makes a list of all the unwritten rules, ranked according to motivators, authorities, levers and 'openness in policy development'.

Interview 2: Unwritten rule - openness

Start interview:
Explain what the protocol of this interview is.
Explain the tables and additional questions.

Interviewer presents interviewee with list of unwritten rules.
Interviewer asks if there are any unwritten rules that can be added.
Interviewer explains the difference between an unwritten rule and a coping strategy.
Interviewer and interviewee again go through the list with unwritten rules.
Interviewer asks:
1. 'What are real unwritten rules and which are more personal coping strategies?'
2. 'What are the most important unwritten rules in terms of internal politics?'

Choose 4. (When testing this protocol, it became clear that in an hour and a half, after the opening questions, on average there is time to analyze 4 unwritten rules using the tables.)

With each of the selected unwritten rules separately, the following 2 main questions are asked in turn:

1. *What is the effect of this unwritten rule on openness in policy development according to you?*
Or: Does this unwritten rule affect the level of openness in policy development?
- Yes/no?
- If yes:
  - Based on the unwritten rule: Who do you involve, or not involve, in policy development? Why (explanation)?
  - What level of participation do you choose? Why (explanation)?
  - What are possible sanctions for violations? (see appendix, table 2)
  - What are possible rewards for violations?

Instruction: Start with open questions to let the interviewee tell you in their own words who they would or would not involve. Then show table 1 (see appendix). The table not only shows WHO may be involved, but also TO WHAT EXTENT their voice is included in the end result.
Check the box that the interviewee is characteristic for the effect of the unwritten rule.
Then ask for explanations (why).

Then ask about potential sanctions for violations.
NB For each of the unwritten rules, fill in both tables separately and ask for explanation (why).

2. Written rules
Also ask: "Which written rule(s) of the formal system do you think is/are underlying the presence of this unwritten rule?'
Indicate that for each of the selected unwritten rules.
After going through the unwritten rules, they are prioritized based on the question: 'Which of the unwritten rules do you think that, after this analysis, have the greatest influence on openness?' Choose five.

3. Coping strategies
Coping strategy = an ordered/structured set of thoughts and actions that help you realize a goal when you encounter problems.
(NB Think: goal and problems are two sides of the same coin)

Suppose you want to create a higher level of openness AND want to use an OMSPD method (Participation level = Consultancy or higher/Who to involve = from level 4 Professional Stakeholders not part of the usual suspects)
- What is a possible coping strategy that can make a higher level of openness possible?
- What are assumptions underlying this possible coping strategy? (operating principles) (Herold, 2012)
- What does the use of such a coping strategy tell you about the convictions of the person applying the strategy?

Finally: **Questions in relation to follow-up research**
What, in your view, are the most important files within the department, within the DG, within the Ministry?
Who within the department/DG, in your view, is good at creating openness in policy development under certain unwritten rules?

Appendix for interview diagram: table relationship unwritten rule and openness.
Unwritten rule = ...
....
....
....
....
....
....

TABLE 1: RELATIONSHIP UNWRITTEN RULE AND OPENNESS

Who to involve?	1	2	3	4	5	6	7	8	9	10
1. Expert administrators own Ministry										
2. Expert administrators other Ministry										
3. Professional stakeholders, usual suspects (not ministry)										
4. Professional stakeholders, not part of the usual suspects										
5. Elected representatives										
6. Lay stakeholders										
7. Random selection										
8. Open targeted recruitment										
9. Open self selection										
10. Diffuse public sphere										

Explanation

- Looking from the unwritten rule: Who do you involve in the policy development and who do you leave out? Why (explanation)?

....
....
....
....
....
....
....
....
....
....
....
....

- Looking from the unwritten rule: What is the level of participation that you choose? Why (explanation)?

....
....
....
....
....
....
....
....
....
....
....
....

Which written rule(s) of the formal system underly/underlies the presence of this unwritten rule?

....
....
....
....
....
....
....
....
....

What is, in your opinion, a realistic sanction when you violate the unwritten rule?
Check (multiple answers are possible).

TABLE 2: REALISTIC SANCTION

a. No sanction	
b. Advice from van colleague ('can I give you a tip').	
c. Colleagues avoid working with you.	
d. Corrective remark by manager.	
e. Increasing number of corrections by managers of your policy memos.	
f. No longer getting important dossiers or projects.	
g. Removal policy dossier from civil servant.	
h. End of career within organization (unable to make a promotion as a result of violating the unwritten rule).	
i. Negative assessment (building file against you).	
j. Censure	
k. Suspension	
l. Dismissal	
m. Other, namely	
n. Other, namely	
o. Other, namely	

What, in your opinion, is a realistic reward for following the unwritten rule?
Check (multiple answers possible).

TABLE 3: REALISTIC REWARD

No reward	
Good assessment	
Compliments from department head	
Compliments from director	
Compliments from the DG	
Compliments from the Minister	
Cooperation	
Special reward	
Other, namely	
Other, namely	
Other, namely	

Appendix 10: Follow-up research

Research generates new questions. In this case, the following thoughts occurred to me.

1. *Openness and (knowledge) integrity*

With regard to the policy development of Ministries, a relationship can be assumed between (knowledge) integrity and openness, as it also exists in the scientific community (Anderson, 2007). Riege & Lindsay (2006: 31) say about that: *'governments also need to approach stakeholders in a heuristic manner with a view to learning rather than adopting quick fix solutions (Adams and Hess, 2001). While policy making is political, outcomes should not be predetermined, and feedback should be provided to stakeholders on how their contributions have been used.'*
Professional, focused OMSPD applications in policy development can give a signal to the outside world that 'no games are being played' and thus promote collaboration between actors and synchronize (network) actions. Further research into the relationship between focused OMSPD applications, (knowledge) integrity and policy development in administrative organizations is recommended.
Speaking about an open government, Meijer, Curtin & Hillebrandt (2012: 25) ask us to consider the following: *'Some social scientists focus on issues of trust and legitimacy whereas others highlight efficiency and effectiveness......... Open government is to be designed and optimized for variety in desirables...... Governments should continuously learn about the effects and side-effects of open government so as to optimize its design.'*
With a focus on focused OMSPD applications/subjects, a concept like 'open government' is also made more concrete and tangible, which also makes it possible to talk in a more focused way about learning, 'effects' and 'side-effects'.
That can include the effects of closed networks on the knowledge production in policy development processes.

2. *'Two layers' – OMSPD*

In various OMSPD trajectories, there is openness on two levels at the same time. One of the practical cases in the Open Master Class From the Outside In of the Academy ECS/SAE/TWM (nowadays called the Learning and Development Square) is the approach used in the SAE program Learning and Working. The program manager involved provided the coordination for the Ministries for EA, ECS and SAE, so that they all worked within the same framework, examining in the basis of equality what the three Ministries had in common, what the underlying common thread was in their separate departmental goals. The results then served as a focus for the account managers of the three Ministries.

These account managers, who worked at a regional level, brought together Education, Government and Entrepreneurs and helped them formulate and realize their own regional goals within the framework of learning, together and successfully.

To generate many regional visions (as opposed to one single vision), a good interdepartmental coordination turned out to be necessary. It was a hard condition.

Professor Roel Bekker pointed me to a similar example involving the development of Schiphol Airport, referring to an important distinction with some policy trajectories between developing a national framework that also makes it possible to develop regional/situational visions through co-creation.

As the number of 'wicked problems' increases, these OMSPD 'two-layered' approaches become more important for Ministries working together and would appear to be a theme for further research: what are successful 'two-layered' approaches and how have they been carried out?

Perhaps lessons can also be learned from the European Union, which, on the one hand formulates frameworks at a European level and, on the other hand, gives countries the opportunity to implement these frameworks at a national level.

3. *'Hijacking' OMSPD for one's own purposes*

If OMSPD approaches are increasingly being applied, are there parties who find ways of using OMSPD for their own ends? What are those possible ways and how can an OMSPD trajectory be organized in such a way as to place the knowledge democracy center stage, and not a one-side lobby/manipulation by various parties? These questions also require further research.

4. *Deliberately exaggerate the complexity of issues or abusing the complexity*

Smidt & Vohen (2013: 51) include a remark by Assange in their book that also deserves attention.

As things become more open, they also become more complex, because people try to hide their bad behavior behind complex structures.'

The examples Assange presents are government bureaucracies and the offshore financial sector. Assange continues:

'Officially, these systems are open but, in practice, they are impenetrable.... At this level, where complexity is legal but is still used to hide things, obfuscation is a trickier problem than open censorship.'

Van Hoesel is quoted in Appendix 2 with a comment about the criterion of simplicity in policy development: *'This criterion may not be obvious, but it is an important condition to be able to meet the other criteria, because complex policy leads to high implementation costs, it is less accessible, abuse is easier, it is more difficult to enforce, it will clash with other policies more quickly and it is harder to implement, which means that the effect is reduced'* (Van Hoesel, 2008: 59).

Looking at the discussion about integrity and the development of the discussion regarding integrity, research into abuse of complexity by civil servants or other influential people is also desirable.

This could vary from complexity as a deliberately applied diffuseness to cover oneself or avoid responsibility, to a creating a deliberate 'fog' for focused abuse.

5. *Outside the political-administrative framework*

It is likely that, especially among large companies (multinational companies and non-governmental organizations) similar processes play a role (with the CEO or the division manager taking on the role of the Minister). This means that similar unwritten rules and coping strategies also play an important role in the business community. A study comparable to this one, among multinational companies would be interesting for two reasons. On the one hand, to validate the research methods we used in this study. This would show that the research methods we used transcend organizations, which is good for the reliability of the methods involved.

On the other hand, it is interesting to see whether the results would be similar, in terms of the relationship between multinational companies and the way they interact with their environment. With the latter, a hypothesis could be whether such large organizations will encounter similar problems in their strategy development as the ones we found with regard to policy development among political-administrative organizations.

6. *Three career paths for civil servants*

Three policy functions have been mentioned: the traditional civil servant, the policy entrepreneur and the OMSPD employee. It is to be recommended to examine to what extent there is room for these career paths within the national government. That would legitimize the application of OMSPD from a functional perspective.

Appendix 11: Declaration of authenticity and quality

Declaration of authenticity and quality

Thesis: 'Dealing with unwritten rules'

As emeritus professor of Applied Policy Studies and former promoter of abovementioned thesis, the undersigned was involved intensively in the execution of the promotional research of Max (E.J.) Herold.
All the interview reports written by the PhD student were directly sent to me by the respondents, along with their declaration that the reports were a correct representation of what was discussed. This applies to both part I and part II of the research.
In my view, the interview reports contain very usable qualitative data with regard to the research question of the study.
I was able to experience the thorough interview method that was used in part II of the research, and the various steps taken to make tacit knowledge explicit myself as a respondent with regard to some other subjects. In my opinion, this method yielded a high validity of the answers given by the respondents.
With the further analysis of the data obtained, I have closely followed the various steps of the PhD students: ordering the material, processes that ultimately led to the four main unwritten rules, establishing the relationship between unwritten rules and level of openness, description of the coping strategies. In my view, these steps were taken in a responsible fashion.
I would like to add to this that this study has an excellent score on what I think is the core of empirical socio-scientific research, namely the quality of the data collection and the analysis, based on the many studies it have assessed as a methodologist.

Prof. dr. P.H.M. van Hoesel   Date: July 16, 2015

Emeritus Professor Applied Policy Studies
Erasmus University Rotterdam